I0799919

IMAGES
of America

BOUND BROOK

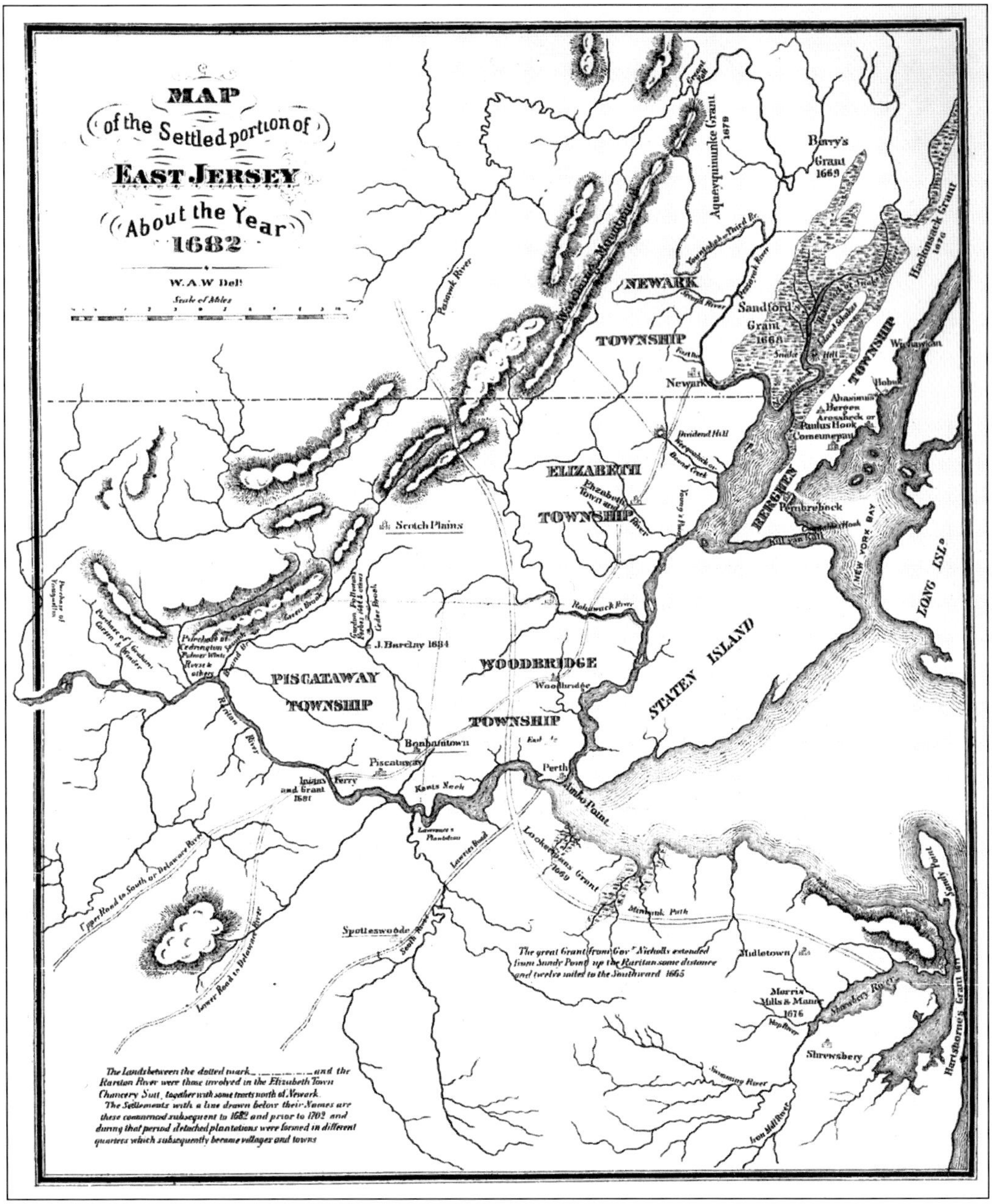
MAP
of the Settled portion of
EAST JERSEY
About the Year
1682
W. A. W Delt
Scale of Miles
NEWARK
TOWNSHIP
Newark
ELIZABETH
TOWNSHIP
Scotch Plains
J. Barclay 1684
PISCATAWAY
TOWNSHIP
WOODBRIDGE
TOWNSHIP
Woodbridge
Bonhamtown
Piscataway
Perth
Ambo Point
STATEN ISLAND
NEW YORK BAY
LONG ISLD
BERGEN
Pembrepock
Kill van Kull
Bergen
Paulus Hook
Comeunepaw
Hoboken
Weehawken
Hackensack Grant 1676
TOWNSHIP
Sandford's
Grant
1668
Berry's
Grant
1669
Aquackanonke Grant
1679
Passaick River
Rahwack River
Raritan River
Inians Ferry
and Grant
1681
Kents Neck
Lawrences Road
Spotteswoode
South River
Mudletown
Morris
Mills & Manor
1676
Shrewsbery River
Shrewsbery
Swimming River
Sandy Point
Hartshorne's Grant
Upper Road to South or Delaware River
Lower Road to Delaware River
Minisink Path
Iron Mill Road
The great Grant from Govr Nicholls extended from Sandy Point up the Raritan some distance and twelve miles to the Southward 1665
The Lands between the dotted mark .... and the Raritan River were those involved in the Elizabeth Town Chancery Suit, together with some tracts north of Newark.
The Settlements with a line drawn below their Names are those commenced subsequent to 1682 and prior to 1702 and during that period detached plantations were formed in different quarters which subsequently became villages and towns

IMAGES
of America

BOUND BROOK

Dorothy A. Stratford and Margaret McKay

ARCADIA
PUBLISHING

ISBN 978-0-7385-0279-3

Published by Arcadia Publishing
Charleston, South Carolina

Printed in the United States of America

Library of Congress Catalog Card Number: 99-69634

For all general information contact Arcadia Publishing at:
Telephone 843-853-2070
Fax 843-853-0044
E-mail sales@arcadiapublishing.com
For customer service and orders:
Toll-Free 1-888-313-2665

Visit us on the Internet at www.arcadiapublishing.com

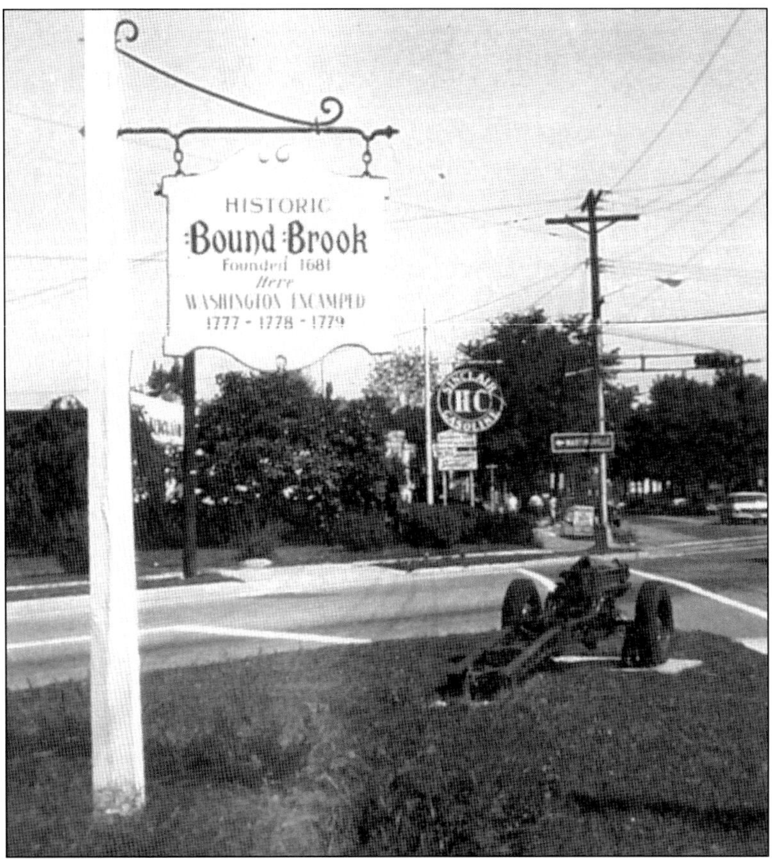

Contents

ACKNOWLEDGMENTS

The authors wish to thank the Bound Brook Memorial Library, which sponsored this publication, and the Somerset County Historical Society and Presbyterian Church for making their respective photographic archives available to us. Thanks are in order to everyone who lent photographs or helped identify them, including Joan Blyth-Lovell, Helen Malloy Collins, Ann Dickinson Kurtz, and Fred Sisser, III. Also, a large vote of thanks goes to Kathy Reser of Copies Now for her expertise and much appreciated advice.

INTRODUCTION

In 1681, 100 pounds of trade goods was the purchase price paid to the Lenape Indians for the land where Bound Brook now stands. Thomas Codrington, who the only Proprietor (one of the English merchants who purchased what is New York from Berkely and Carteret families) actually to build a house and reside on his land, received 877 acres of the purchase. A settlement grew on this tract, and Bound Brook became the first settled town in Somerset County. Several of the early settlers purchased tracts of 1,000 acres each. The Raritan River was the first means of transportation for the early settlers, but in time the Great Raritan Road and Old York Road offered transportation for people and supplies.

Over the next century, the town grew slowly, in spite of the constant threats of the floods and freshets of the Raritan River. At the time of the Revolutionary War, the town had grown to 35 families. Both the British and Continental Armies conducted forays in and about town for needed supplies. Washington's army was encamped twice at Middlebrook. On April 13, 1777, the British stationed at New Brunswick sent a force to attack the outpost manned by General Lincoln's troops. On October 26, 1780, Colonel Simcoe and his troop of Loyalist Cavalry conducted a sweep through the area, destroying boats at Van Veghten bridge and burning both the Dutch Reformed Church along the river west of town and the Somerset Court House at Millstone. Recuperating from the ravages of the war, the town experienced slow growth until 1806, when the New Jersey Turnpike Company began construction of a toll road from New Brunswick to Phillipsburg via Bound Brook and Somerville. This road was heavily used by farmers moving their products to New Brunswick. Some days, the gatekeeper could count up to 500 wagons moving produce to New Brunswick. The Swift-Sure Stage Line established before the Revolution made three trips each week from New York to Philadelphia via the Old York Road in 1826.

Another factor in the town's growth was the building of the Delaware and Raritan Canal, begun in 1830 and completed in 1834. The canal was open from April through December, and an unending stream of barges traveled the waterway day and night, carrying more freight than any other U.S. canal. In 1867, 3 million tons of cargo were transported via this waterway. All traffic ended on the canal in 1933. Yet another factor in the town's growth was the coming of the railroad. Begun in 1831, the Elizabethtown and Somerville Railroad reached Bound Brook in 1838, supplying a new mode of travel to the area and bringing new residents and industries to town. At this time, there were 80 dwellings, and 566 inhabitants called Bound Brook home.

In the years after the Civil War, the Reading Railroad and Lehigh Valley Railroad ran lines through town. The availability of an hour's ride to New York City enticed many New York businessmen to build homes and move their families to the attractive small town within commuting distance of their places of business. Some 100 passenger and freight trains passed through town in a day during these years, and the town became a hub of railroad business with roundhouses and turntables servicing the five lines that passed through the area. Another innovation was the trolley lines that came to town in 1887, later to be electrified in 1897. All these travel conveniences brought industries to town, changing its tenor from a sleepy farm village to a busy small industry town.

In 1855, John Smalley & Company built farm machinery in a factory at the corner of John and Church Streets. The Herberts ran a thriving gristmill on Easton Turnpike west of town. In 1880, the Einstein Brothers opened their Woolen Mills, employing 300 workers. In addition to these, other small businesses drew in new residents so that in 1898, 2,600 people resided here.

The rising population brought the need for additional educational facilities. For more than two centuries, there had been a succession of one-room schools presided over by consecutive schoolmasters. In the 1870s, Lafayette School was built and boasted 189 students. Likewise, population growth brought the need for additional churches. Until 1846, the Presbyterian church was the only one in town. The Methodist, Episcopal and, in 1876, the Roman Catholic denominations all had congregations and had built places of worship.

Floods and fires seem to be the town's nemesis, for almost annually the Raritan River would flood, causing damage to the center of town. In 1881, a disastrous fire destroyed all the buildings in a block of Main Street. In 1896, flooding caused the lime in the L.D. Cook lumberyard to ignite by spontaneous combustion. Fanned by strong winds, the fire spread to and destroyed the Presbyterian church building erected in 1829. The 1881 conflagration brought about the formation of a fire department. Since the town lacked a fire department of its own, it was necessary to bring fire equipment by railroad flatcar from Somerville to fight the disastrous conflagration.

As the town grew, so did the need for a local paper. Several were printed in Somerville, but the deficiency was corrected by the publication of the short-lived *Argus*, the *Rock*, and the *Family Casket*. The *Family Casket* was begun in Whitehouse Station but was moved to Bound Brook in 1877 by owner Andrew Shampanore, who also changed its name to the *Chronicle*. In 1884, W.B.R. Mason purchased the newspaper from Shampanore and ran it for 53 years until he sold it to Irving Reimer in 1937. There was also a short-lived German-language newspaper published in town.

William R. Whiting became the first mayor when a borough form of government was adopted on February 10, 1891, after severing the town from Bridgewater Township. At this time, there were no paved streets, no sidewalks, and kerosene supplied the lights to the more than 3,000 residents. Amenities came with expansion: a public library in 1897; a hospital in 1927; police force in 1917; two theaters, one boasting a fine stringed pit orchestra; and three additional schools—a high school in 1907, LaMonte School in 1914, and Smalley School in 1951.

As the 20th century arrived, Bound Brook's population continued to increase. This was because the town remained a railroad hub with 30 trains running daily to and from New York City as well as direct service to Philadelphia. In 1917, a round-trip fare to New York City was $8.80. Such easily available transportation lured additional factories to the area that depended on the local workforce for staff.

World War I saw 500 men and women from Bound Brook, South Bound Brook, and Middlesex serve their country overseas. During World War II, the number of Bound Brook service personnel was many times larger. The industries that had located in the area during the time between the wars worked around the clock producing products for the war effort. This increased activity brought about a great population boom and a housing shortage.

Today, the large industries are gone, and the railroad only employs a small number of people. Moreover, faces in town have change to reflect a more diverse population. Only time will tell what the 21st century has in store for the little village on the Raritan, settled first more than 300 years ago.

As work on this publication was winding down, on September 17, Hurricane Floyd inundated our town with floodwaters over 20 feet deep. It was the worst disaster ever sustained here. More than one-third of the area was affected by the destructive water. In recovery, our town may never be the same again. We hope that our publication will preserve the memories of what our world here was like before the terrible floods took away much of our past, and certainly some of our future.

One

THE TOWN

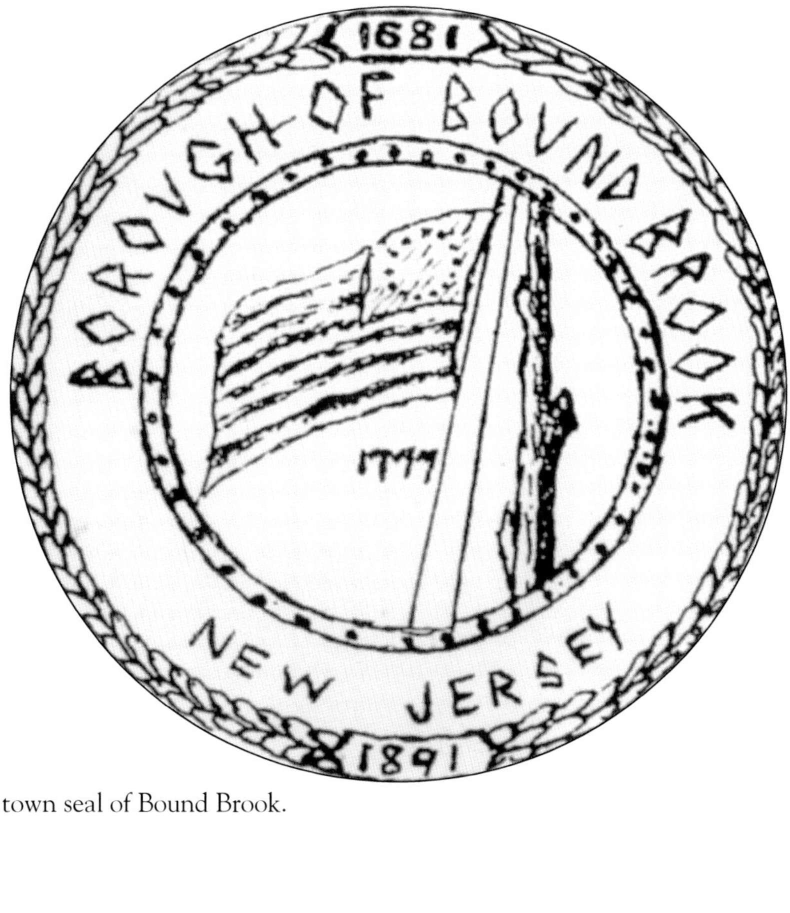

This is the town seal of Bound Brook.

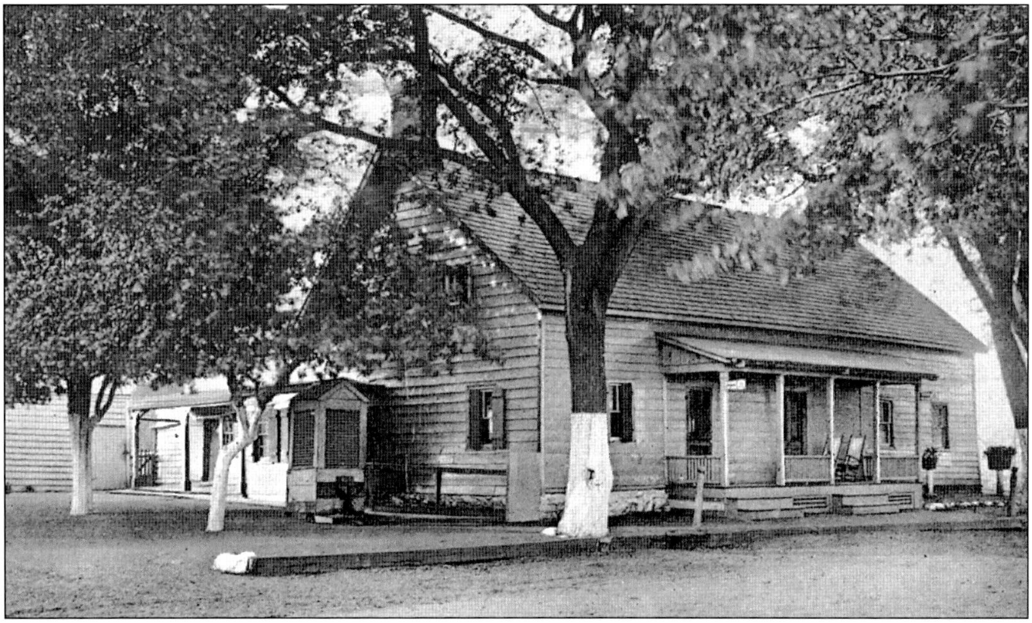

George Washington attended Masonic meetings at the Fisher Hotel in Middlebrook. The historic hotel served as the stagecoach stop and local meeting place for nearly two centuries. However, it fell into disrepair and was torn down in the early 1920s.

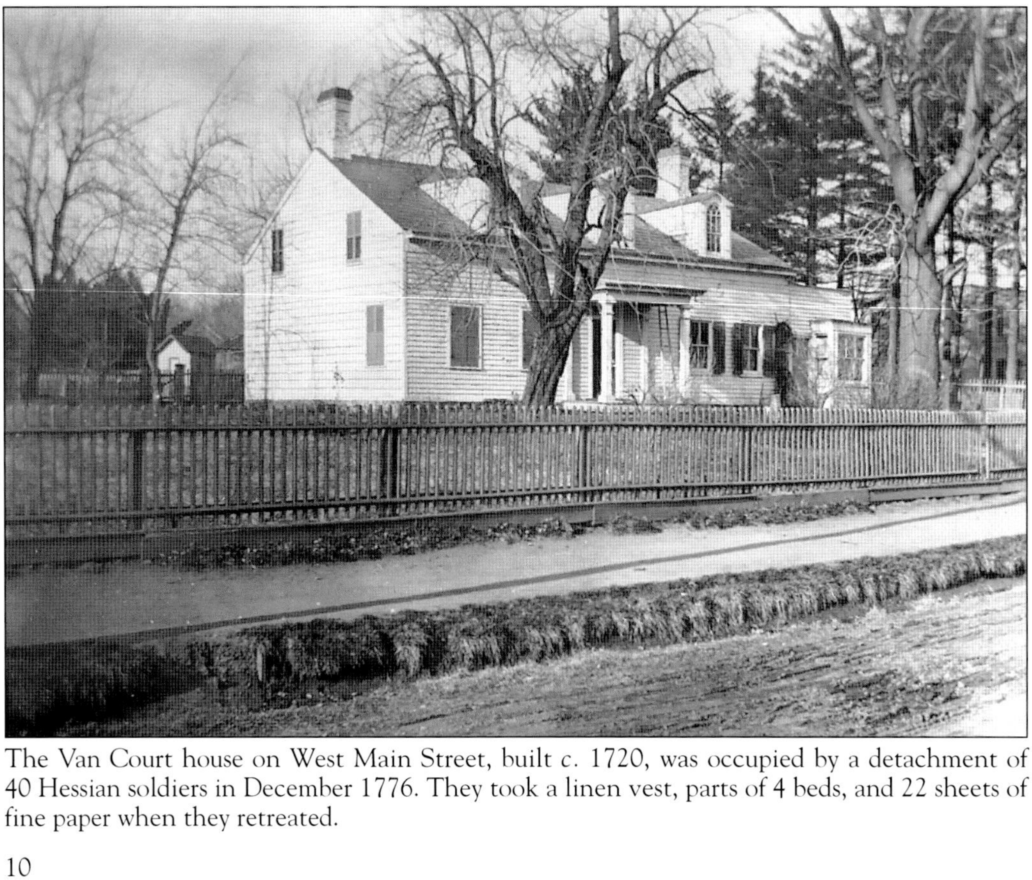

The Van Court house on West Main Street, built *c.* 1720, was occupied by a detachment of 40 Hessian soldiers in December 1776. They took a linen vest, parts of 4 beds, and 22 sheets of fine paper when they retreated.

A pre-1883 view of Main Street shows, from left to right, ACVN Mollison's Store, the Harpending house with Dr. Matthews' Apothecary Shop, and E. Casterline's Harness Shop. The Harpending House was also known as the Frelinghuysen Tavern.

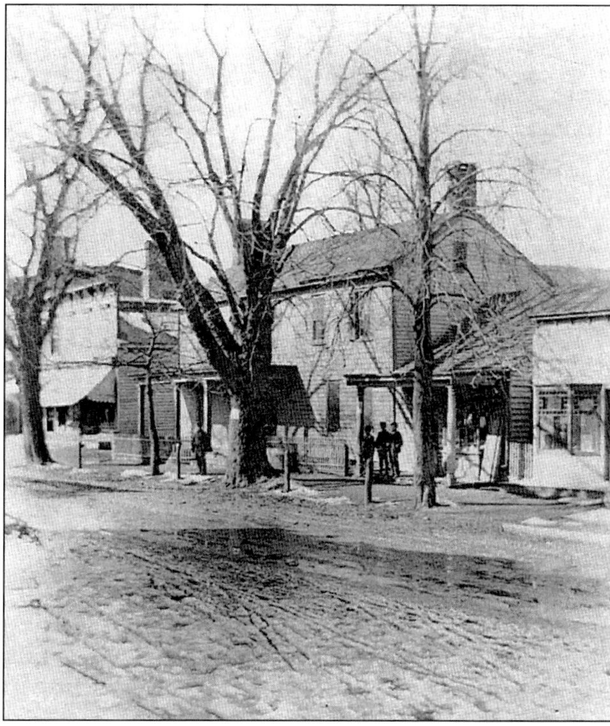

Dr. William McKissack, a Revolutionary War veteran, purchased this property from Dr. John Griffith. The house stood on the south side of West Main Street in Middlebrook near the intersection with LaMonte Avenue.

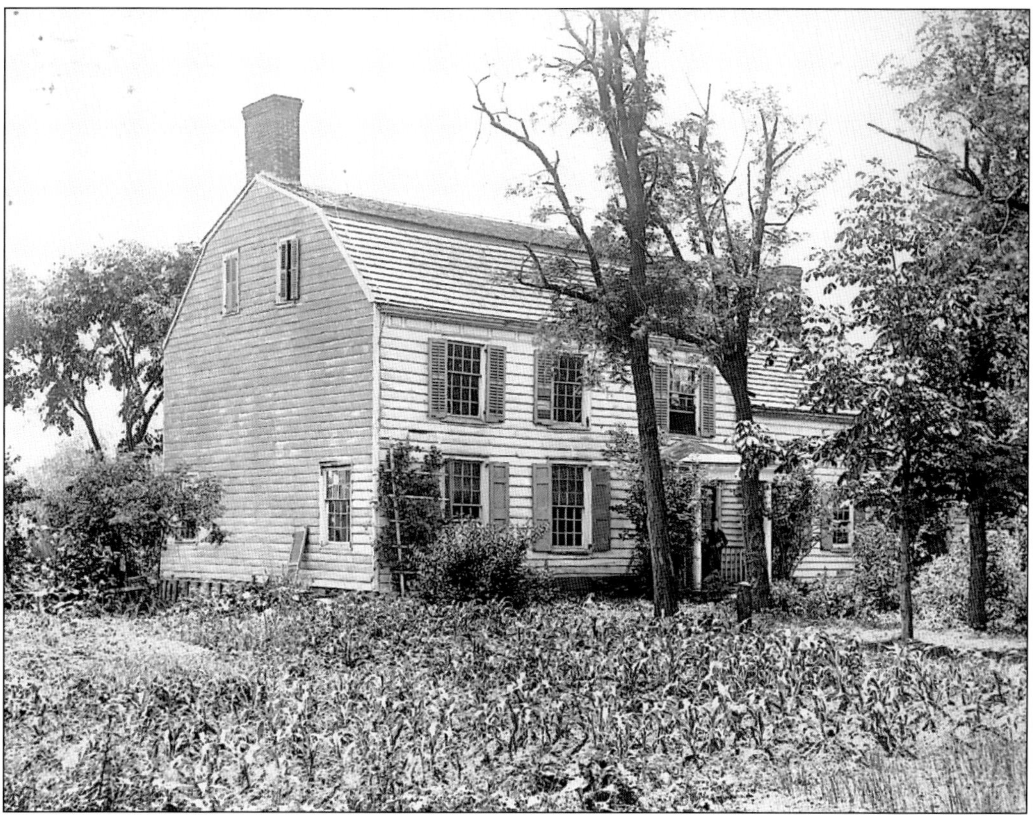

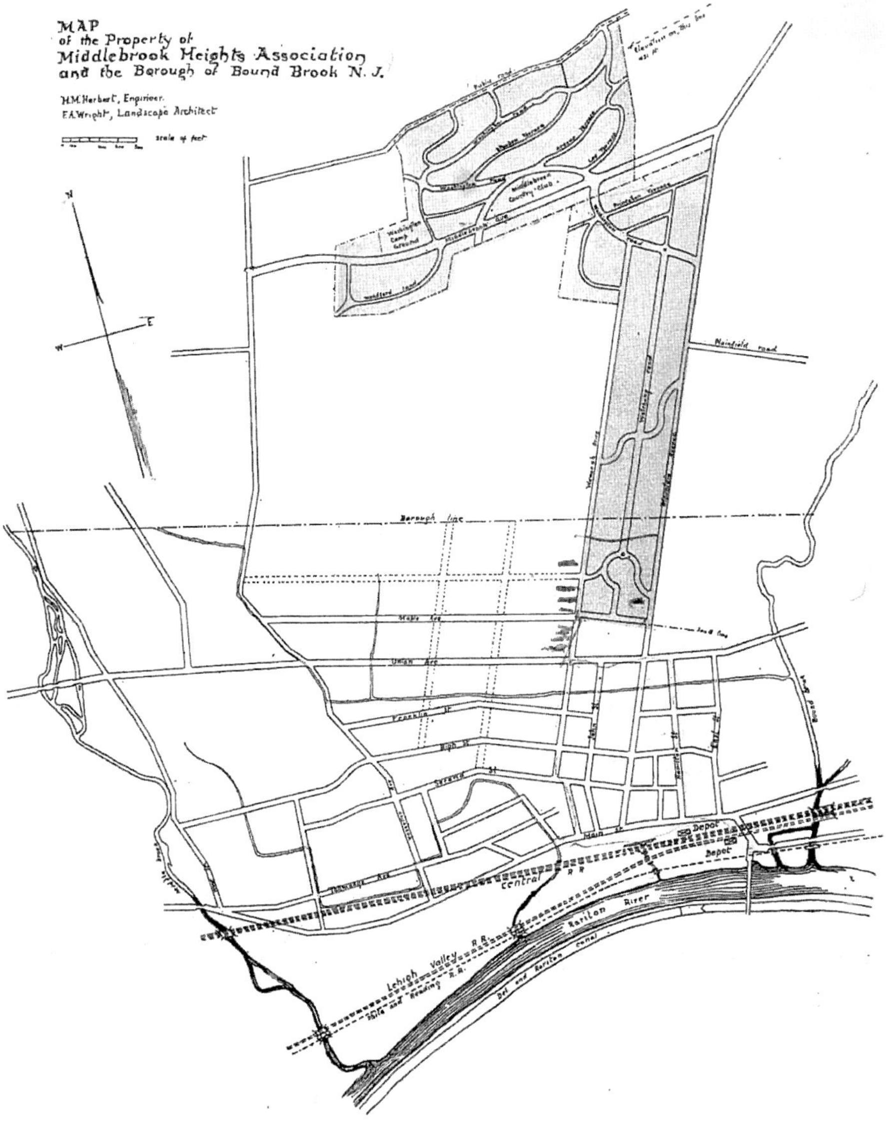

THE HEIGHTS AND THE TOWN.

George LaMonte and a group of investors known as the Middlebrook Heights Association purchased a large plot of land adjoining the town for development. This map shows their proposed layout.

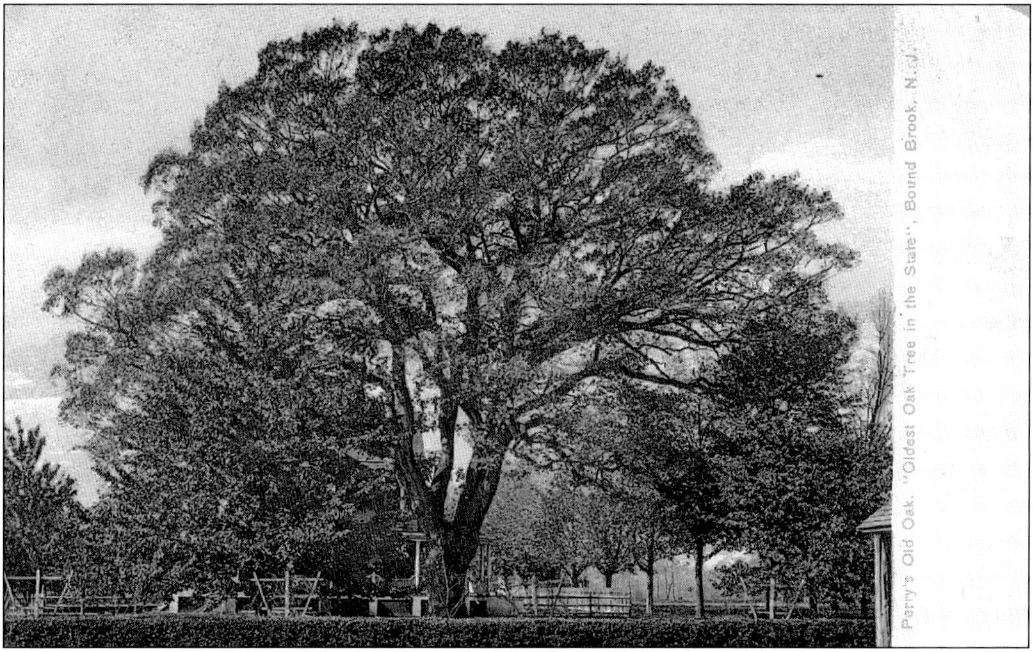

This tree, believed to be one of the oldest oak trees in the state, was called Perry's Oak until Dr. Hird became owner of the property. Since that time, it has been known as the Council Oak.

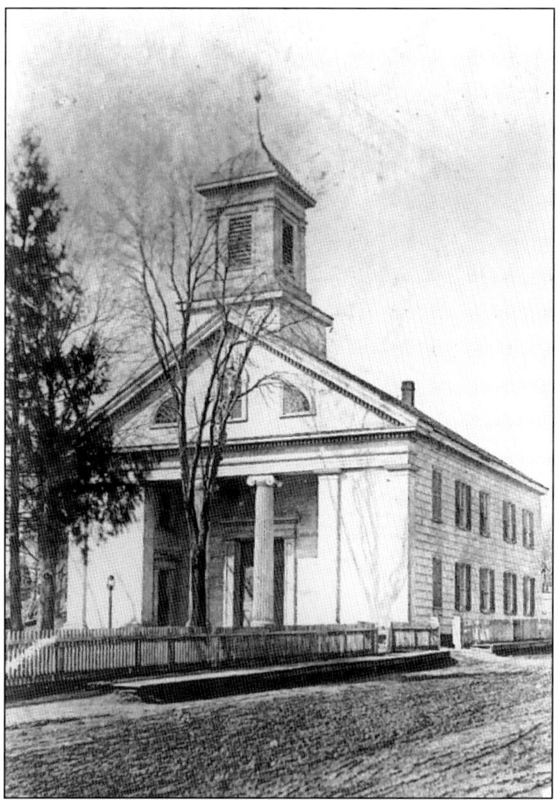

The Presbyterian denomination built this church in 1829 and enlarged it in 1851 after a lightning strike. It was the fourth structure on the site. The building faced Main Street at East Street and was destroyed by fire in 1896.

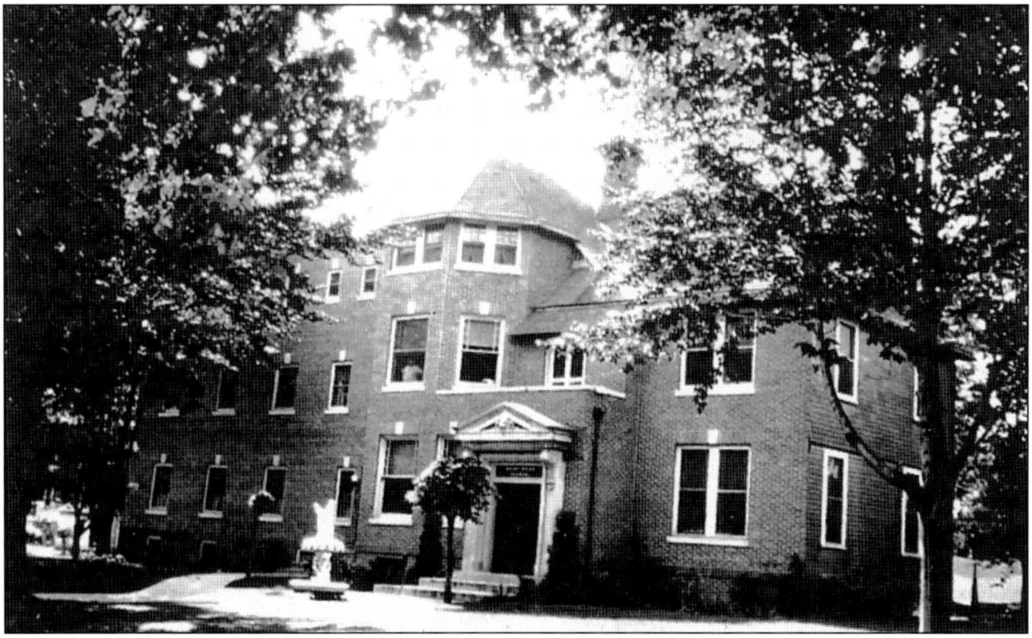

Bound Brook Hospital served the community for more than one-quarter of a century. It was owned and operated by the Borow family of physicians and occupied the northwest corner of West Maple Avenue and Church Streets.

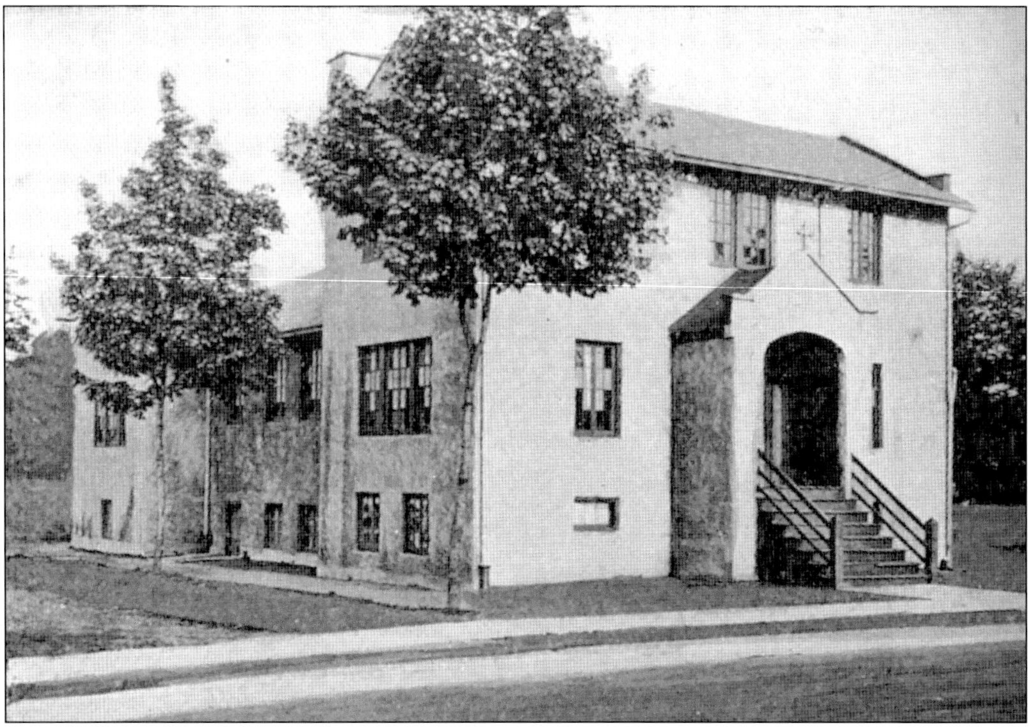

Another LaMonte family benefit, the Settlement House initially served the immigrant families of the West End. It later became the first home of St. Mary's Catholic Church congregation. Greenbrook Academy currently occupies the building.

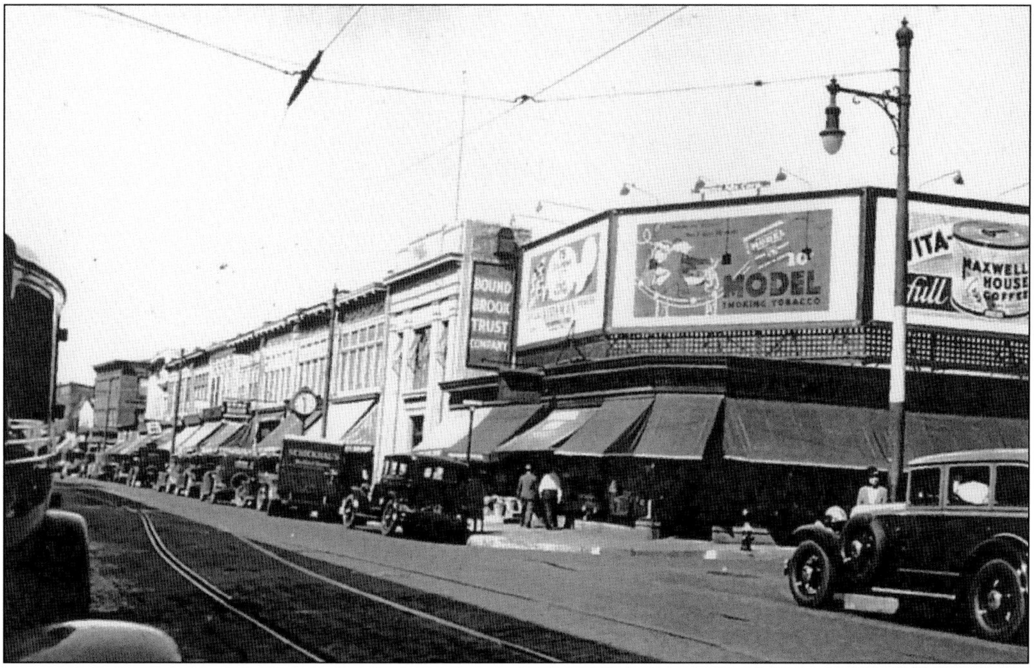

Advertising billboards graced the roofs of the stores on the corner of Maiden Lane and Main Street in the late 1930s and early 1940s.

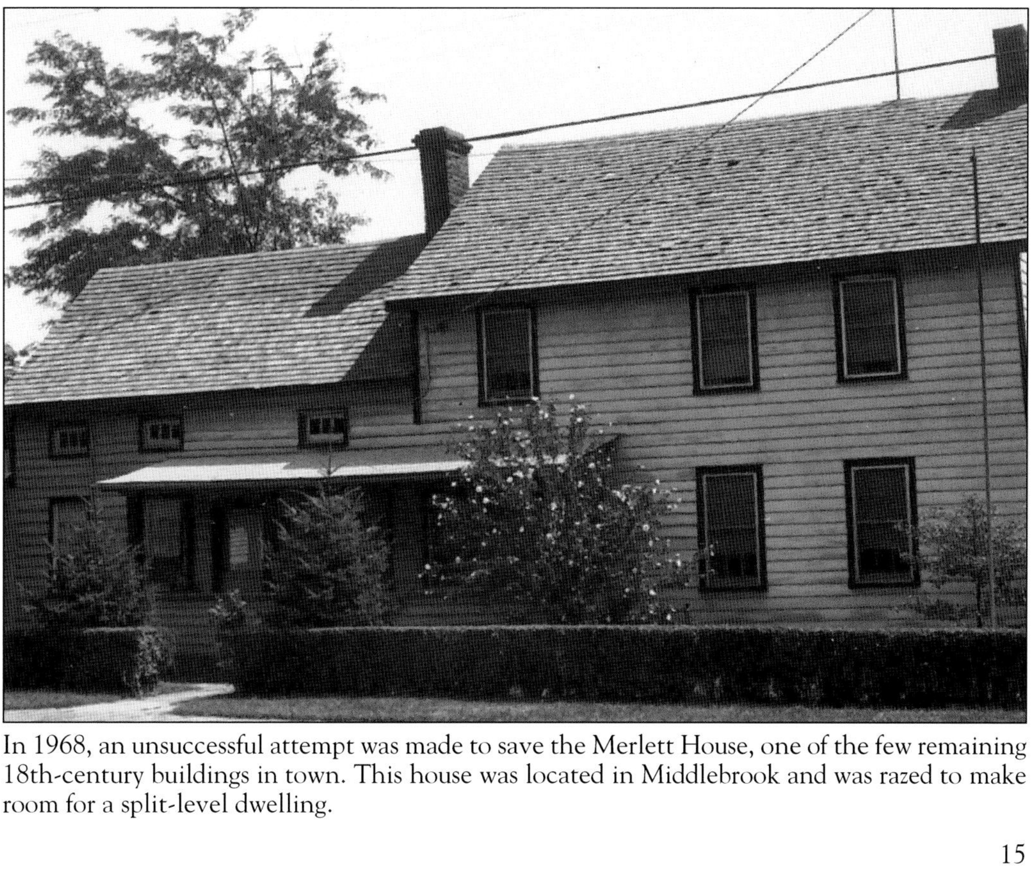

In 1968, an unsuccessful attempt was made to save the Merlett House, one of the few remaining 18th-century buildings in town. This house was located in Middlebrook and was razed to make room for a split-level dwelling.

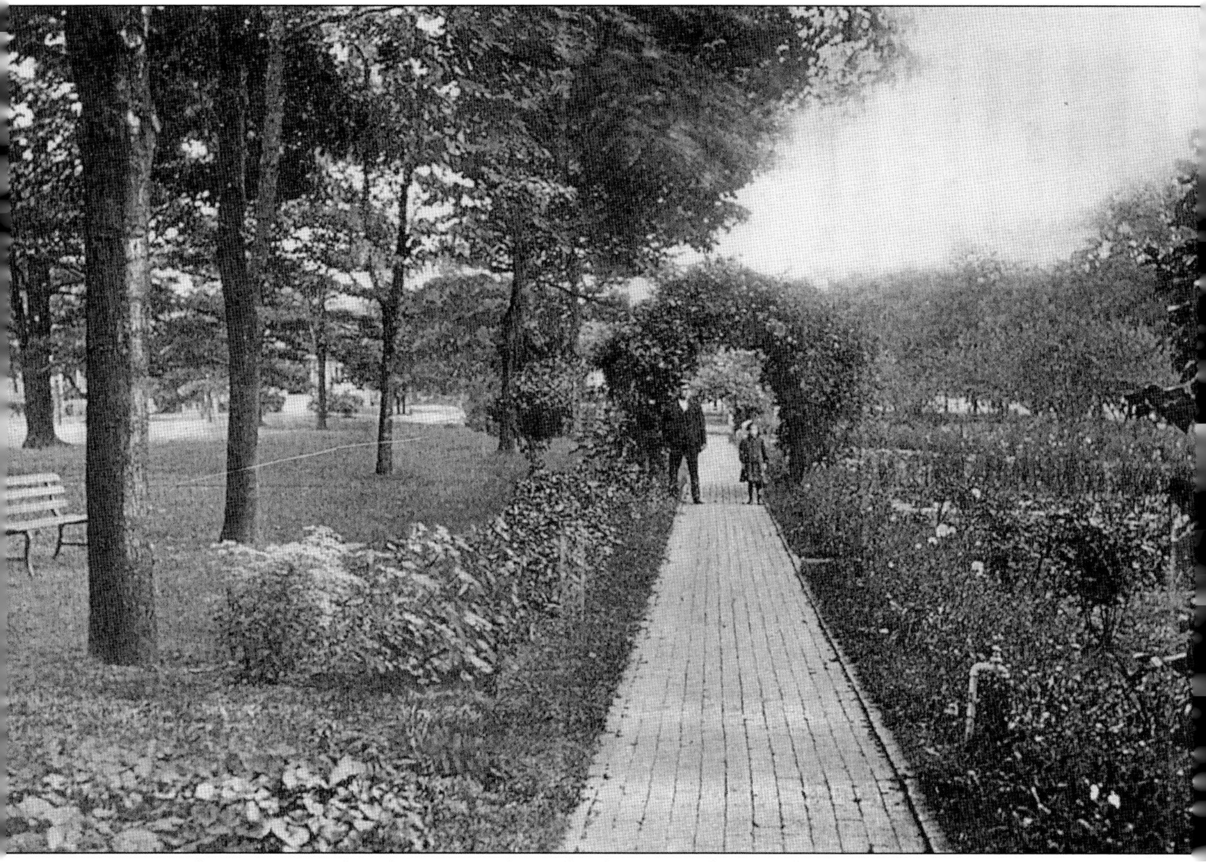

During the LaMonte family's ownership, the house and grounds of the Evergreens became a local showplace, as these well-kept gardens show.

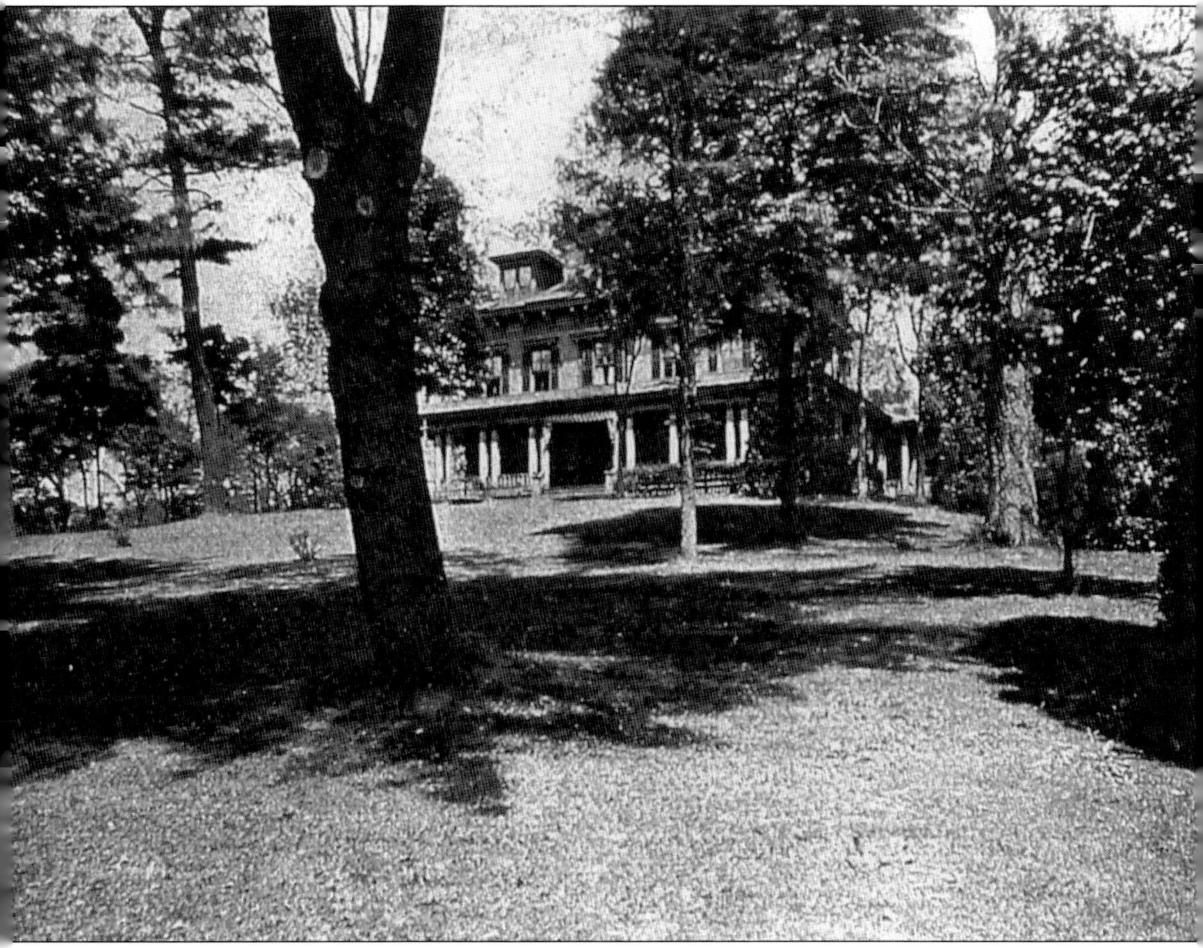

Daniel Talmage built this imposing residence on the foundations of Bound Brook's first house. He called the property Evergreen Hill. It was later sold to George LaMonte.

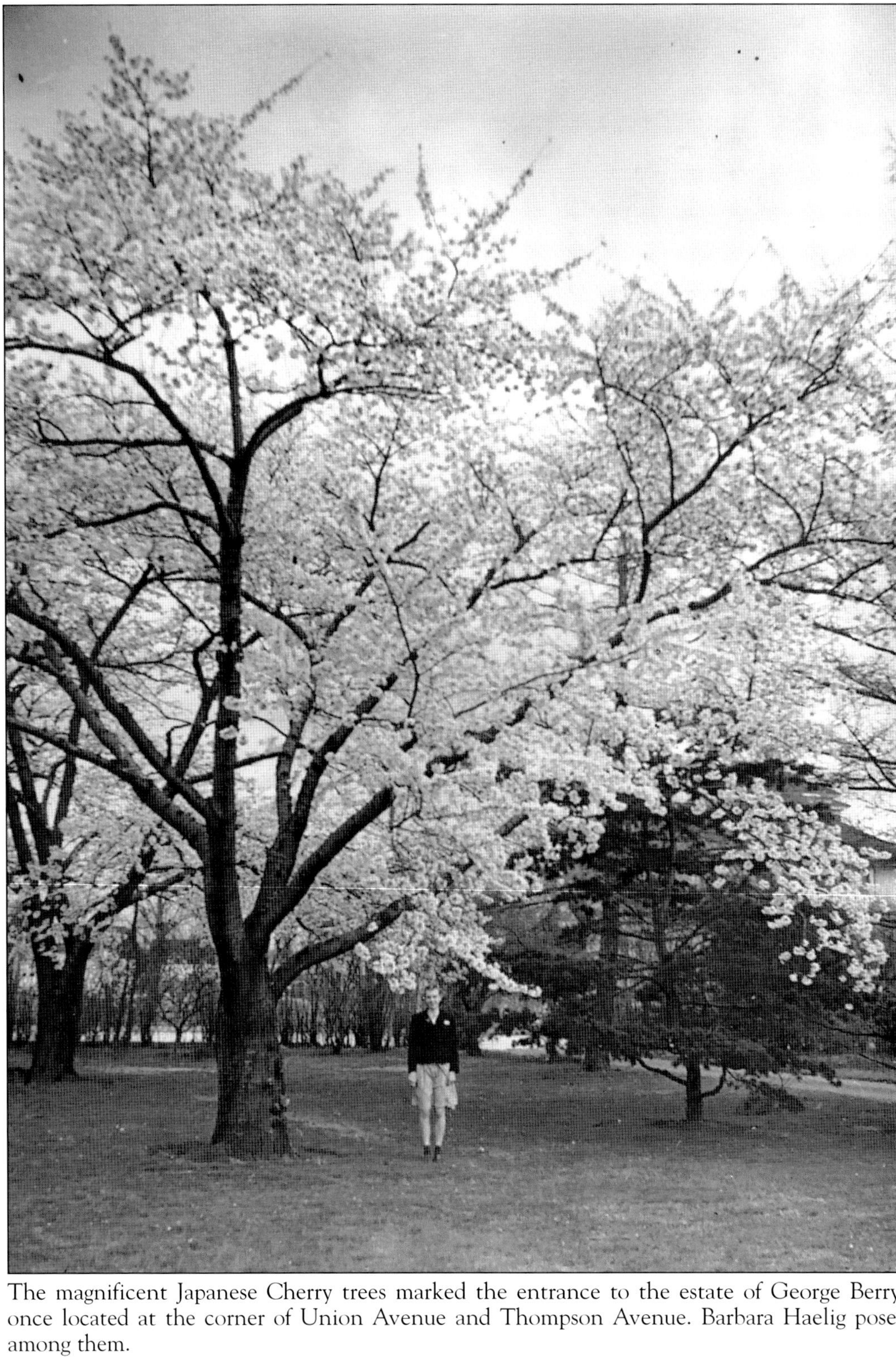

The magnificent Japanese Cherry trees marked the entrance to the estate of George Berry, once located at the corner of Union Avenue and Thompson Avenue. Barbara Haelig poses among them.

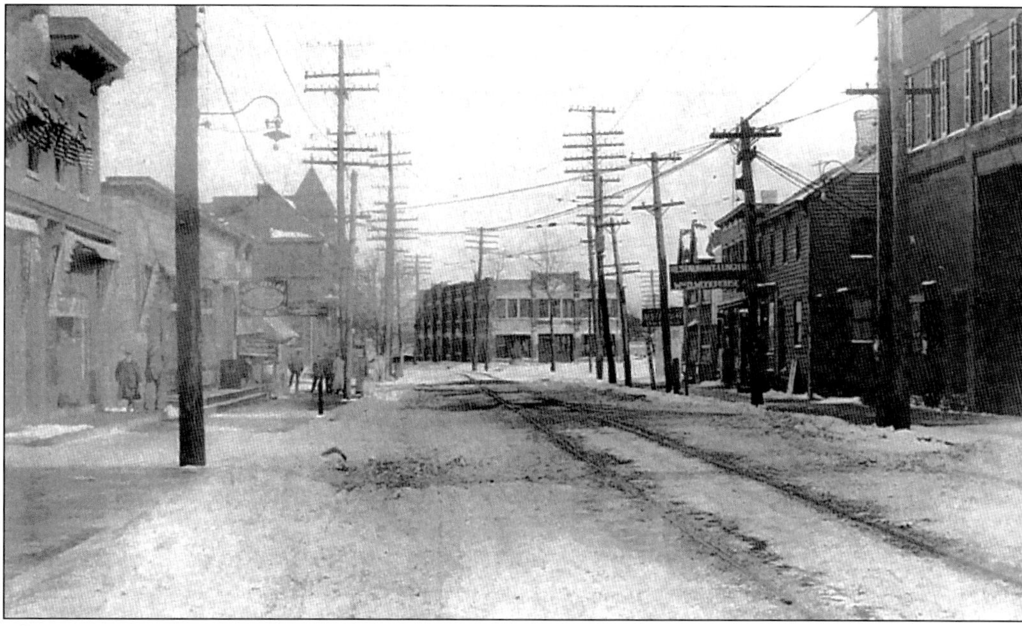

This snowy scene depicts lower Main Street at the turn of the 19th century. Bolmer's garage fills the background. Many of the other buildings on the right were demolished to make room for the trolley barn.

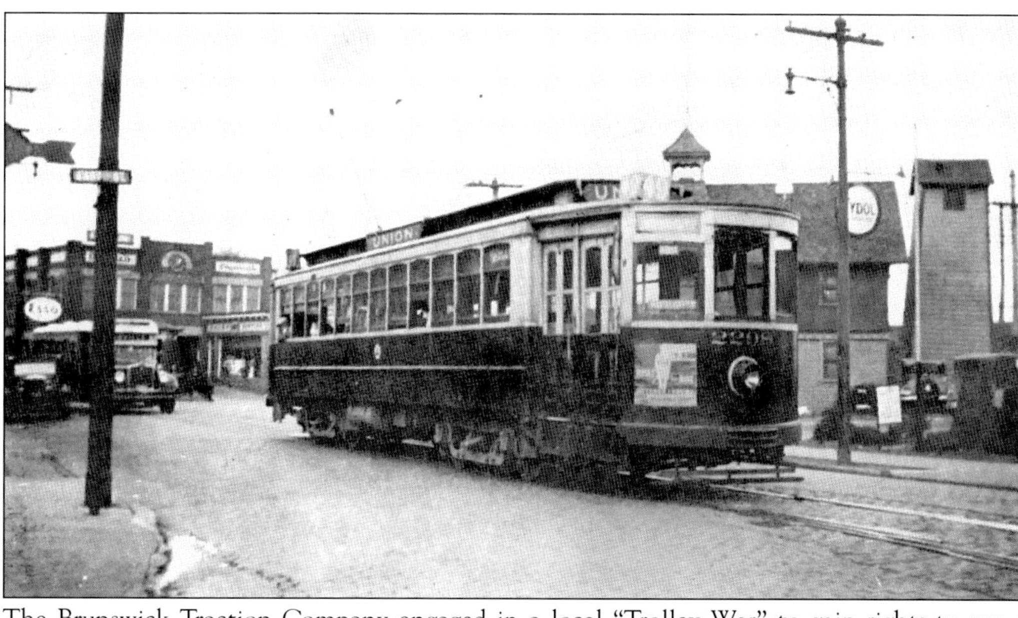

The Brunswick Traction Company engaged in a local "Trolley War" to gain rights to run a trolley line to Bound Brook from New Brunswick.

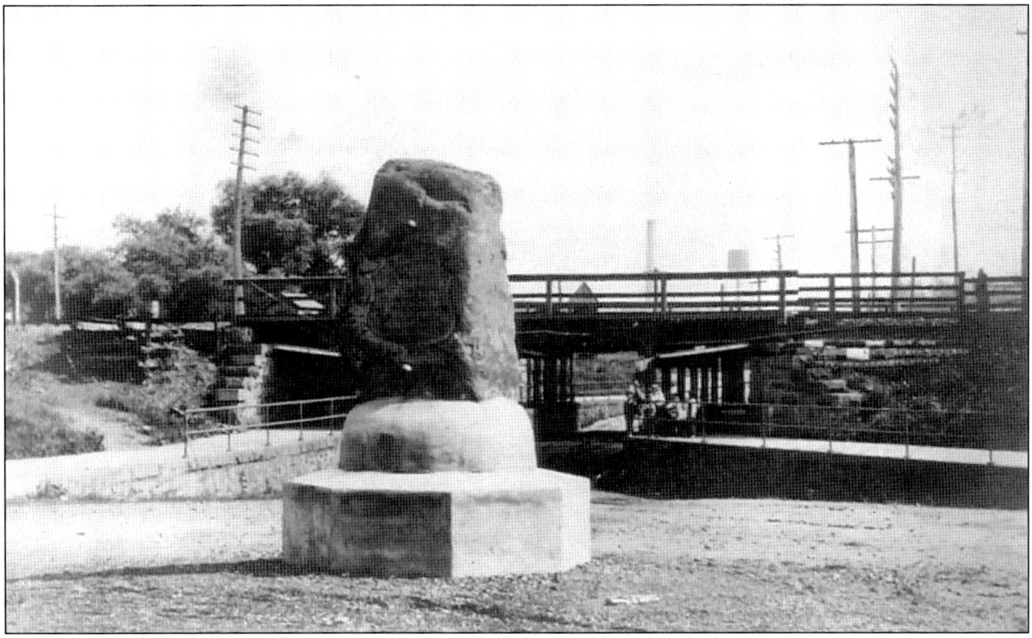

The boulder was excavated from the bed of the Delaware and Raritan Canal during its construction. The Battle Monument, seen here at its original site, was prepared and mounted by Essex Yawger, a local stone cutter.

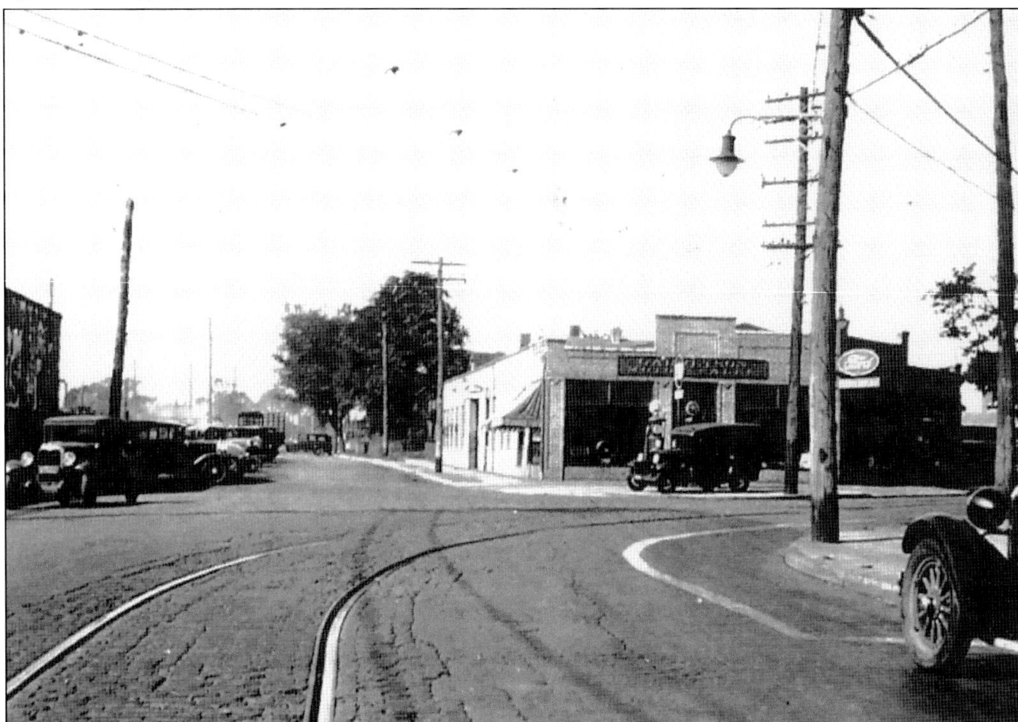

For almost one-quarter of a century, Garretson's Ford Agency occupied the familiar corner of Columbus Place and West Main Street. The railroad crossing to Middlebrook is no longer open.

IF WE SHOW IT, ITS RIGHT

DRY GOODS. : R.M.SCHEID : FANCY GOODS.

THE UNIQUE EMPORIUM

:NOTIONS: GENT'S FURNISHINGS : NOVELTIES.

415 East Main Street, Next door to P. O. BOUND BROOK, N. J.

ALFRED A. BILLIAN

Electrical and Chandelier Contractor

ELECTRICAL WORK OF ALL
KINDS PROMPTLY DONE
AT SHORT NOTICE

ESTIMATES CHEERFULLY GIVEN

107 EAST MAIN STREET
BOUND BROOK, N. J.
L. D. Telephone 8-J

WILLIAM EDGERTON,

FUNERAL DIRECTOR,

24 MAIDEN LANE

'PHONE 133-L BOUND BROOK, N. J.

RESIDENCE, 338 MOUNTAIN AVE.

'PHONE 157.

BELL PHONE No. 11-J HOME PHONE No. 17

JAMES TAGGART

LIVERY AND BOARDING
STABLES

COACHES, COUPES AND
LIGHT CARRIAGES TO HIRE

Hamilton St. cor. Second
Rear of Berkeley Hotel

BOUND BROOK, NEW JERSEY

JOHN D. GILES

Dealer in

Choice Groceries and Provisions

TEAS, COFFEES
FLOUR, SPICES

Specialties: Elgin Creamery Butter
and Full Cream Cheese

SOUTH BOUND BROOK, N. J.
Telephone Connection

The Berkeley

Leon W. DuFour, Prop.

THE LEADING HOTEL BETWEEN
NEW YORK AND EASTON

Tel. 28 Bound Brook, N. J.

At the turn of the 19th century, there were many prospering businesses in town, typified by this page of local advertising.

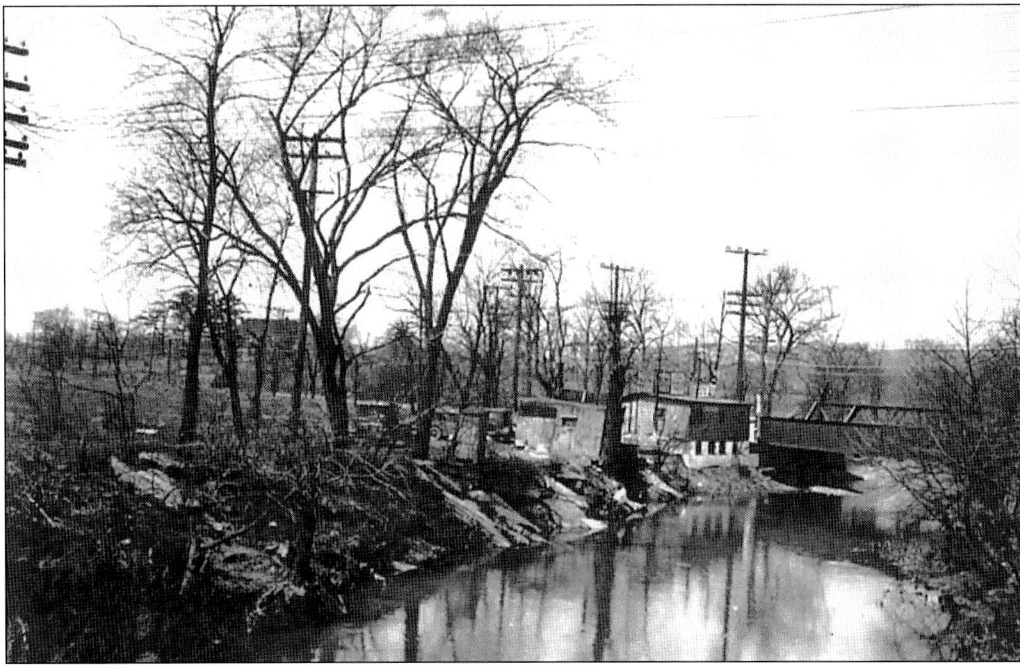

On the Bridgewater side of the Middlebrook, Daniel Conroy Sr., the father of the late Mayor Daniel Conroy, sold tobacco, newspapers, and candy in this small shop along the trolley line.

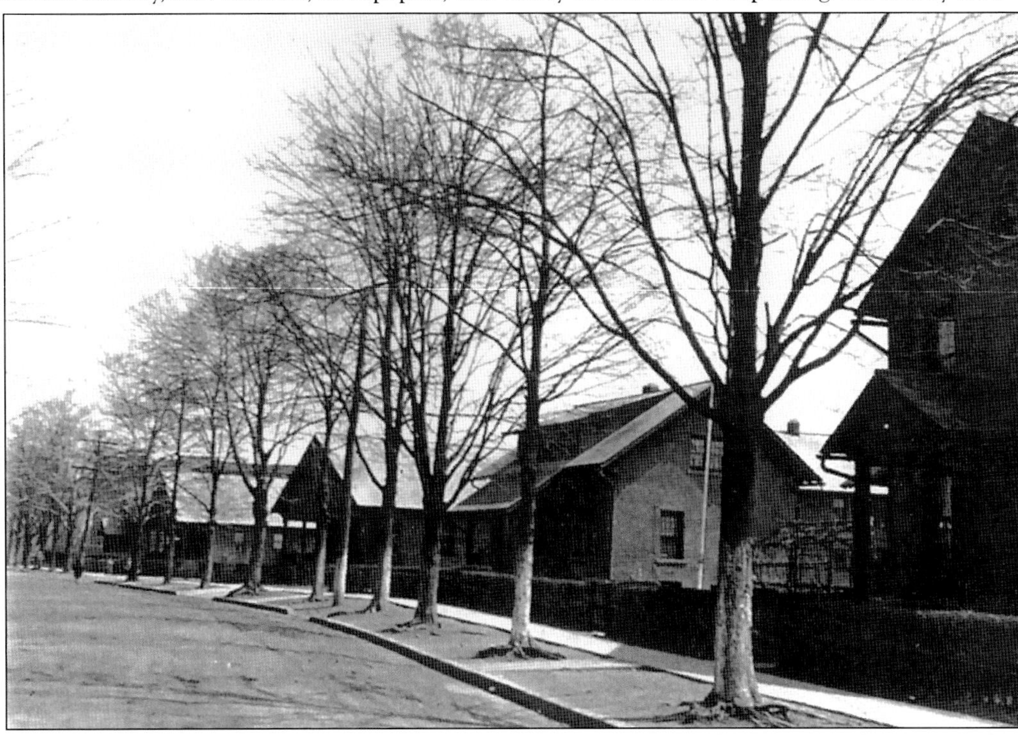

Westerly Gardens, an experiment in low-income housing, was the project of Miss Caroline LaMonte. The buildings are still part of West Second Street, Romney Road, North Street and New Hampshire Lane.

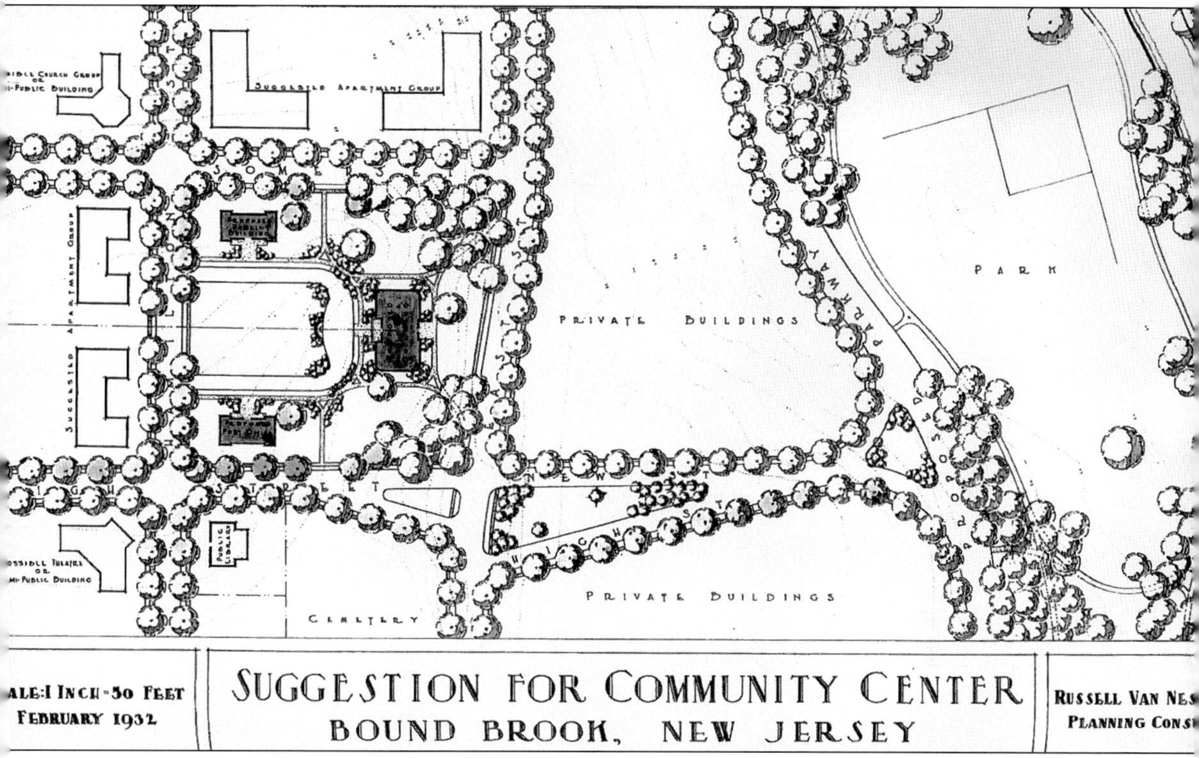

At the height of the Great Depression, this layout for a community center was prepared for the town by Russell W.N. Block.

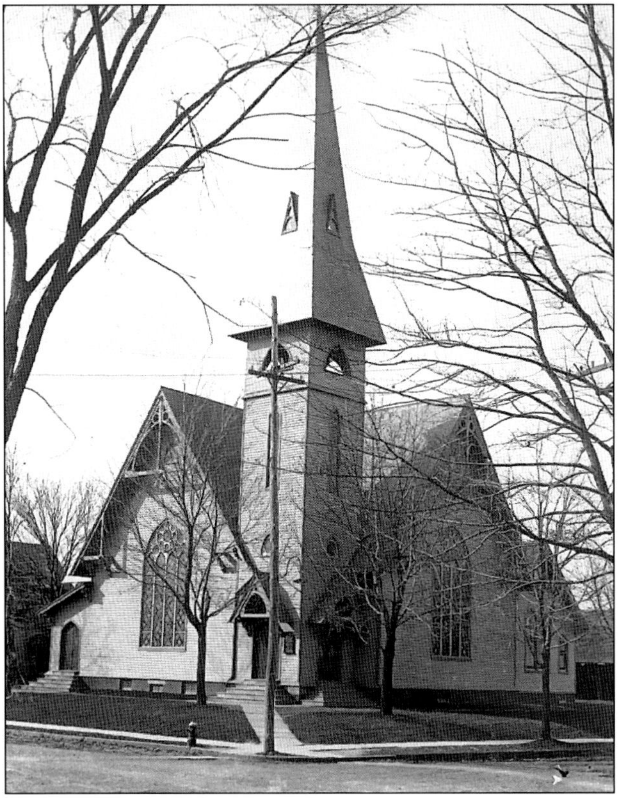

The Congregational church at West High and Church Streets no longer has the graceful tower shown in this photograph.

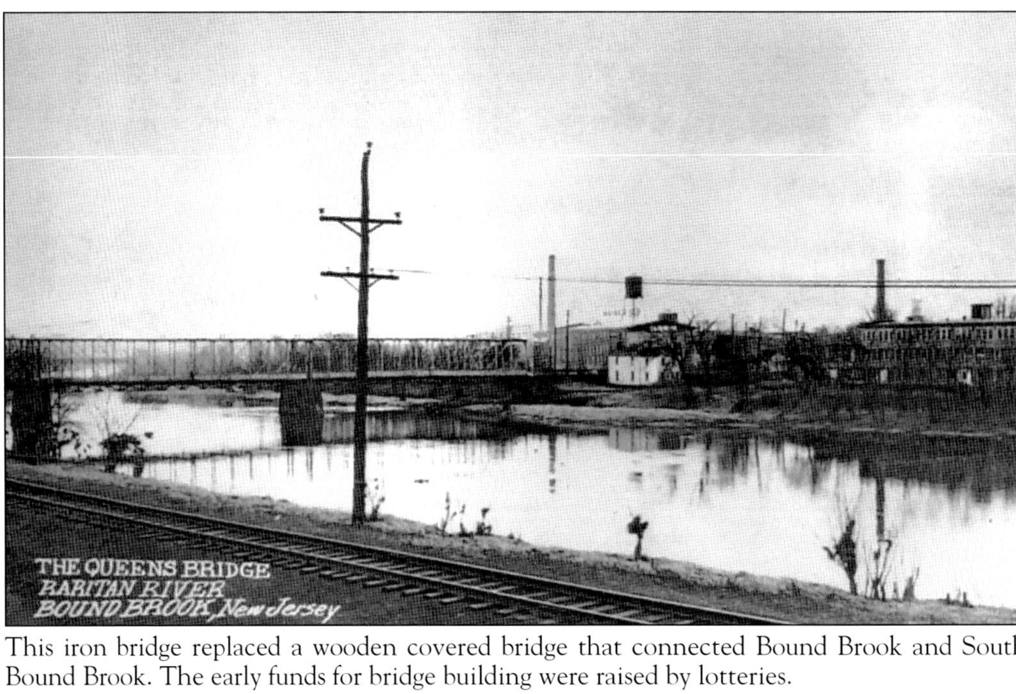

This iron bridge replaced a wooden covered bridge that connected Bound Brook and South Bound Brook. The early funds for bridge building were raised by lotteries.

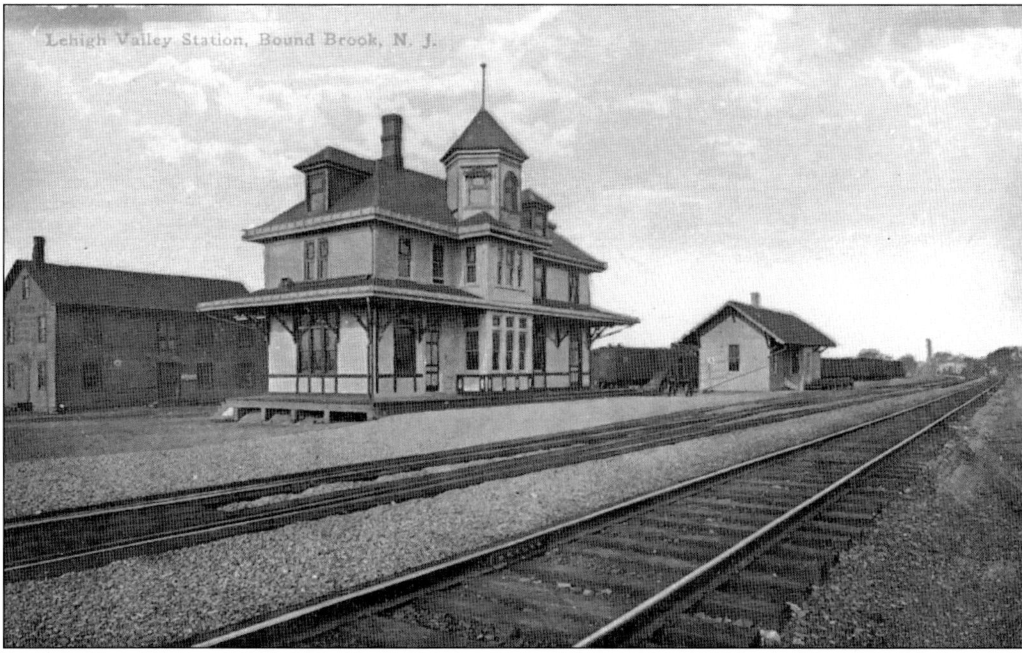

The Lehigh Valley and Central Railroads had Victorian-style stations in town. This one, belonging to the Lehigh Valley Railroad, was razed. The Central Station was replaced by the present building, which now houses George's Railroad Restaurant.

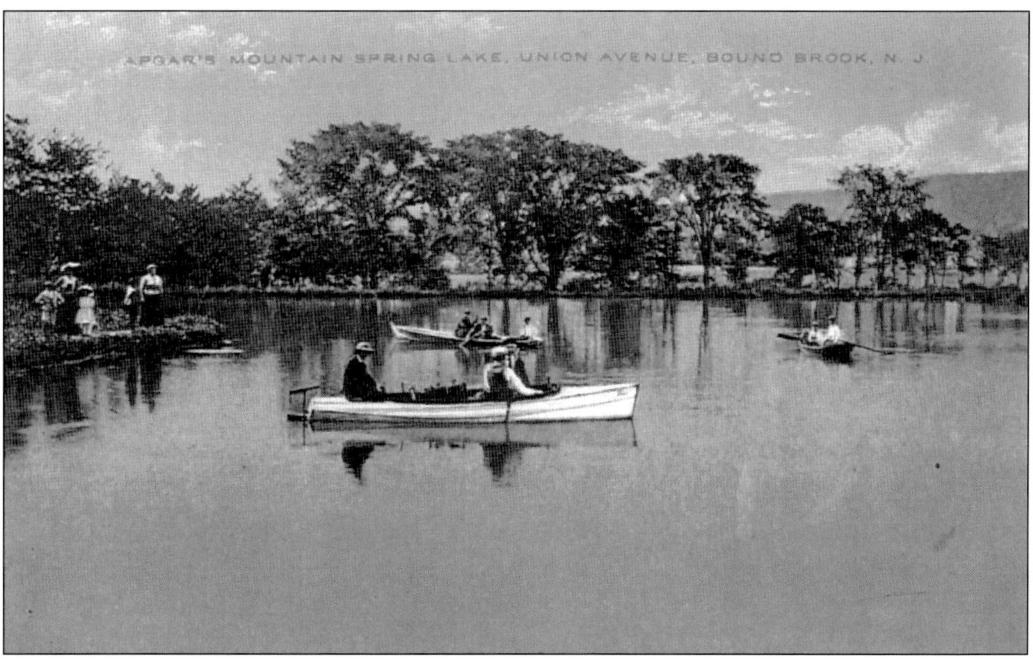

Apgar's Pond on Route 28 in neighboring Bridgewater Township was the scene of ice-skating and boating parties as well as a lucrative source of winter ice production. The site, now filled in, contains a number of homes.

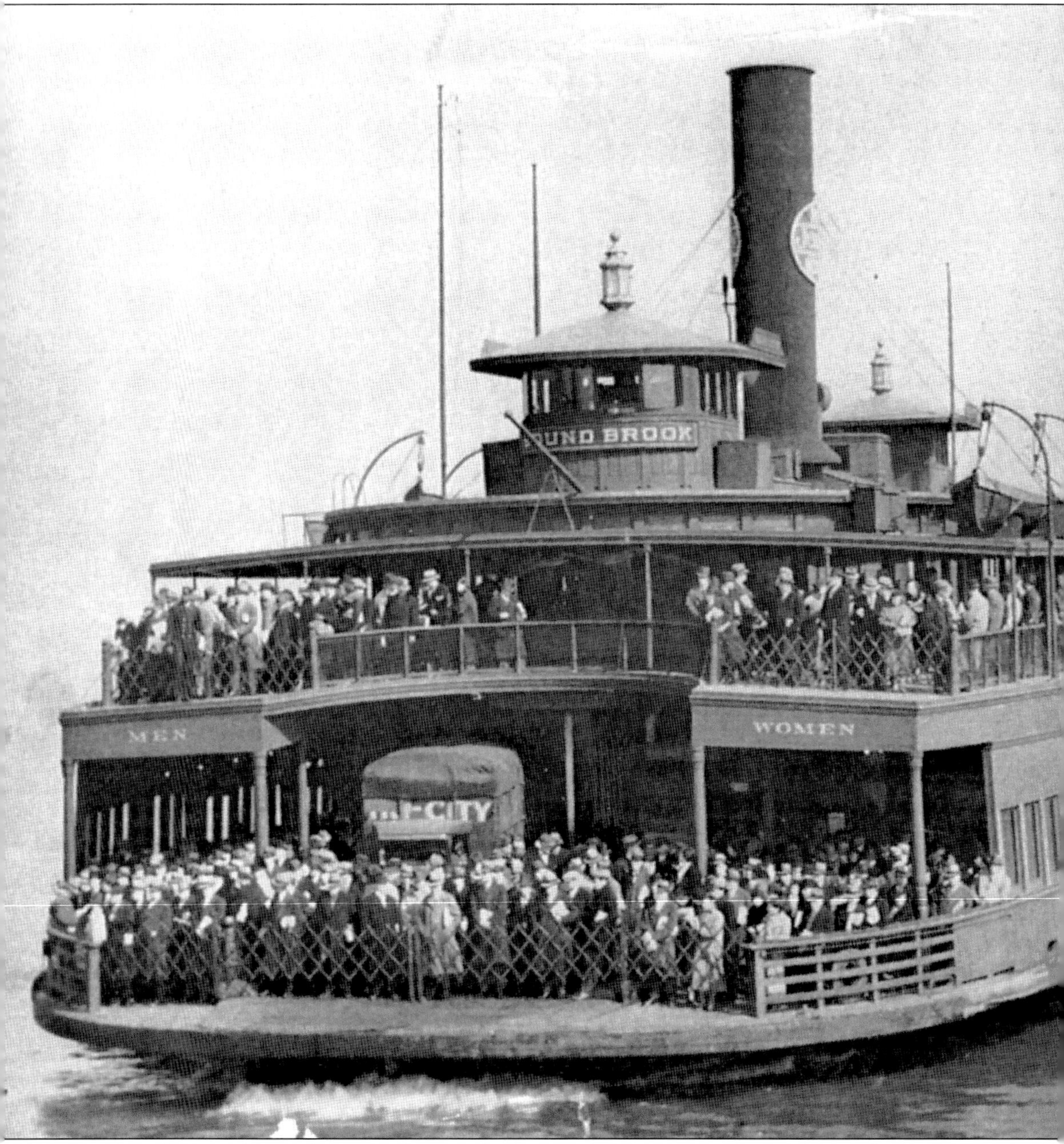

The Central Railroad ran a fleet of ferries on the Hudson River, providing a connection from Jersey City to New York. The ferries were named for local towns. Here, our namesake ferry, *Bound Brook*, transports a boatload of city-bound commuters.

Caught with no fire companies when the fire of 1881 destroyed most of the town's business area, the town fathers quickly remedied the defect with the fire companies shown here.

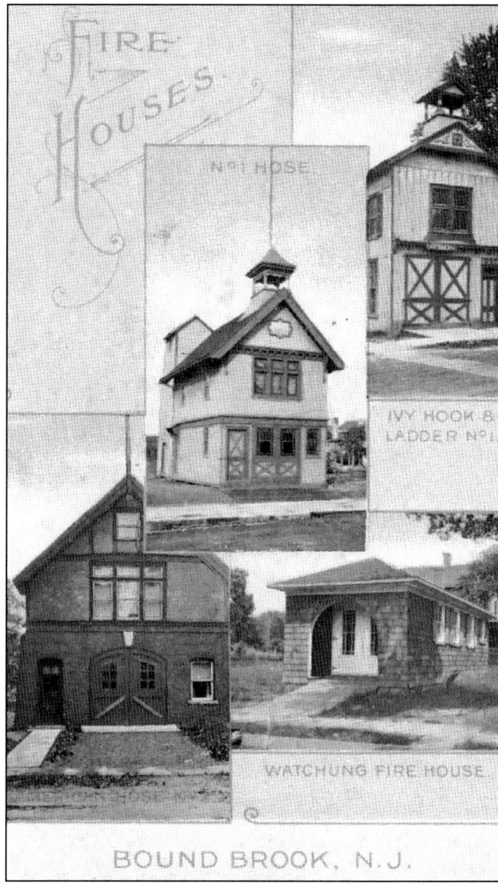

The Einstein Brothers sold their interest in Woolen Mills in Somerville and built the Mills in Bound Brook. This brought experienced mill workers from the New England states and provided jobs for a number of local residents.

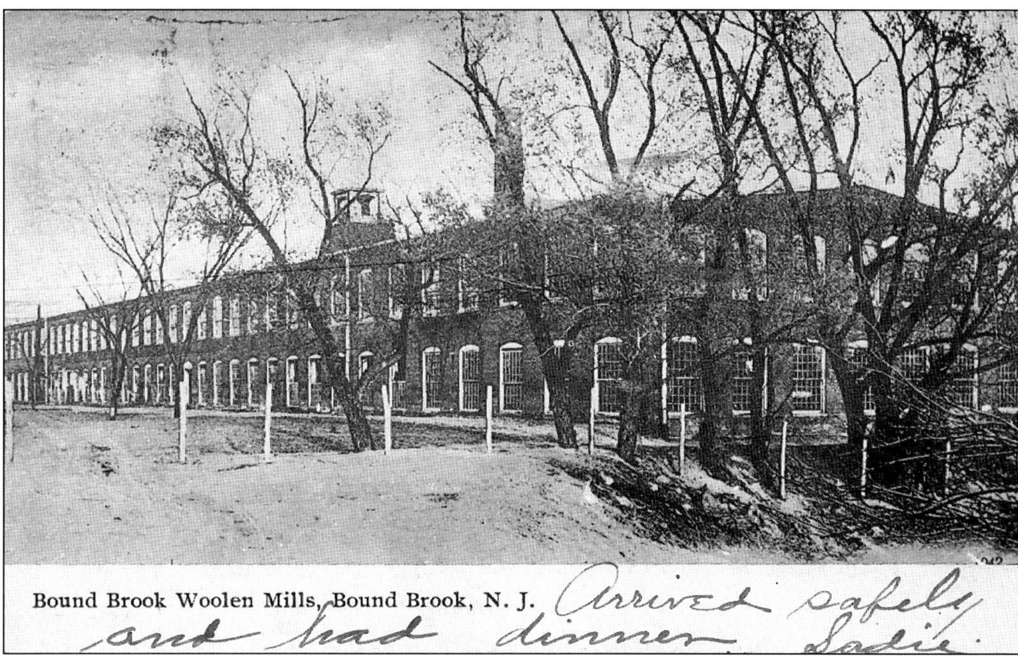

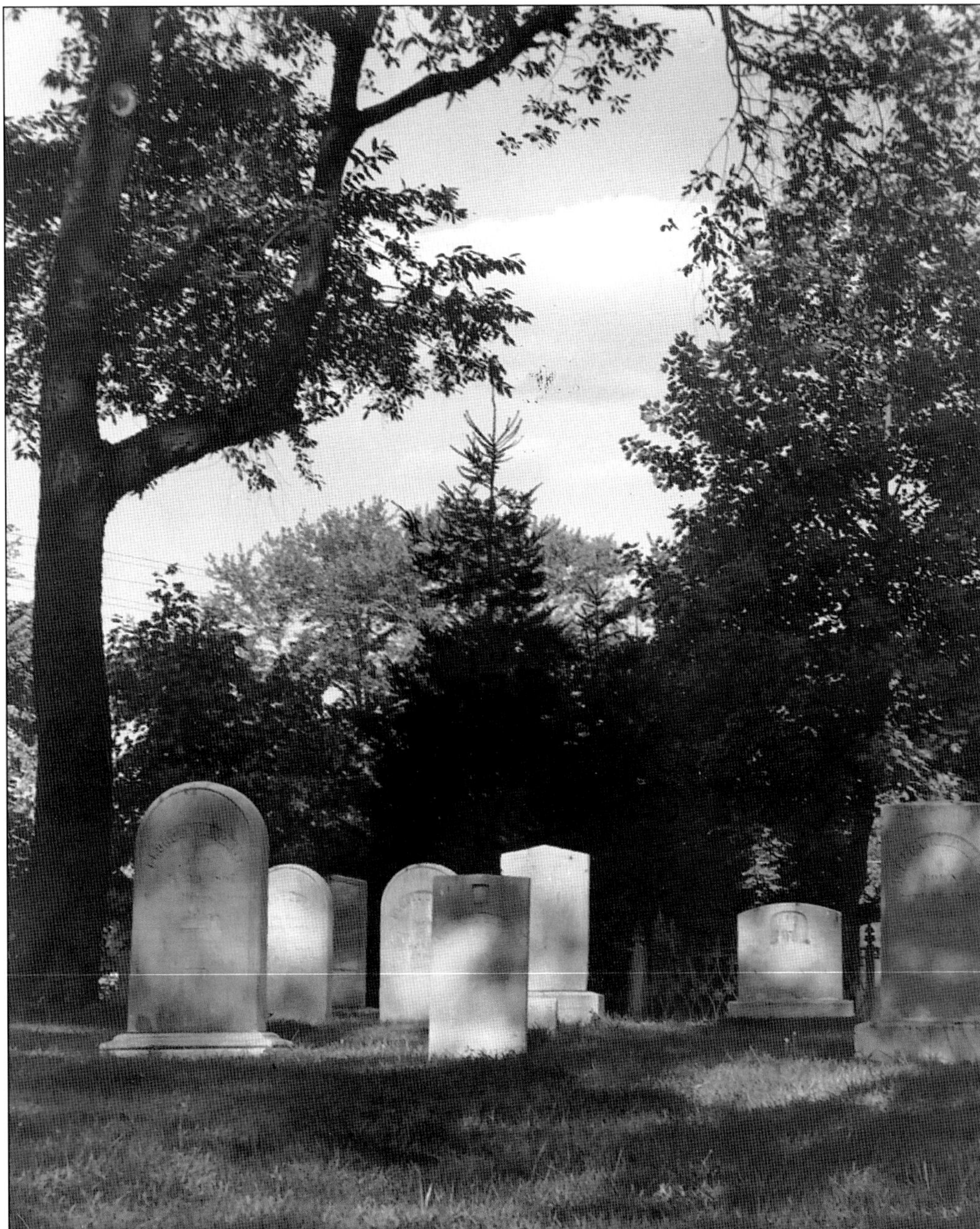

The old Presbyterian Burying Ground was the final resting-place of many soldiers of the American Revolution. George LaMonte bought the cemetery from the Presbyterian Church and designated the Daughters of the American Revolution as caretakers of the property.

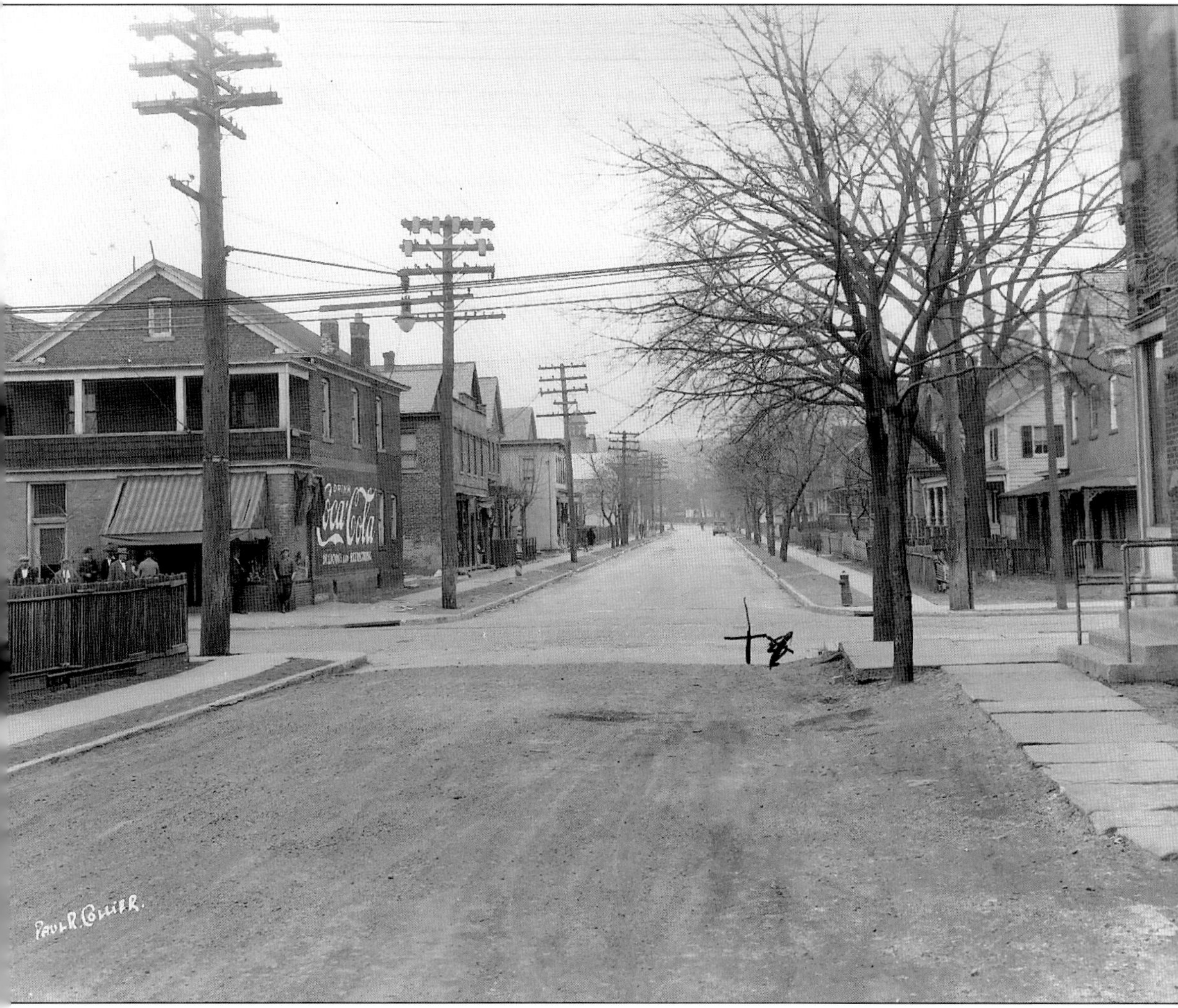

This 1929 photograph shows a view of the intersection of Vosseller Avenue and Talmage Avenue. St. Mary's Church steeple is in the background, and a number of small stores line Vosseller Avenue.

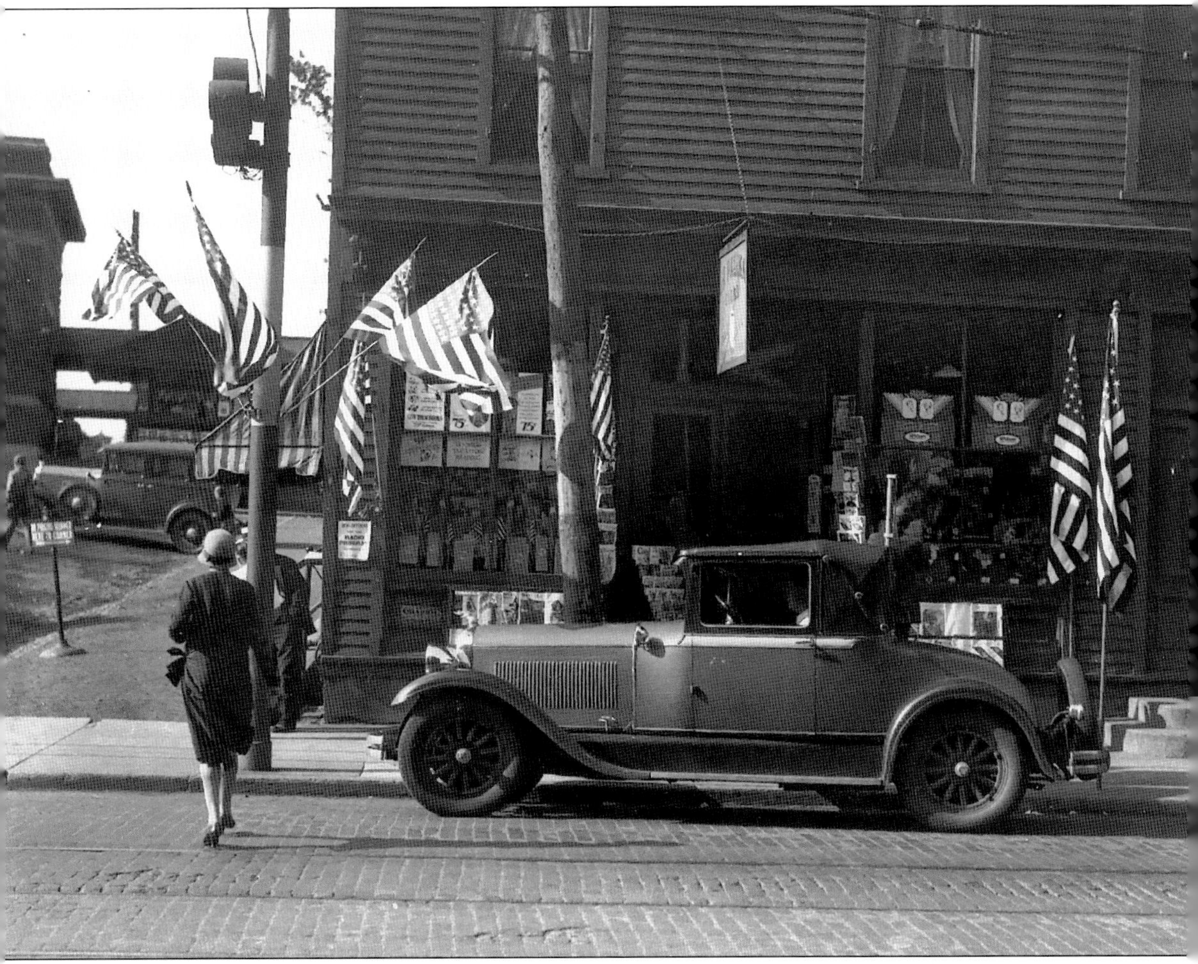

Brick pavement and trolley tracks are in full view in this flag-bedecked shot of Main Street near the train station in 1932. Hoagland's newspaper and bookstore form the backdrop.

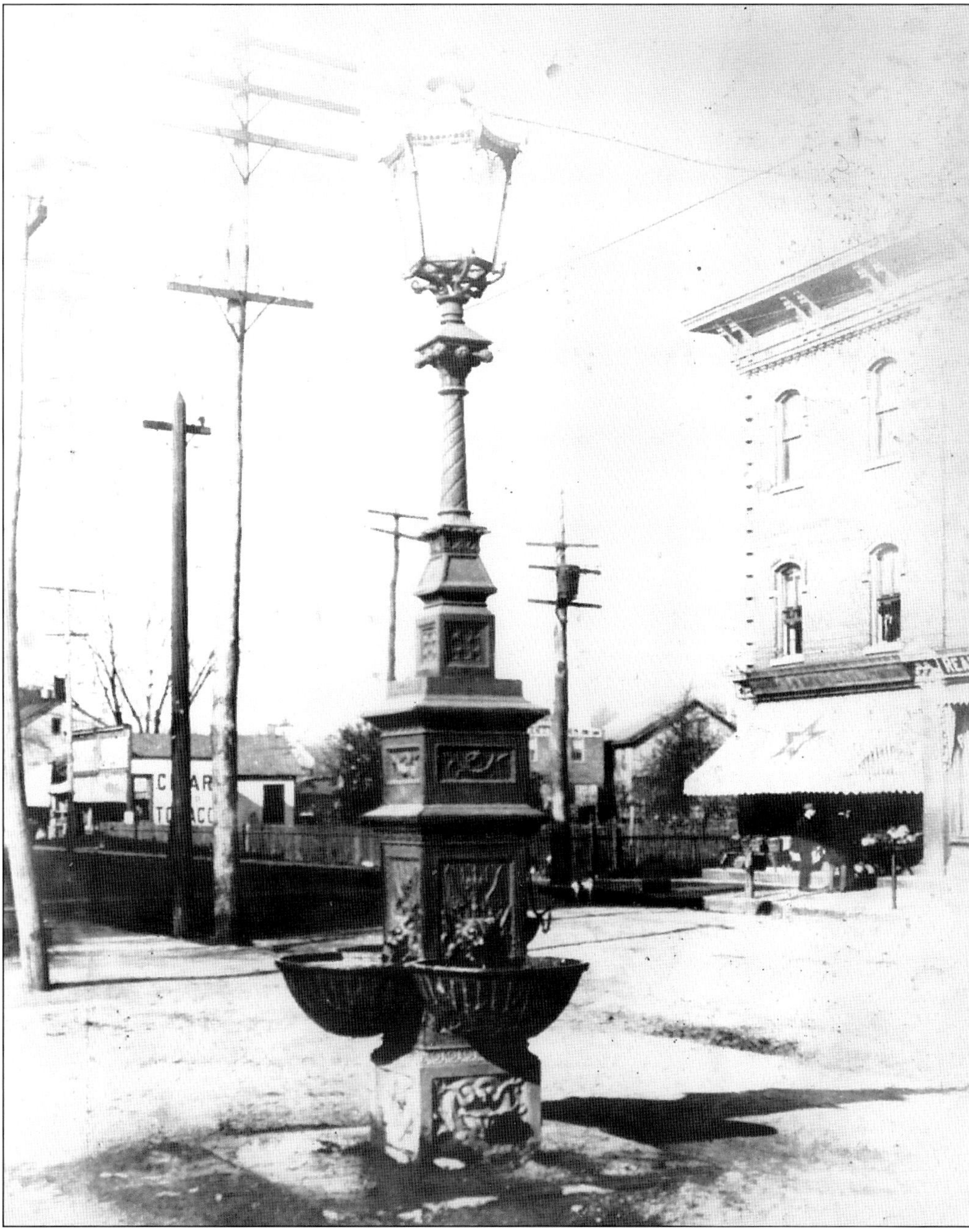

In 1896, the Camp Middlebrook chapter of the Daughters of the American Revolution raised $860 to purchase and maintain this fountain supplying "good water for man and beast." The structure was dismantled and sold for scrap in 1900, after it sustained extensive damage by horses and heavy wagons.

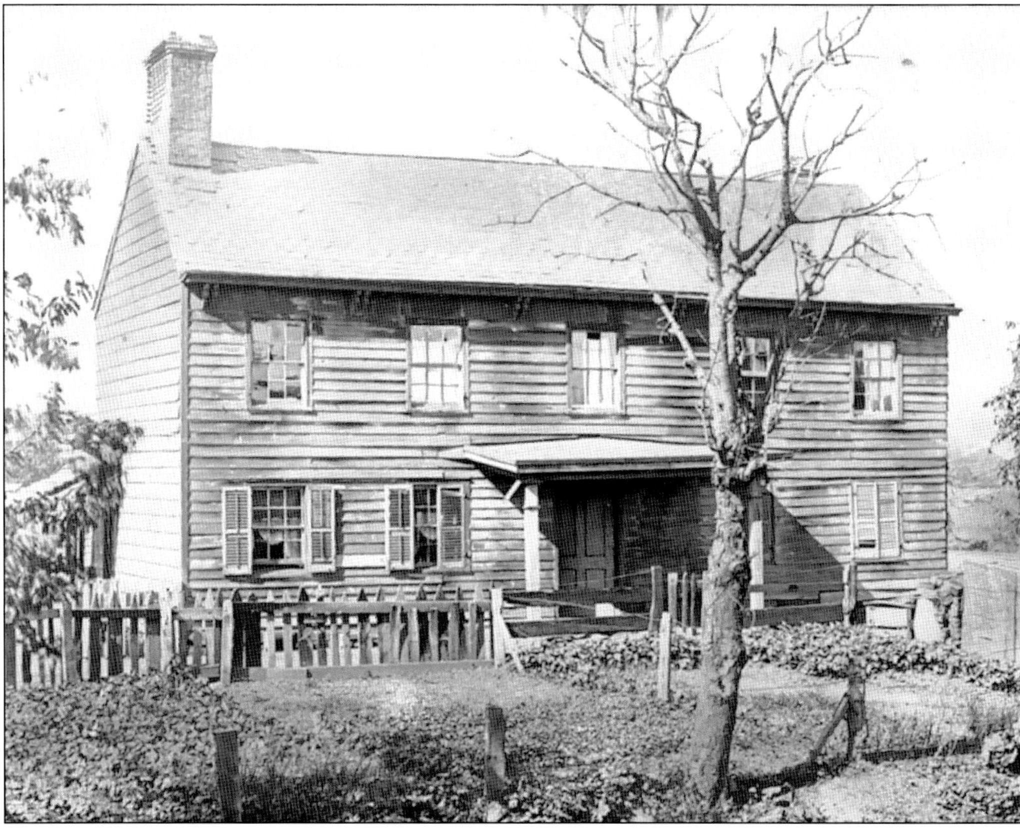

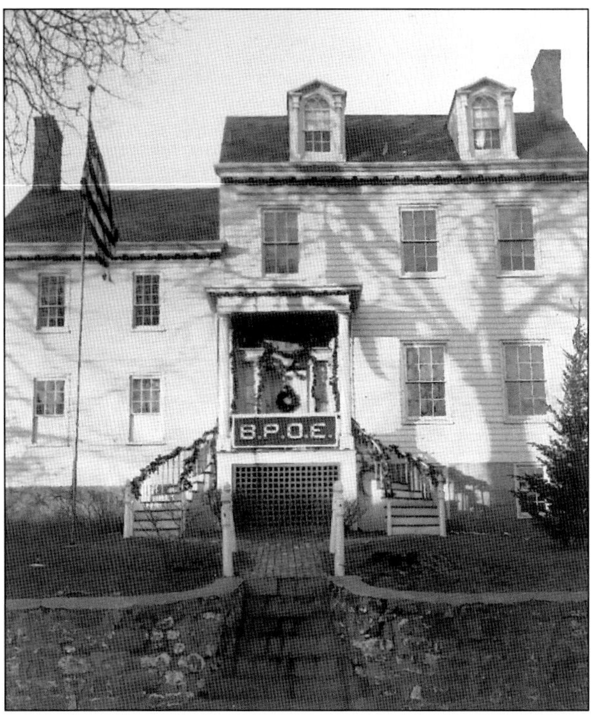

The Battery, or Williamson House, once stood on the site of the Bolmer Motor Company building. It served as part of the defense of the village from British attack. Later, it served as stone yard for Ellis Yawger.

The Ball House occupied the northeast corner of Second Street and Maiden Lane. Purchased by the Board of Trade for their headquarters, it was subsequently sold to the Elks and razed to make room for their new clubhouse.

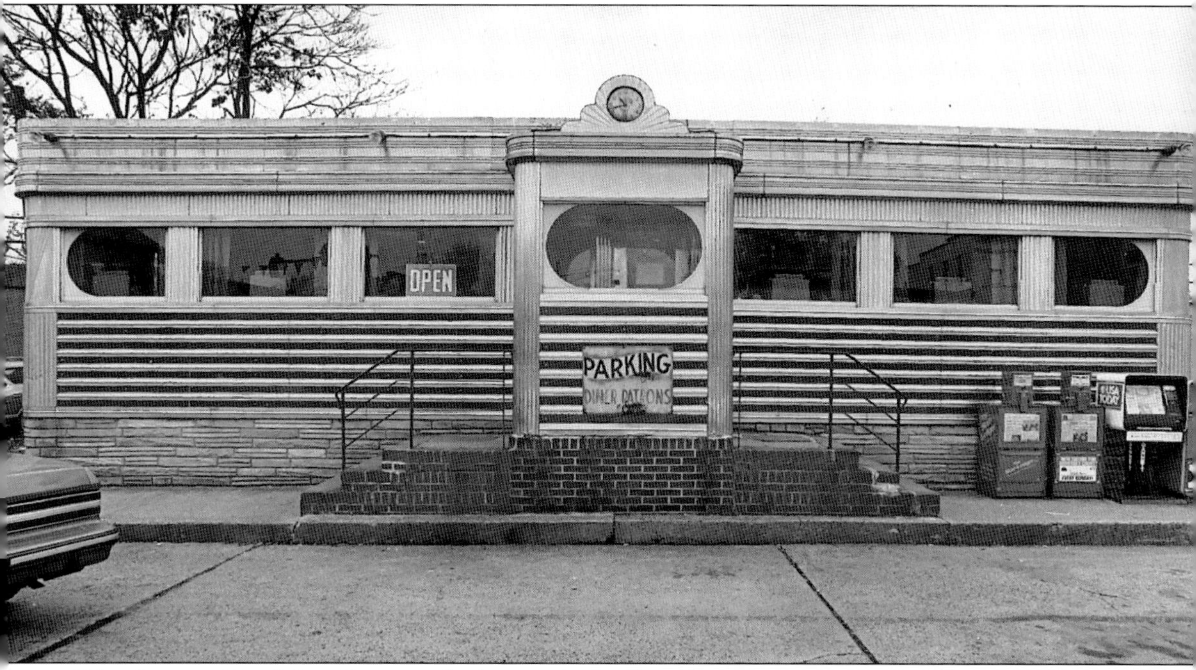

The diner on East Main Street is the latest of several similar eateries to occupy the site. In diner architecture, it is "an unassuming little gem" to those in the know.

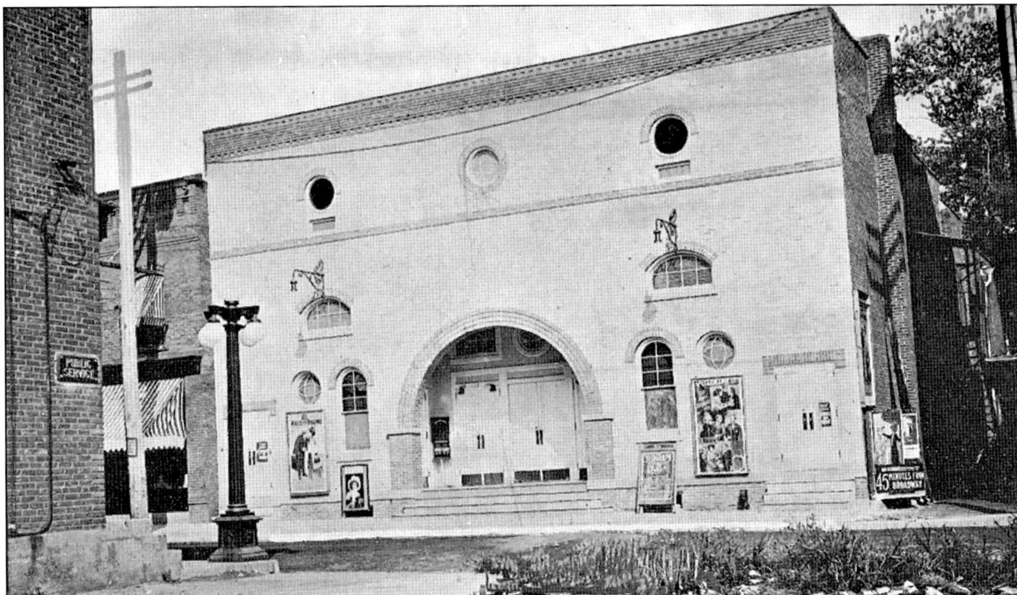

NEW PALACE THEATRE, Bound Brook, N. J.

The Palace Theater on Maiden Lane offered a variety of entertainment—minstrel shows, live plays, silent movies—and eventually replaced Bound Brook Hall and Voorhees Hall as a venue for these productions. In its heyday, it boasted a fine pit orchestra.

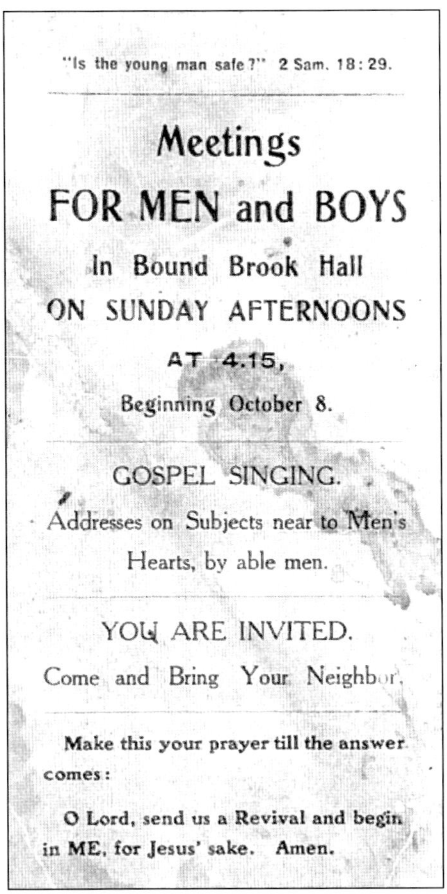

"Is the young man safe?" 2 Sam. 18:29.

Meetings

FOR MEN and BOYS

In Bound Brook Hall

ON SUNDAY AFTERNOONS

AT 4.15,

Beginning October 8.

GOSPEL SINGING.

Addresses on Subjects near to Men's Hearts, by able men.

YOU ARE INVITED.

Come and Bring Your Neighbor.

Make this your prayer till the answer comes:

O Lord, send us a Revival and begin in ME, for Jesus' sake. Amen.

In addition to operating a library and public reading room, the Men's Reform Club also held weekly meetings for men of the town—especially those who came to Bound Brook to work in the mills and factories in the late 19th century.

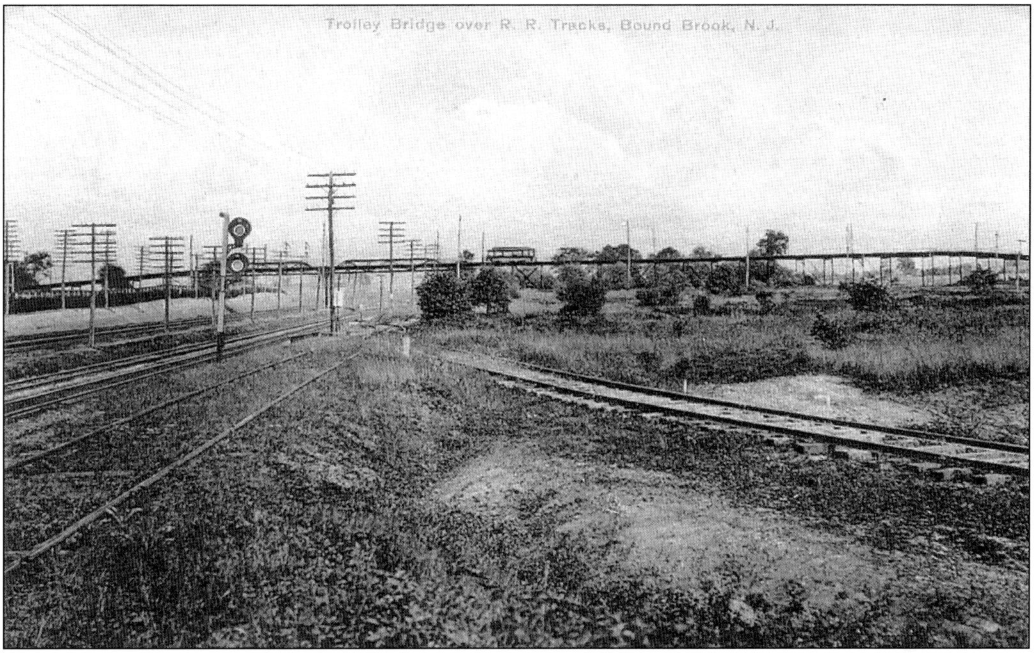

The Brunswick Traction Company erected this wonderful elevated roadway to provide transit for trolleys over extensive railroad tracks east of town.

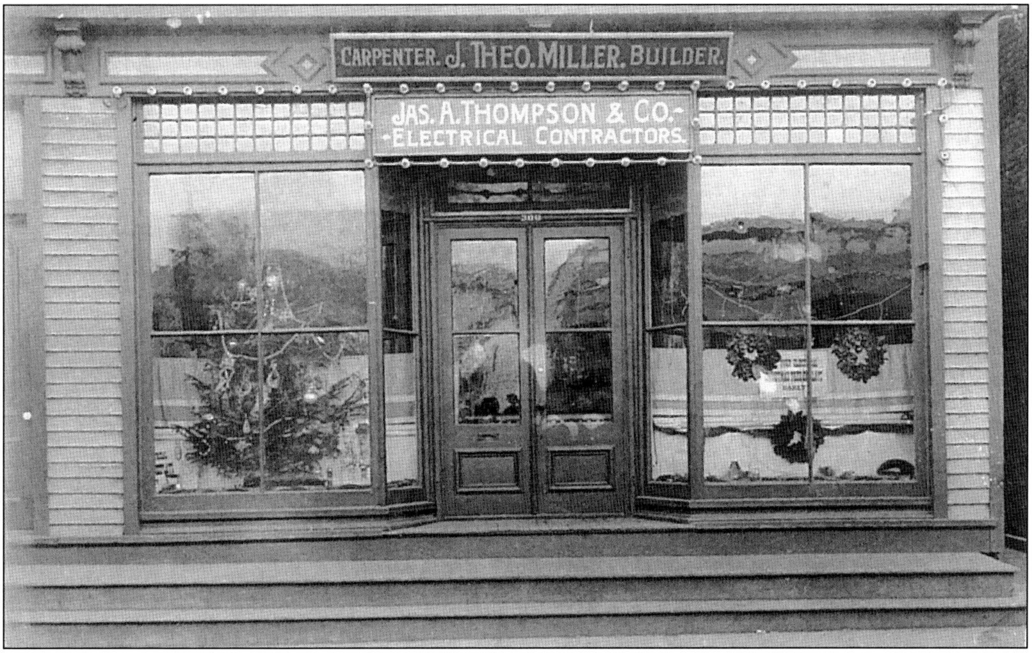

J. Theodore Miller had a construction business office in the building that also housed the post office. Located on East Main Street, it is seen here decorated for the holiday season.

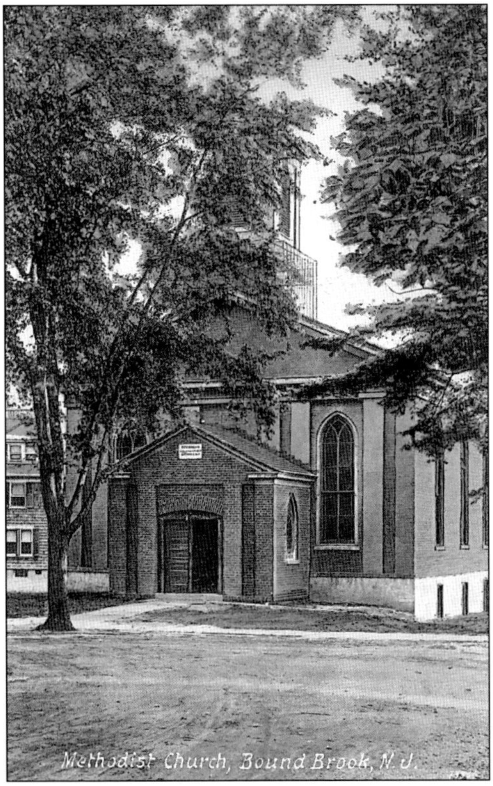

Facing Main Street for the first four decades of its existence, this Methodist church building was moved to Second Street when the original site became too commercial. The Methodist Church later sold the building to the Masonic Order and rebuilt on Union Avenue.

In the early years of the 20th century, this house and property on Mountain Avenue was offered for sale at $12,000. Once known as the Garretson property, it has been the home of the Prugh family most recently.

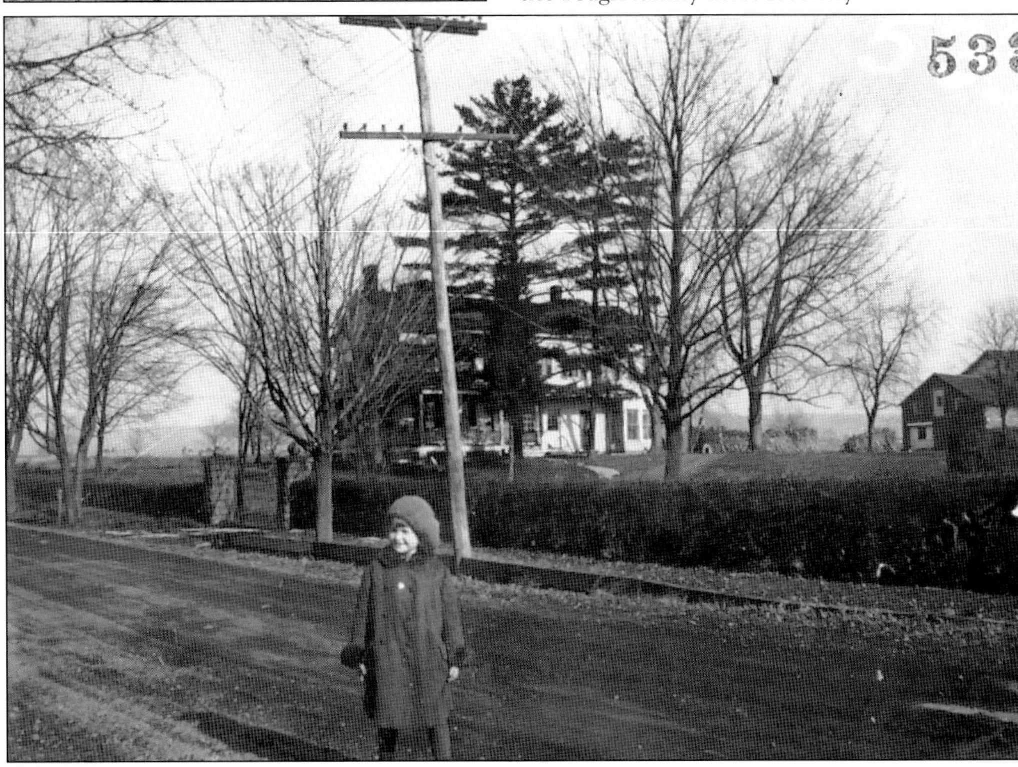

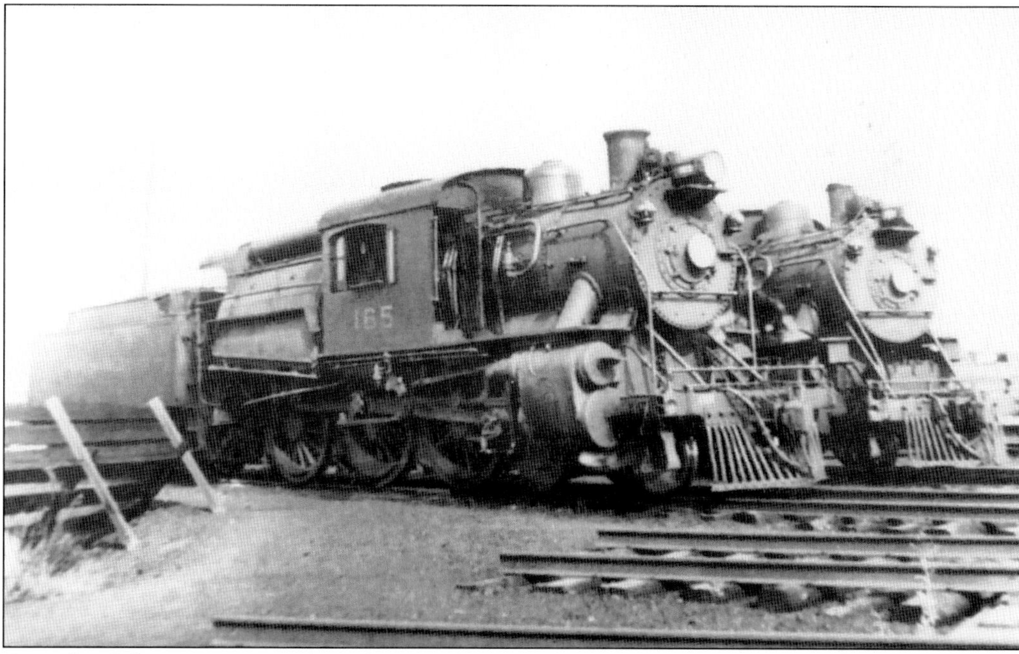

Camelback locomotives, such as the pair shown, were common sights in the pre-WWII years in Bound Brook, even as the town's busy railroad era was rapidly ending.

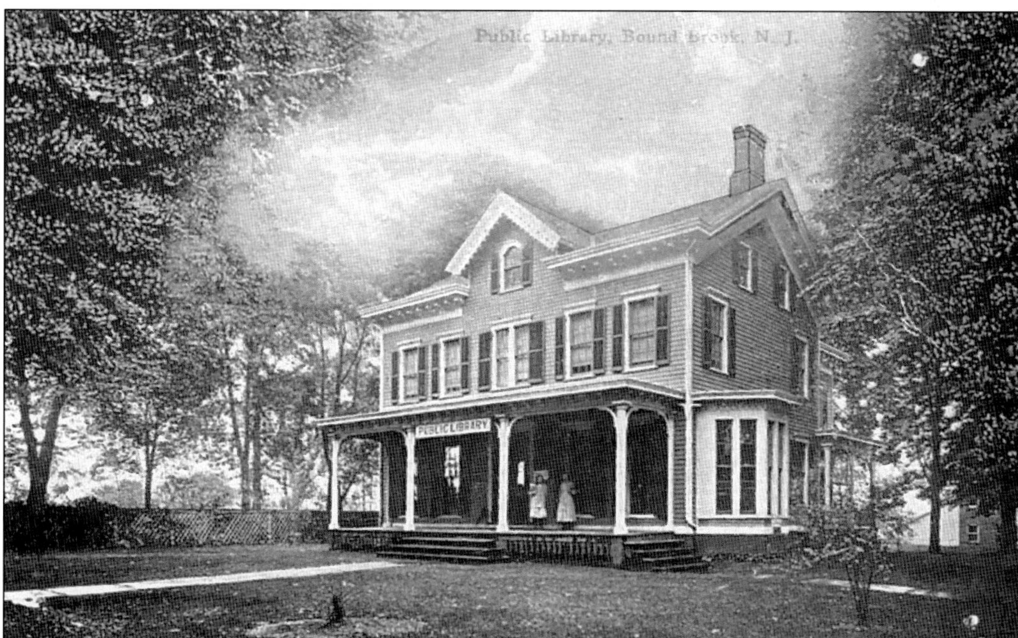

The Taylor family home on the corner of High and Hamilton Streets was purchased by George LaMonte and given as a home for the public library. The library was operated at the time by the Woman's Literary Club. Early librarians cleaned the lamps, swept the floors, and kept track of the books.

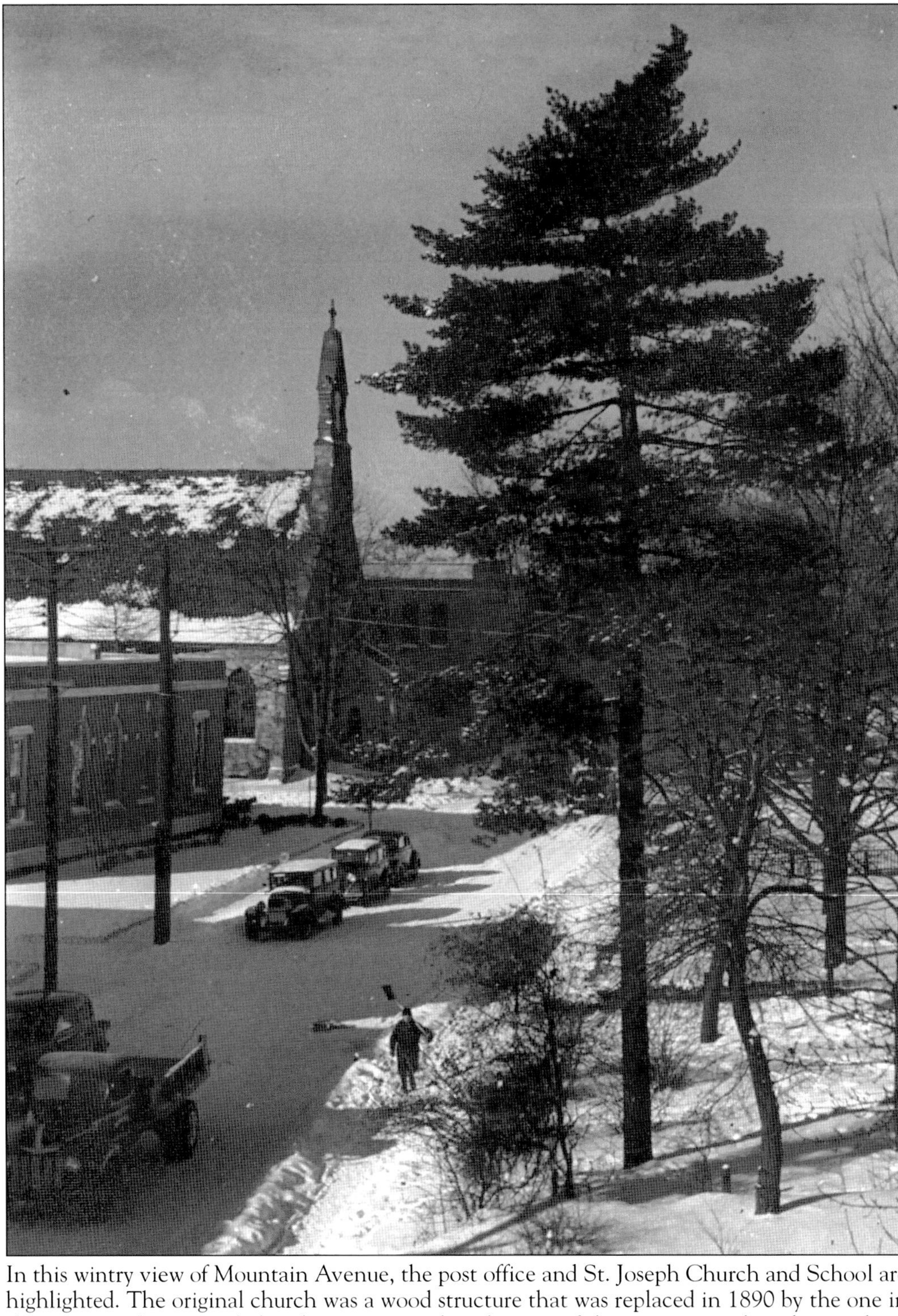

In this wintry view of Mountain Avenue, the post office and St. Joseph Church and School are highlighted. The original church was a wood structure that was replaced in 1890 by the one in the picture. The original church was removed to the rear of the property and used as a school by the parish.

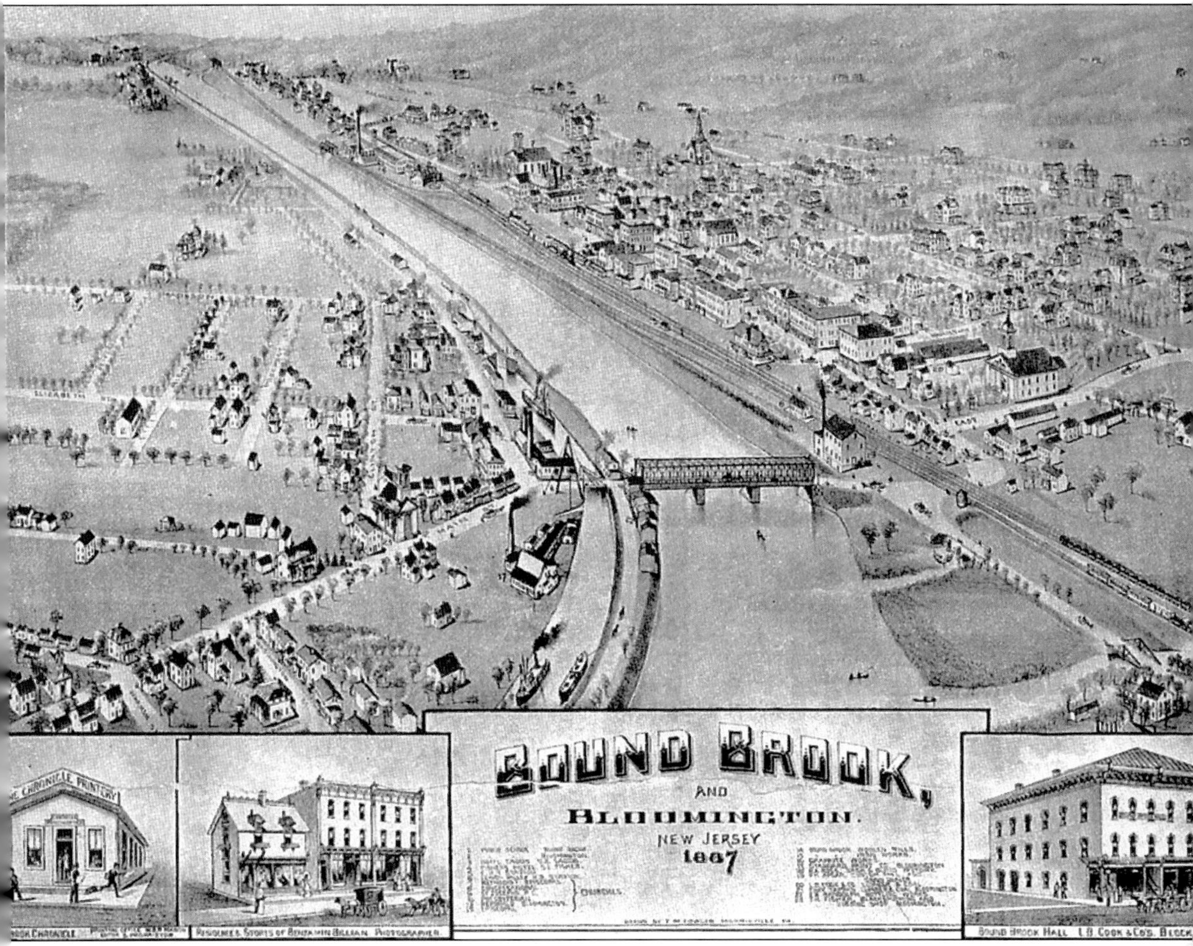

By 1887, Bound Brook had grown from a sleepy village to an important railroad town and a budding manufacturing site. This was due to its close proximity to the Delaware and Raritan Canal, Raritan River, and rail access. This map depicts the location of the businesses and residences of the time.

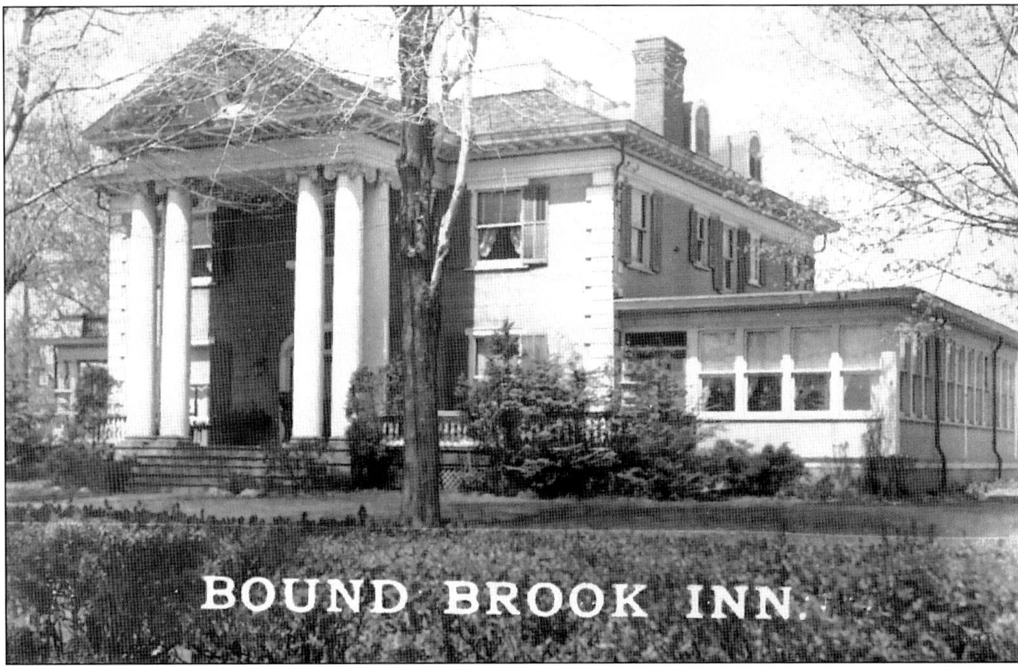

William Robeson purchased 3 acres of land and an existing house on West Union Avenue in 1900. Alterations and additions produced the look shown here. Alfred Nangeroni bought the property in 1922 and ran the popular Bound Brook Inn on the site.

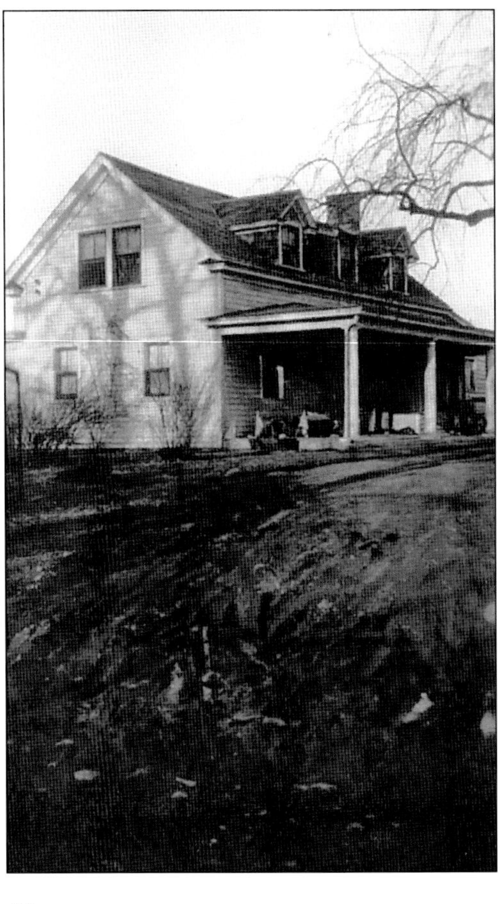

The Jonathan Smith house stood on the east side of Tea Street, a short distance north of Union Avenue. Built c. 1800, it was destroyed by fire not long after this 1922 photograph was taken. The Bound Brook apartments now occupy this site.

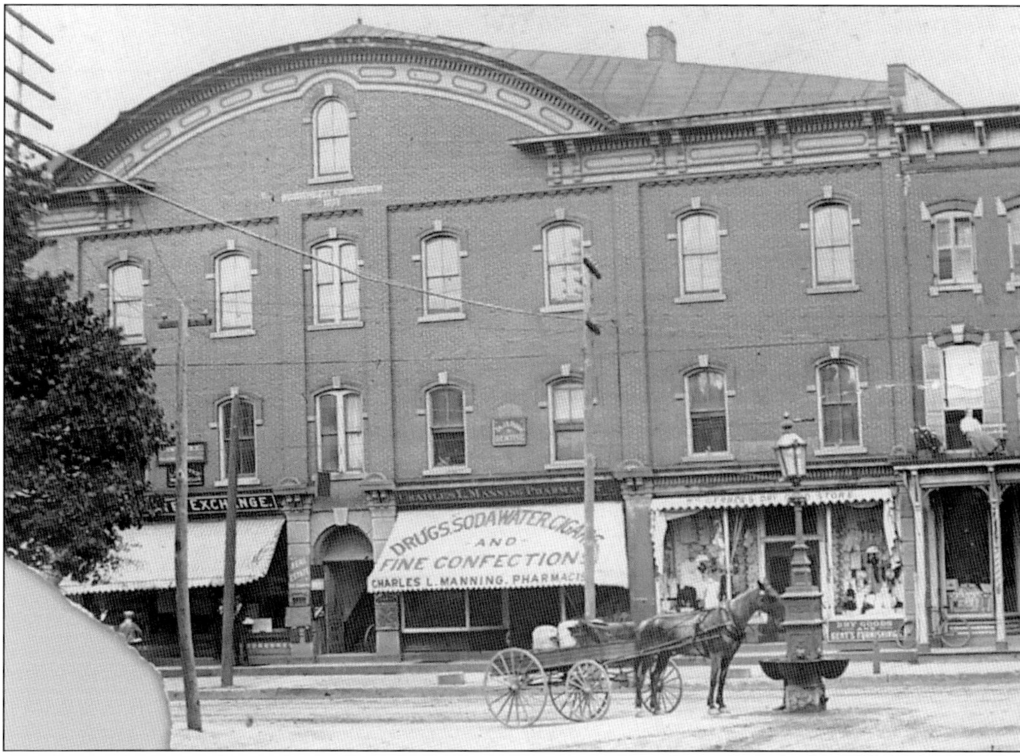

The Voorhees building's distinctive architecture makes it a local landmark. Constructed on the block destroyed by fire in 1881, the third-floor ballroom was the site of many local functions. The Daughters of the American Revolution fountain is seen in the foreground.

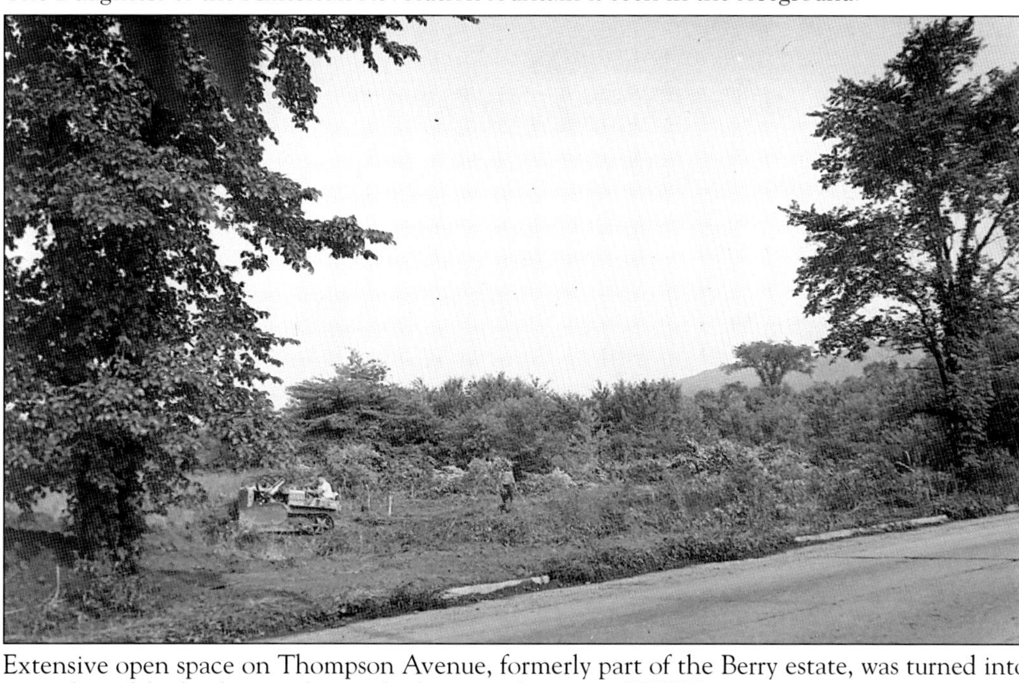

Extensive open space on Thompson Avenue, formerly part of the Berry estate, was turned into a number of duplex houses during the housing shortage of WWII.

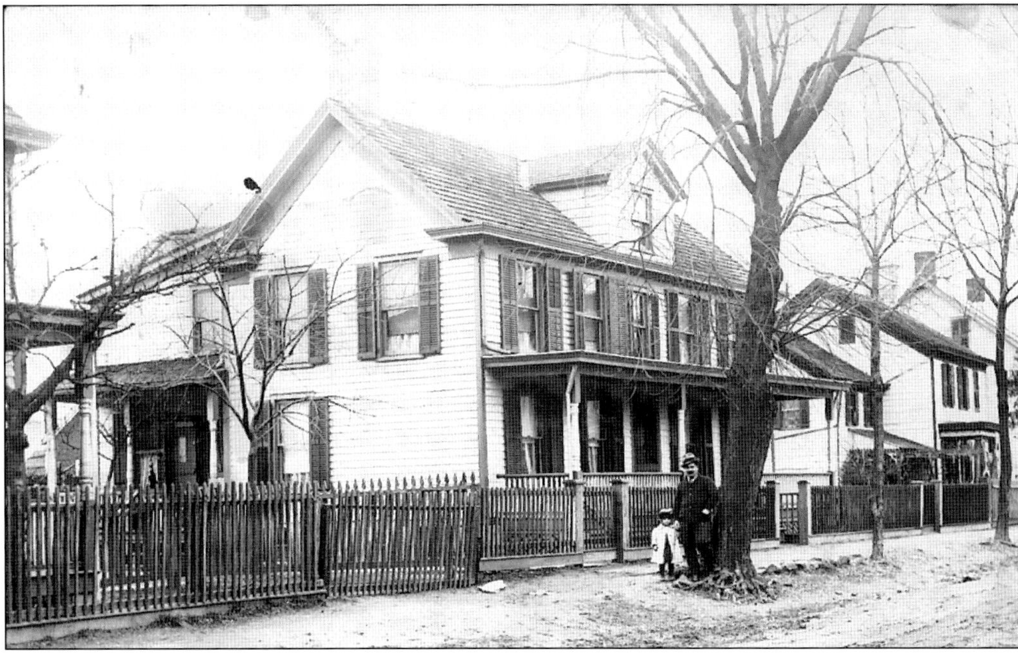

Frank Ciccone purchased this house on West Main Street (Middlebrook) in 1890. Anthony and Theodora Ciccone pose there in this 1912 photograph.

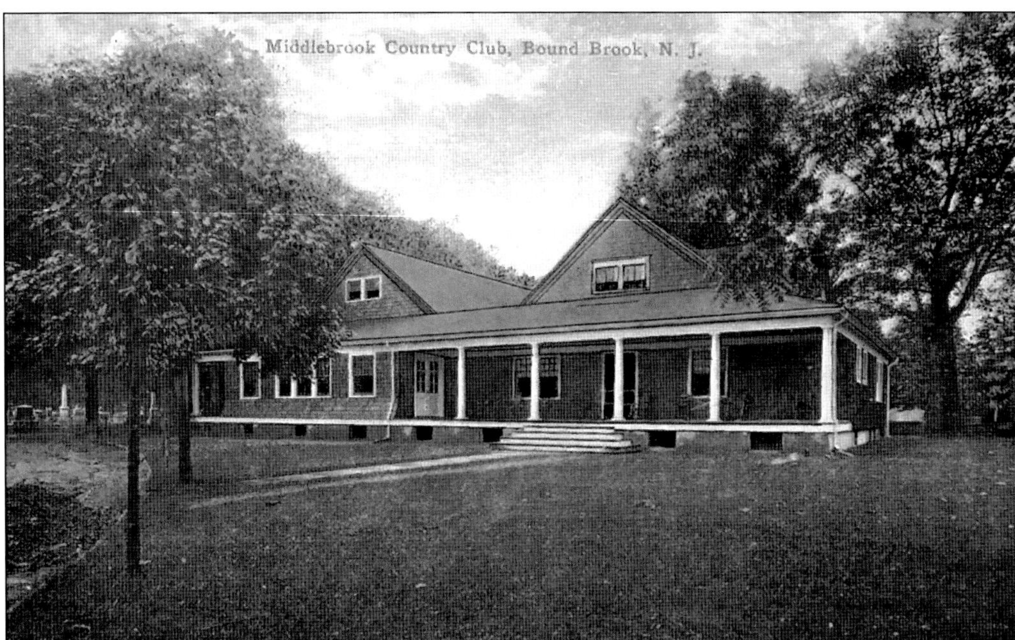

Middlebrook Country Club, included as part of LaMonte's Middlebrook Heights project, was constructed with many large timbers that were felled on the property. A golf course was also part of the facility for a number of years.

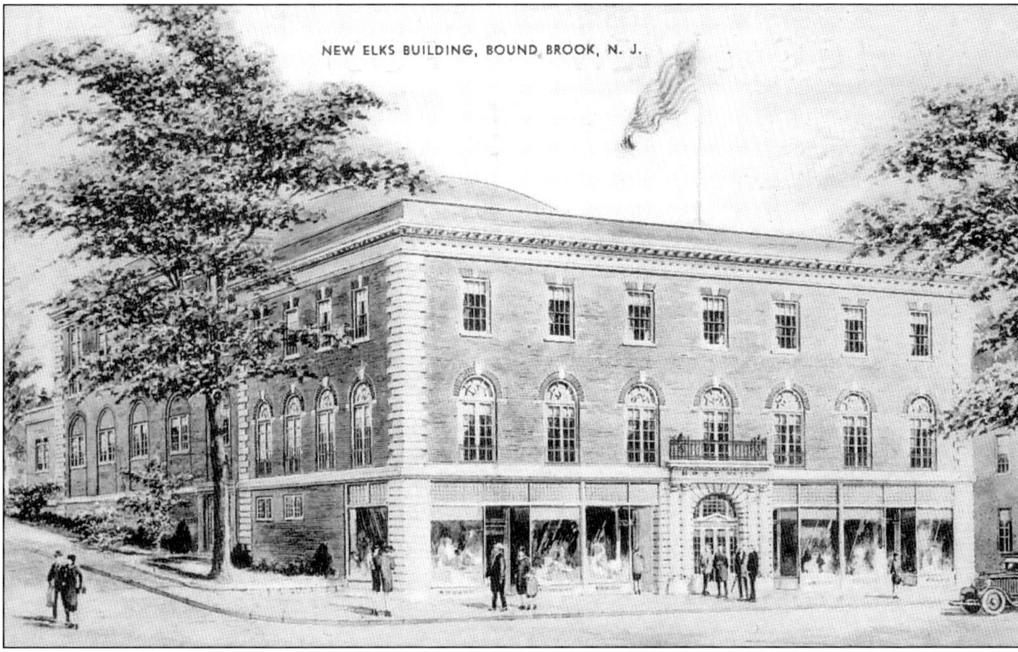

Located on the northeast corner of Second Street and Maiden Lane, the Elks building was constructed on the site of the Ball House.

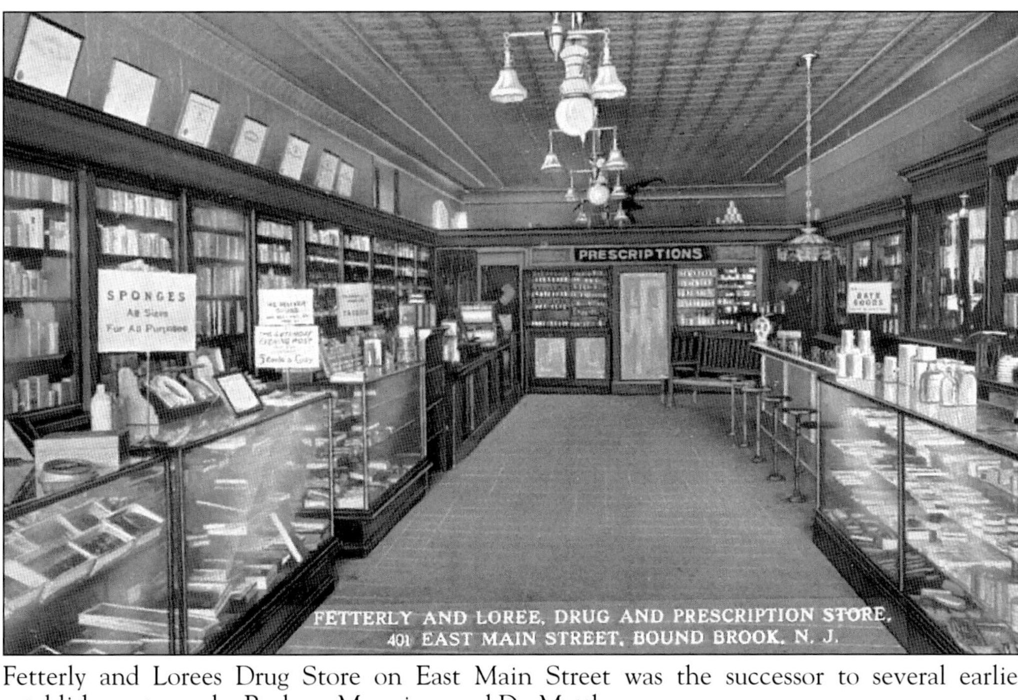

Fetterly and Lorees Drug Store on East Main Street was the successor to several earlier establishments run by Brokaw, Manning, and Dr. Matthews.

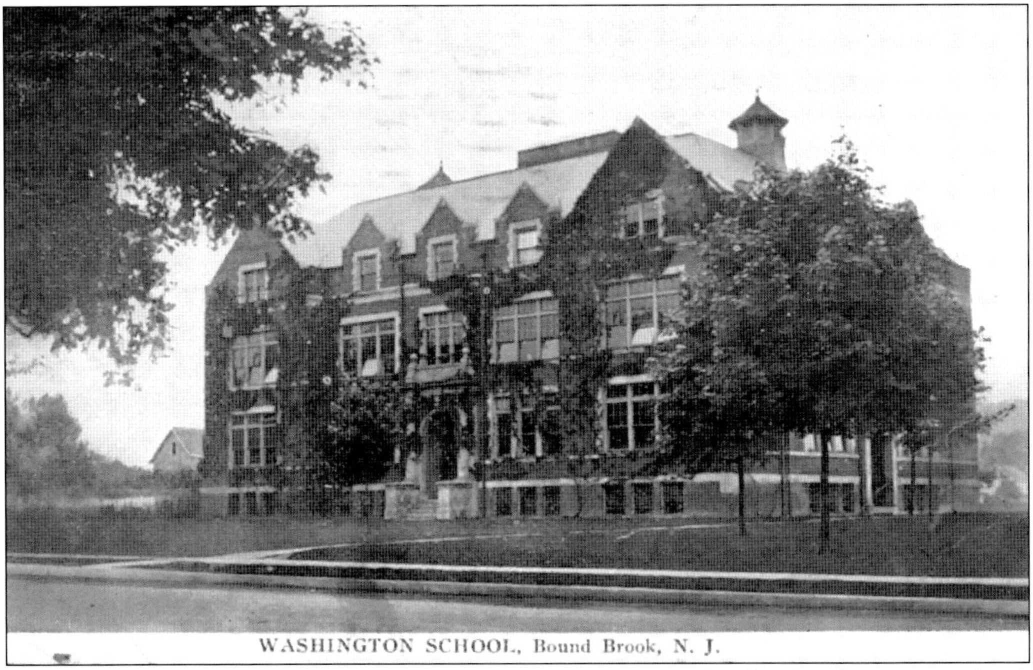

Washington School, completed in 1907, was the home of the high school and grammar school. At the time, it was a state-of-the-art building. Students commuted from as far away as Belle Meade and Weston by train.

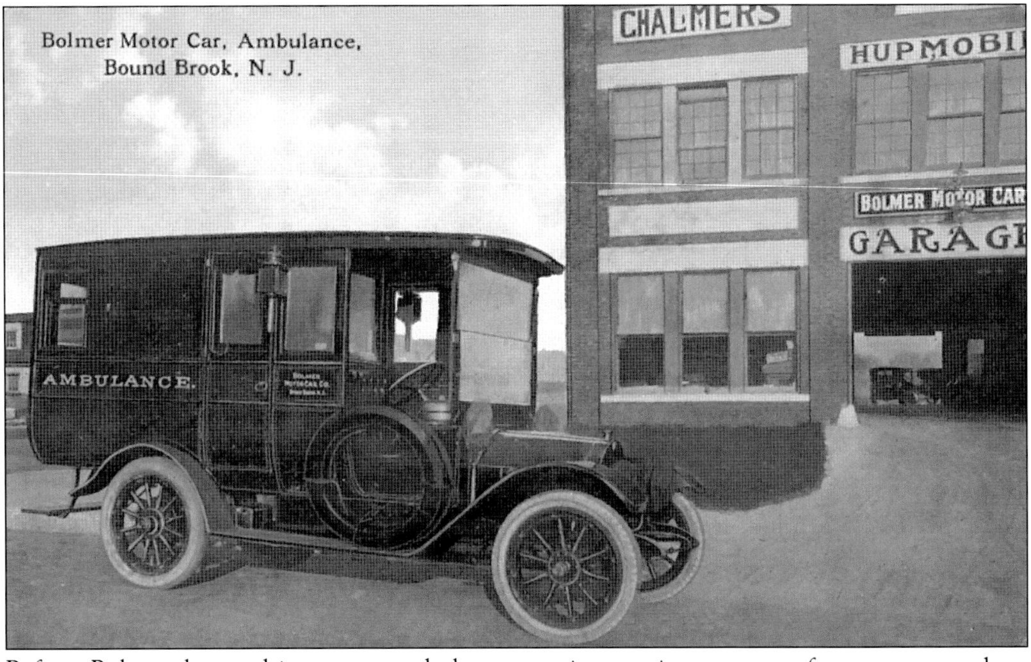

Before Bolmer began his motor ambulance service, patients were often transported to Muhlenberg Hospital via the railroad after being treated at the scene by local physicians.

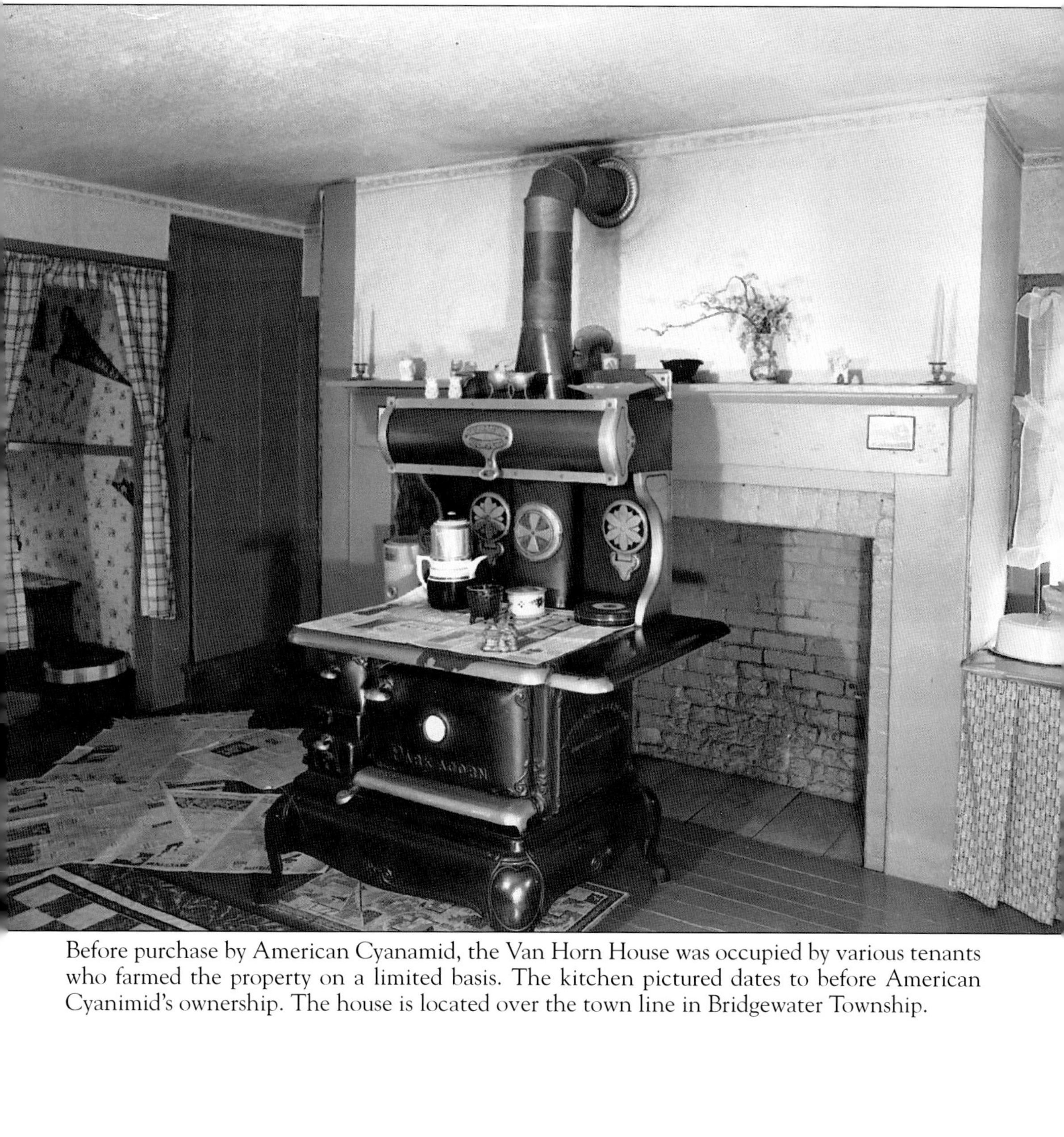

Before purchase by American Cyanamid, the Van Horn House was occupied by various tenants who farmed the property on a limited basis. The kitchen pictured dates to before American Cyanimid's ownership. The house is located over the town line in Bridgewater Township.

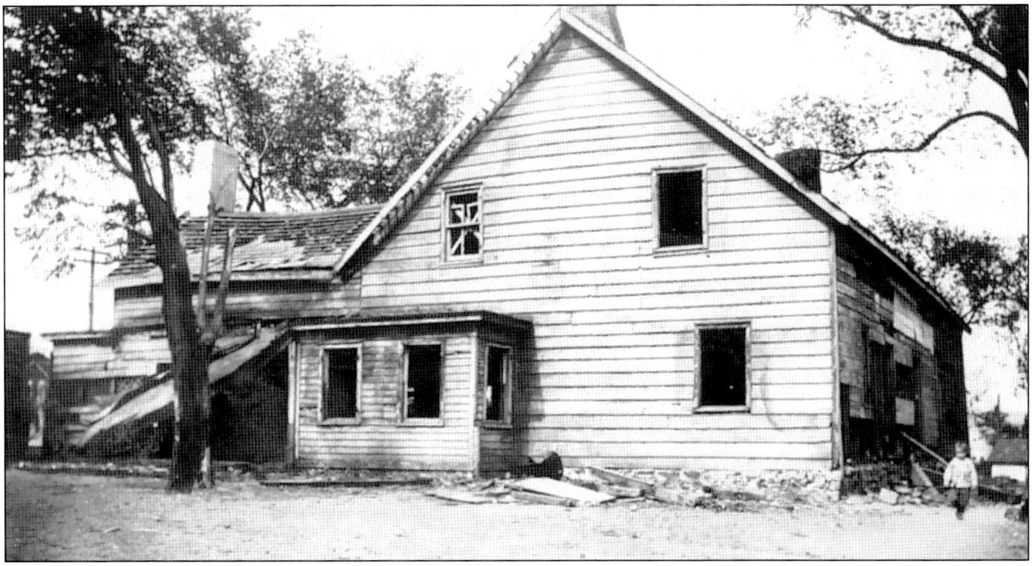

A derelict Fisher's Hotel is shown just before being razed in the 1920s. This was truly a sad ending for the once busy hostelry, whose death knell was sounded first by the railroad and later by Prohibition.

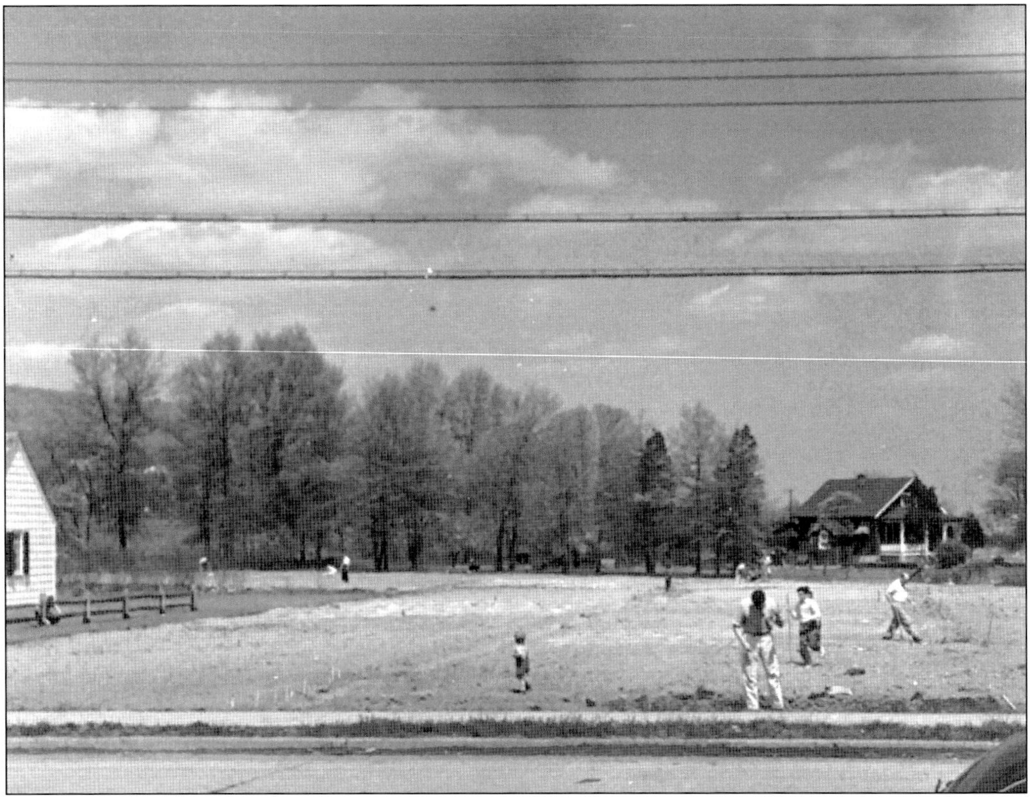

Victory Gardens were a part of the local scene during WWII, when everyone was encouraged to grow as much food as possible. Open plots of land on Thompson Avenue were used for this purpose as shown in this 1944 view.

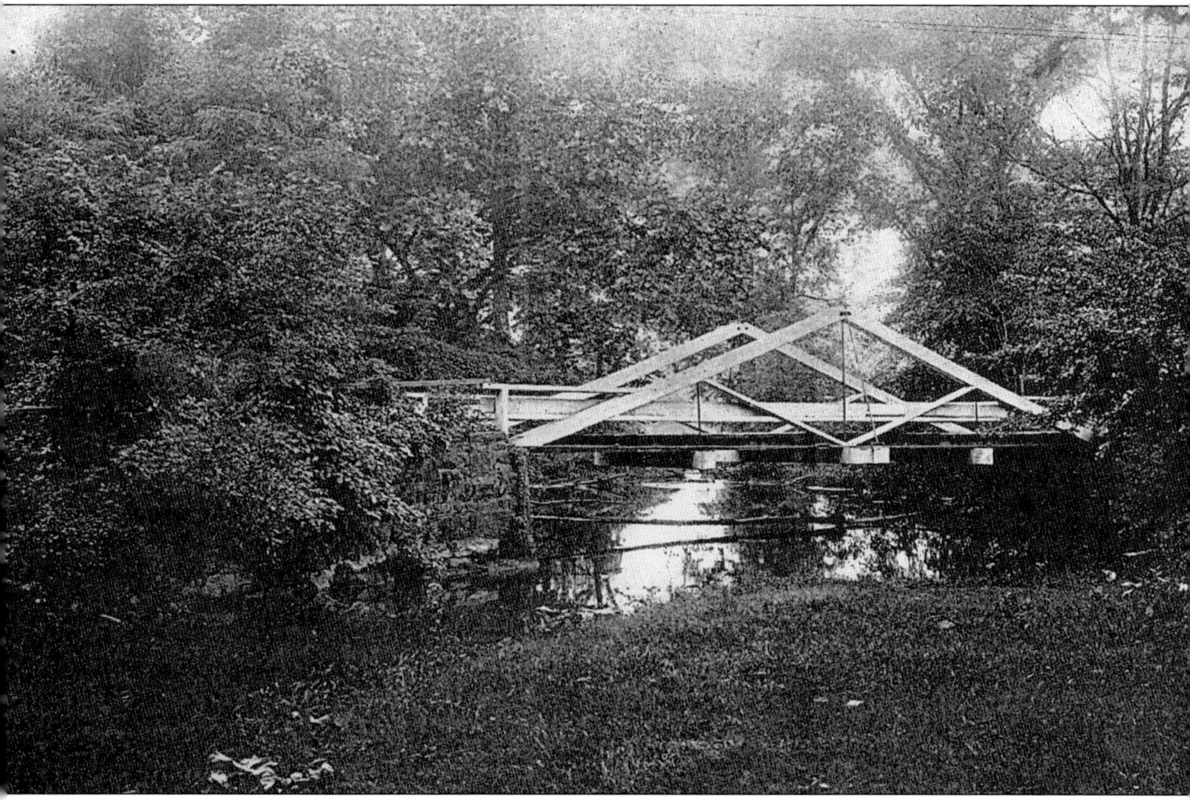

This iron bridge over the Green Brook on Shepherd Avenue has been replaced by a modern structure. The Shepherds were early settlers of this section of Middlesex Borough bordering Bound Brook. They owned many acres of fine land on which they raised purebred horses at one time.

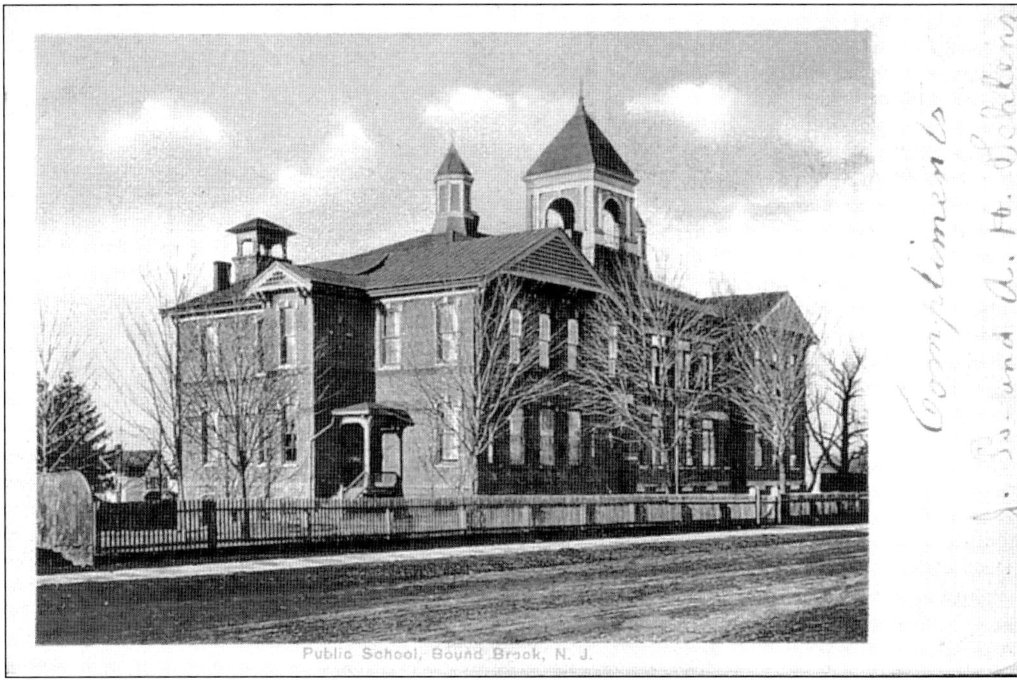

Lafayette School, completed in 1883, was the first modern school in town. Earlier, much smaller schools had been located in several parts of the village, including the Willow Grove School over the Middlebrook west of town, which still stands as a dwelling house on Talmage Avenue. The building pictured was replaced in 1961 following a fire.

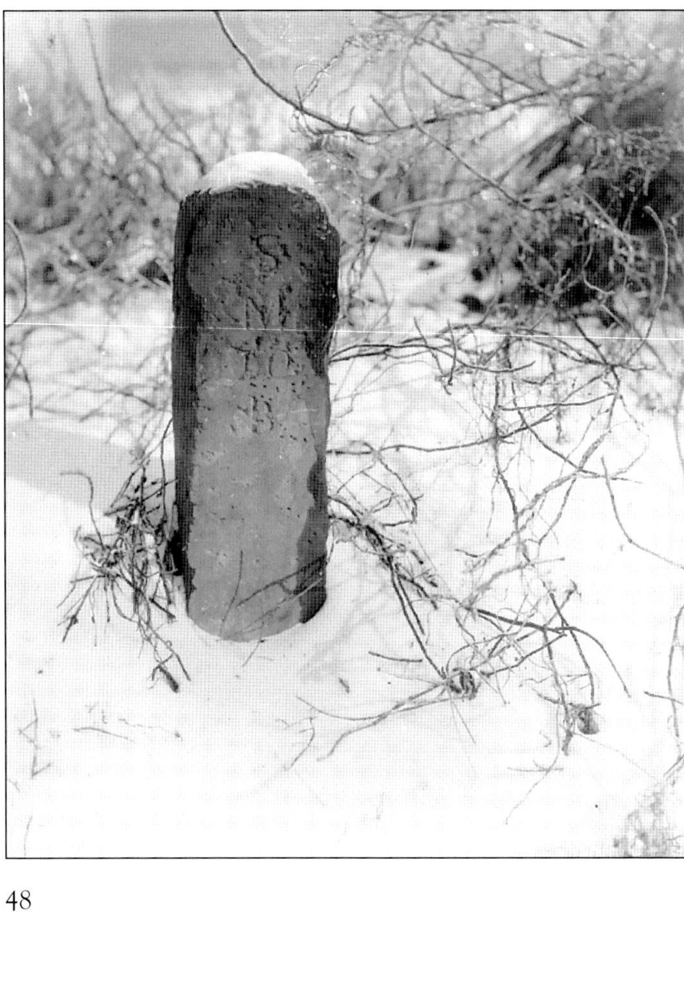

In 1806, construction was begun on the original New Jersey Turnpike from New Brunswick to Phillipsburg. Mile markers such as this one were installed along the road to aid the traveler. This one was located on the road just west of town, not far from the tollgate.

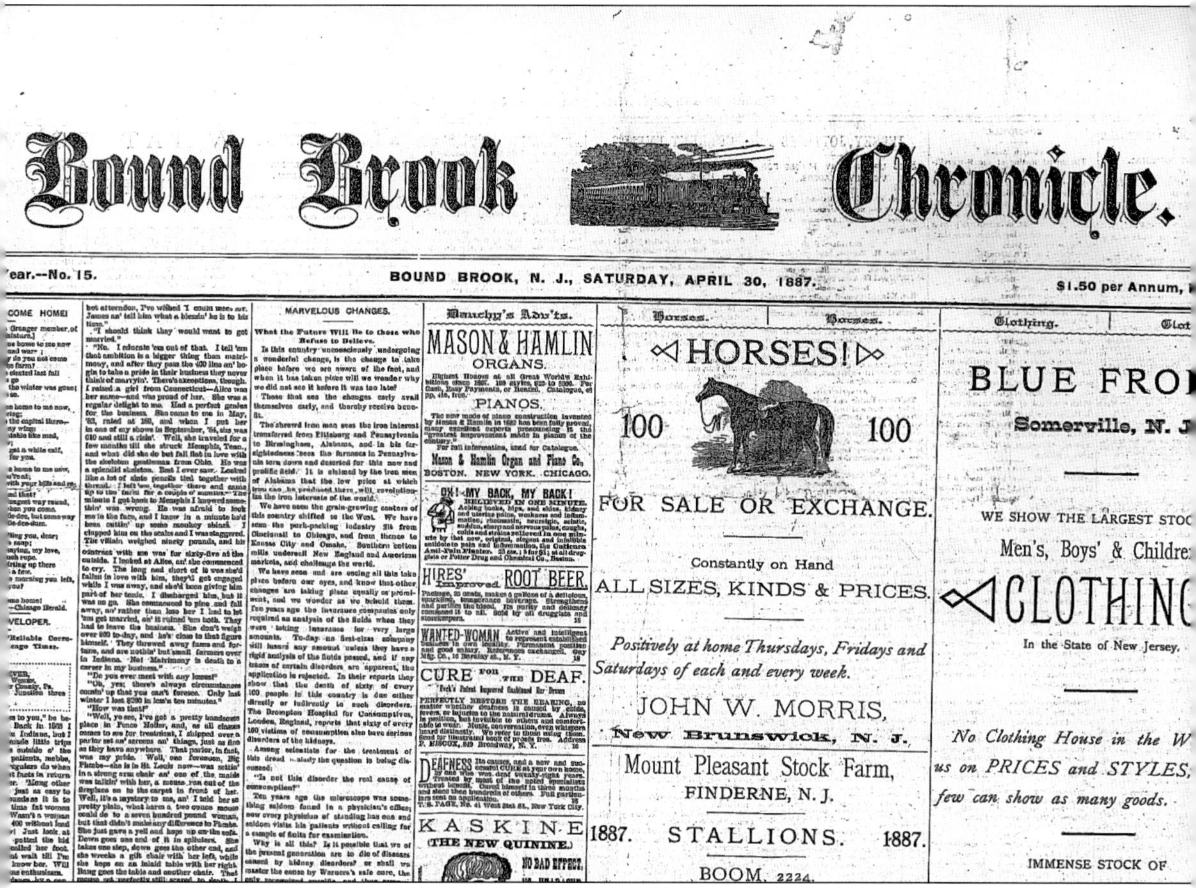

Bound Brook Chronicle.

'ear.--No. 15. BOUND BROOK, N. J., SATURDAY, APRIL 30, 1887. $1.50 per Annum,

MARVELOUS CHANGES.

Mauchy's Adv'ts.

MASON & HAMLIN ORGANS.

PIANOS.

Mason & Hamlin Organ and Piano Co., BOSTON. NEW YORK. CHICAGO.

OH!-MY BACK, MY BACK!

HIRES' Improved ROOT BEER.

WANTED-WOMAN

CURE FOR THE DEAF.

DEAFNESS

KASKINE (THE NEW QUININE.)

NO BAD EFFECT.

Horses. Horses.

HORSES!

100 100

FOR SALE OR EXCHANGE.

Constantly on Hand

ALL SIZES, KINDS & PRICES.

Positively at home Thursdays, Fridays and Saturdays of each and every week.

JOHN W. MORRIS,

New Brunswick, N. J.

Mount Pleasant Stock Farm,

FINDERNE, N. J.

1887. STALLIONS. 1887.

BOOM, 2224.

Clothing.

BLUE FRO

Somerville, N. J

WE SHOW THE LARGEST STOC

Men's, Boys' & Childre

CLOTHIN

In the State of New Jersey.

No Clothing House in the W us on PRICES and STYLES, few can show as many goods.

IMMENSE STOCK OF

As a reporter for a local newspaper, W.B.R. Mason came to town on a railroad flatcar with the Somerville fire apparatus during the 1881 conflagration. He returned the following year and purchased the newspaper from William Shampanore and served as its owner-editor for more than a half century. The locomotive in the masthead implies the importance of the railroad to the local economy.

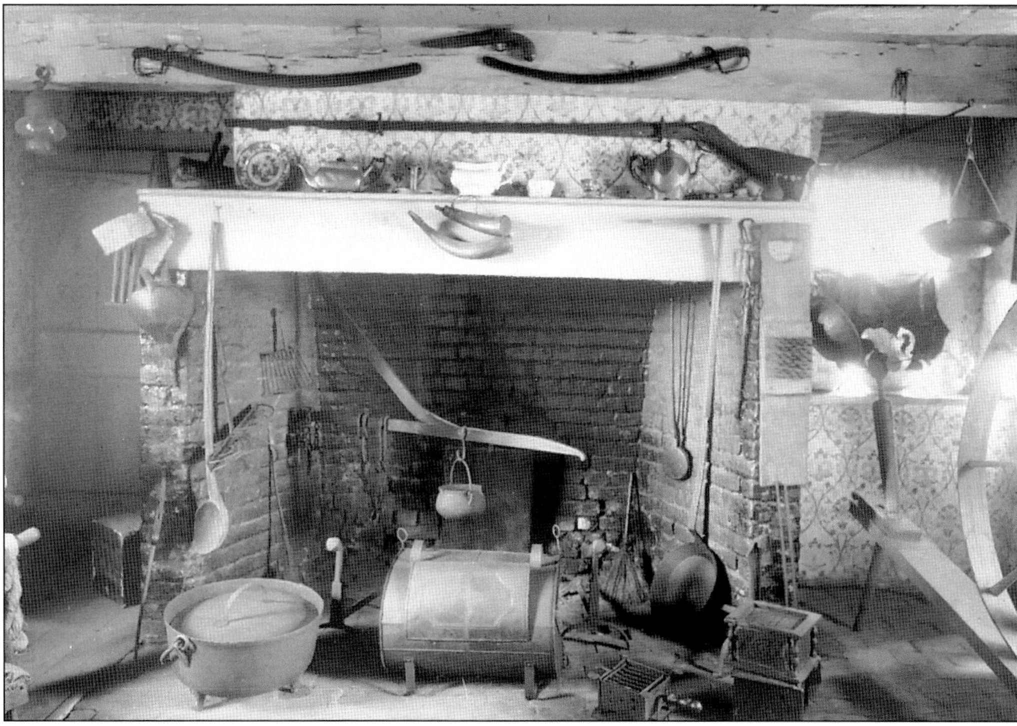

Shown is the kitchen of the Staats House. The Staats House was in continuous ownership of the same family from 1738 to 1935. The property originally consisted of 300 acres along the Raritan River in present South Bound Brook. It served as the headquarters of Baron Von Steuben during the Middlebrook Encampment in 1779.

WOMAN'S LITERARY CLUB AND LIBRARY ASSOCIATION OF BOUND BROOK

PROGRAMME OF LITERARY WORK---JANUARY 9th TO APRIL 24th, 1899

::: OFFICERS :::

PRESIDENT--MRS. PETER STRYKER.
SECRETARY--MISS M. BOYLE.
TREASURER--MISS ADDIE TAPPEN.

The Woman's Literary Club, founded in 1885, first met in its members' homes. The group later enlarged its activities to benefit the entire community, establishing the public library in 1898, the Visiting Nurse Service in 1908, and working as an auxiliary to the Red Cross in WWI and II.

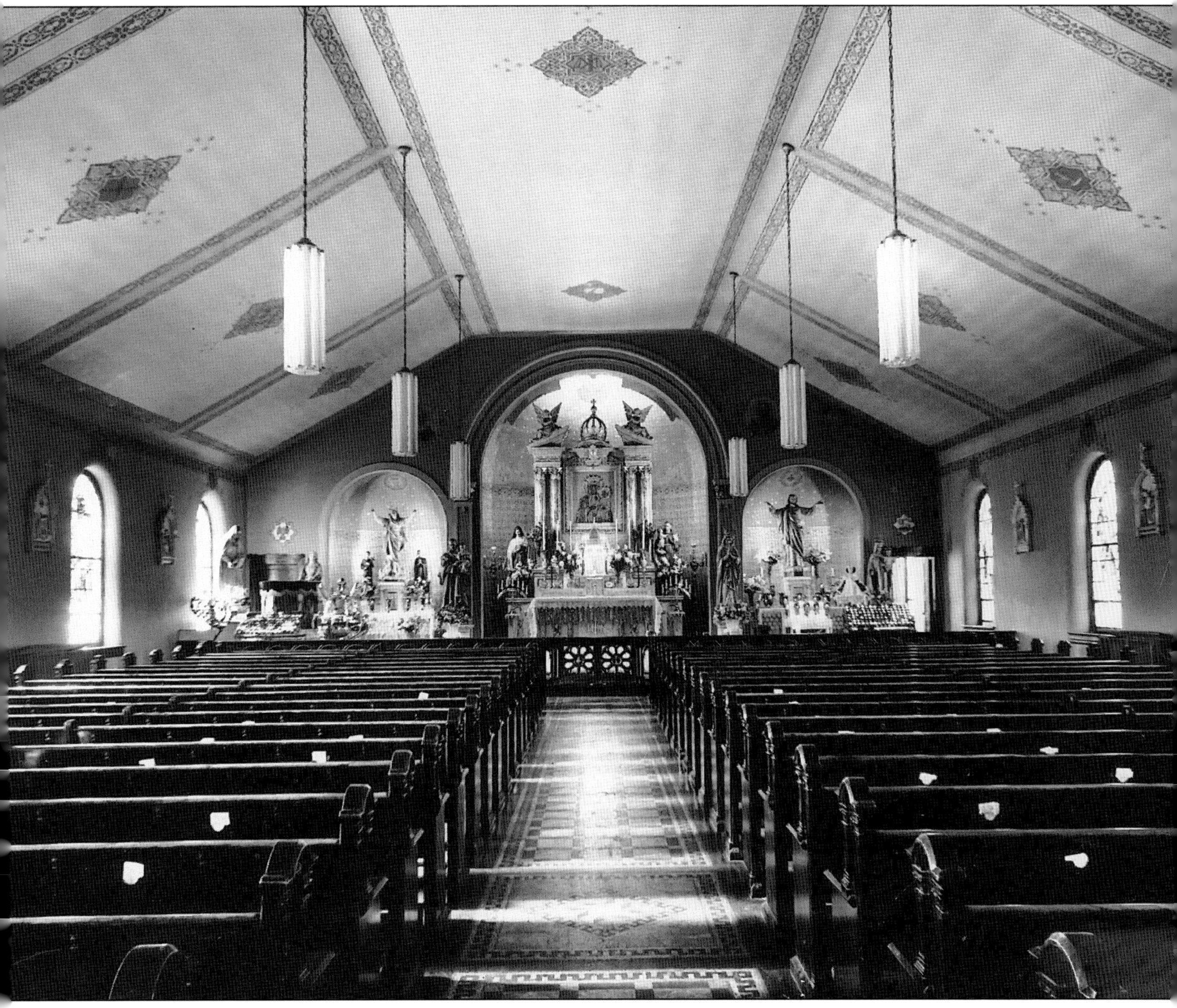

Before 1914, all Bound Brook Catholics worshipped at St. Joseph Church. In 1915, the Polish Catholic congregation purchased land at the corner of Second Street and Vosseller Avenue from the LaMonte family and built a church there, the sanctuary of which is shown in this photograph.

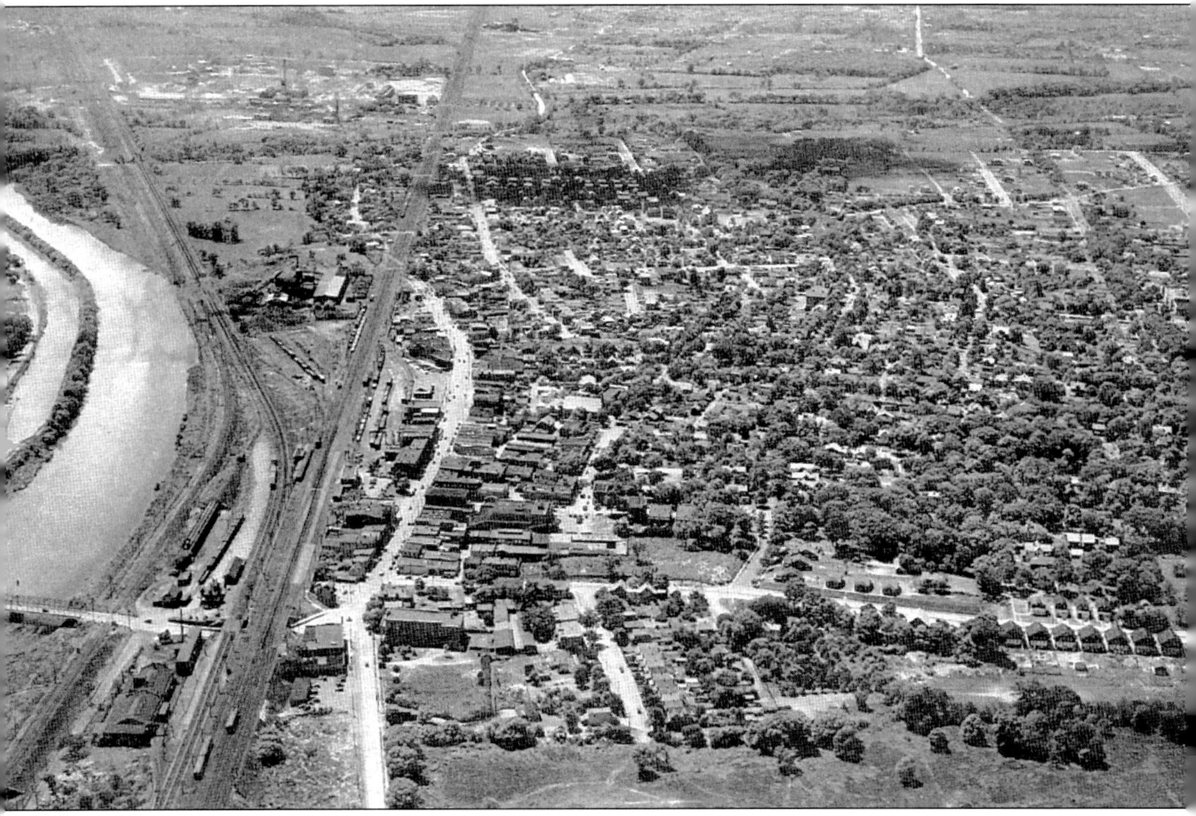

The aerial view of Bound Brook, taken in 1930, demonstrates the town's growth from a tiny riverside village to a busy industrial site. It was touted as the county's foremost center of industry.

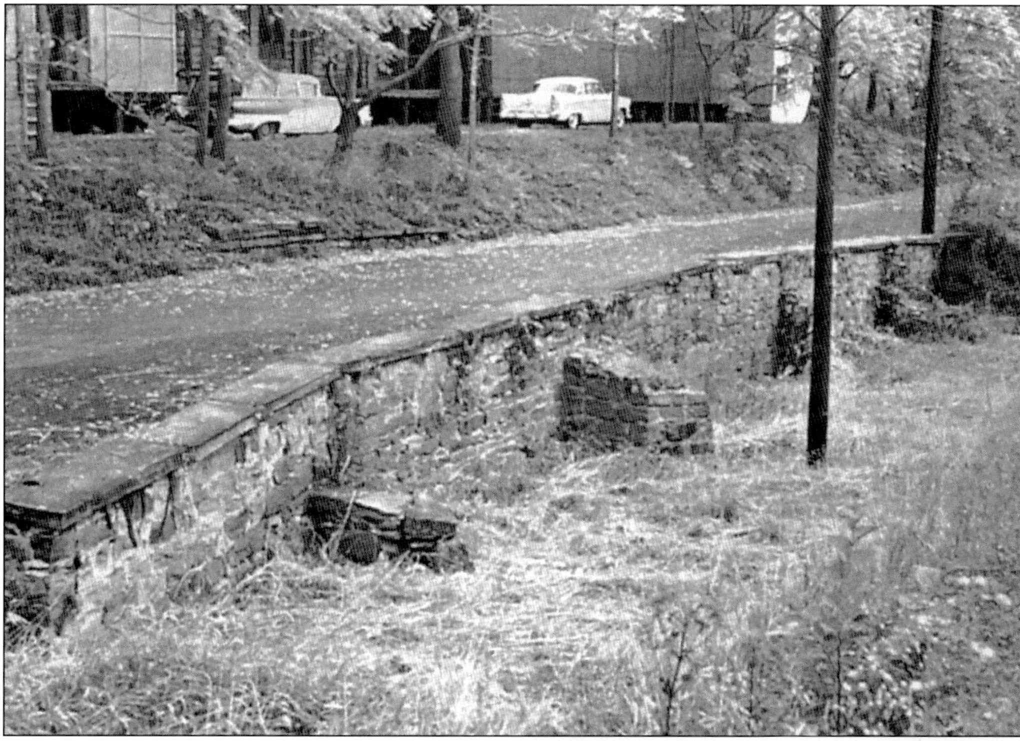

Shown is Stone Bridge. The Colonial Assembly passed an amended bill in 1730 ordering the construction of the stone bridge over the Bound Brook on this section of the "Road up Raritan." The cost was to be shared by Somerset and Middlesex Counties. Today, the bridge is in great disrepair and its location nearly forgotten.

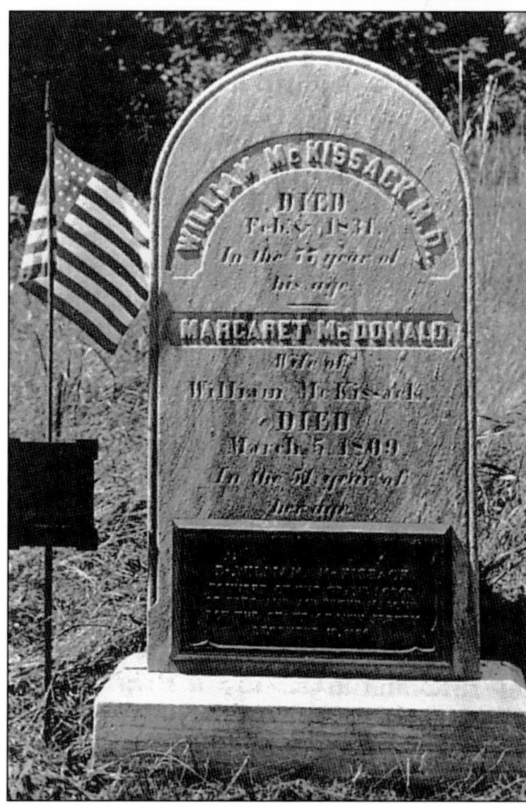

During service in the Revolutionary War, Pennsylvania native Dr. William McKissack was stationed in this area. He returned after the war, marrying Margaret McDonald and remaining to practice medicine in the county. He is credited with founding the first Masonic lodge in the county. His gravestone in the Old Presbyterian Cemetery bears a commemorative plaque honoring his Masonic work.

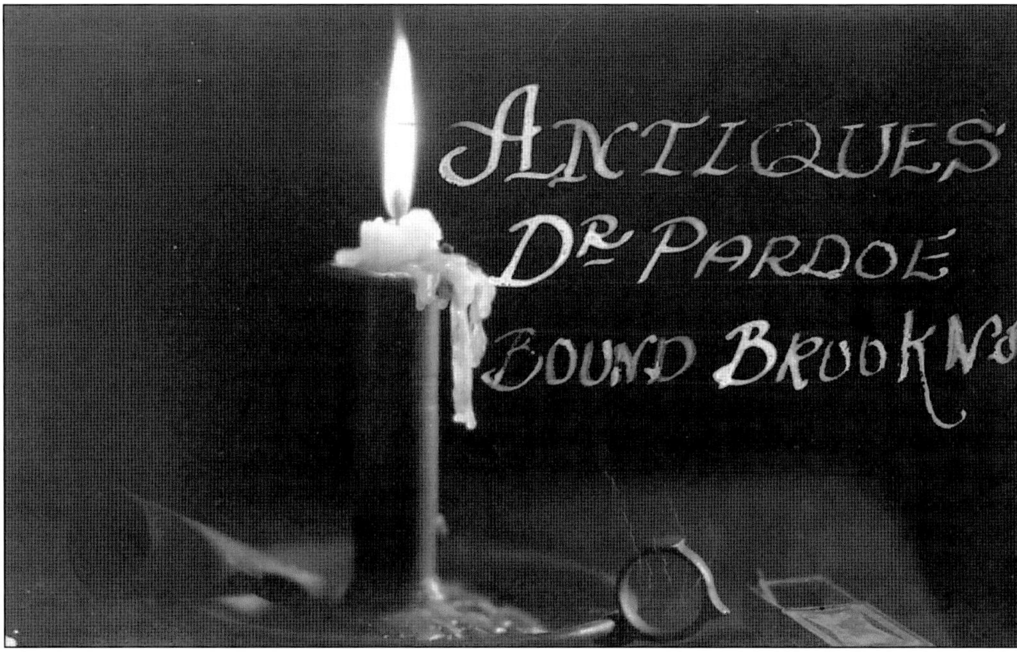

In addition to his dental practice and avocation of prize-winning photography, Dr. Jonathan Pardoe also bought and sold antiques, as illustrated by this advertisement.

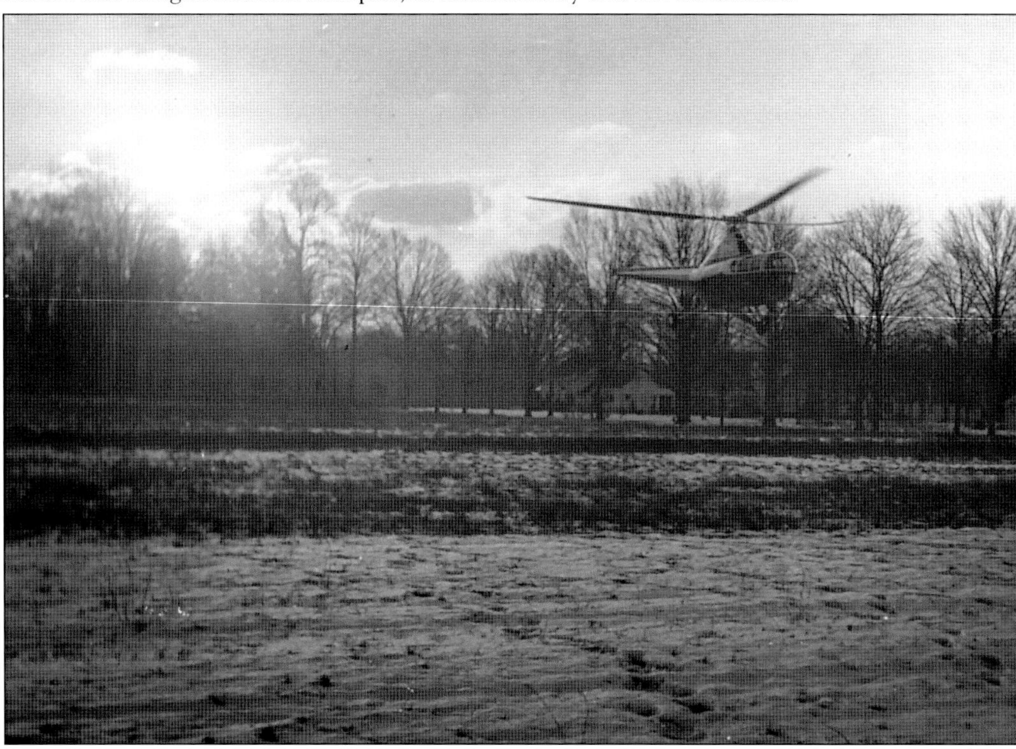

Helicopter Airmail Service came to this area after WWII. This 1946 view shows the helicopter landing on the northeast corner of Mountain and Shepherd Avenues. There was also a landing field on Cyanamid property behind the Van Horn house.

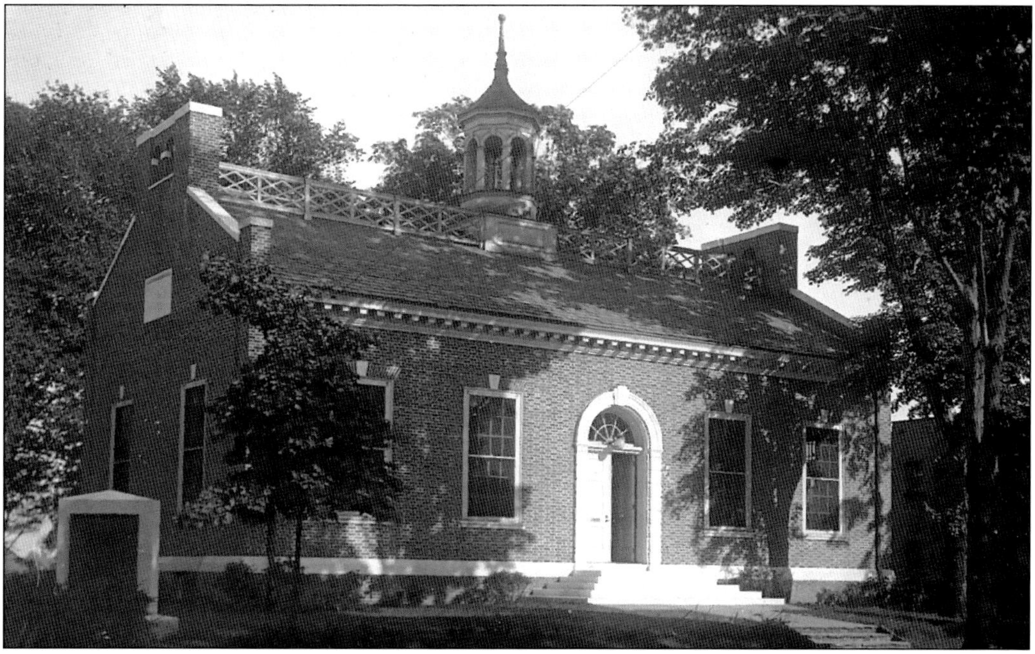

In 1924, the existing building was razed and replaced by the present library structure. The building was financed by public subscription and erected as a memorial to honor WWI service men and women. The building was dedicated on December 20, 1924.

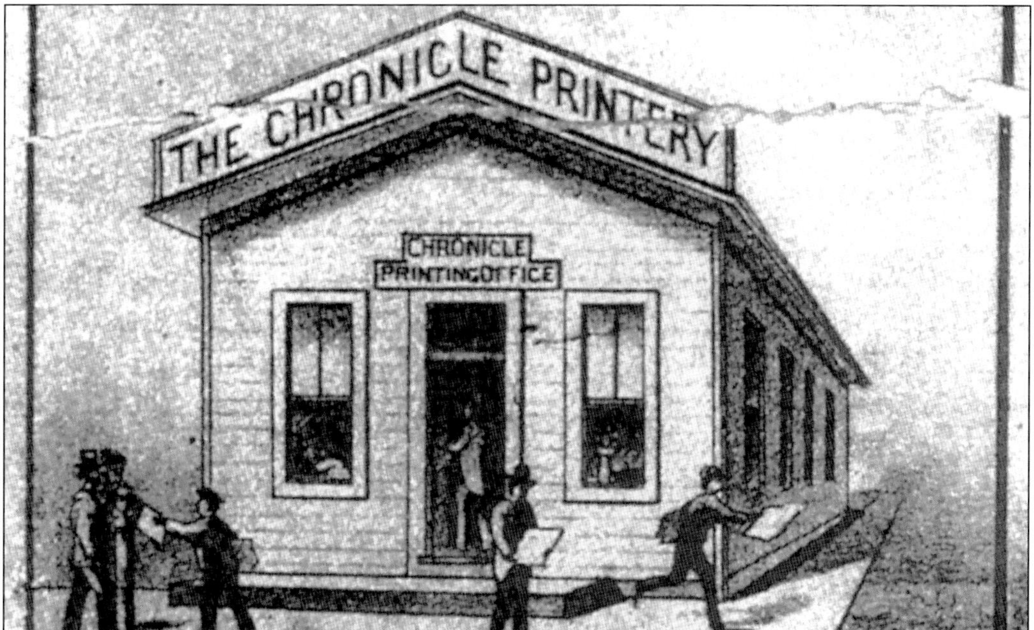

The Chronicle printing office, shown in this woodcut, was located on Maiden Lane and destroyed by fire on December 31, 1891. This building, along with the *Chronicle* newspaper, was purchased by W.B.R. Mason from William Shampanore in 1882. The operation was relocated to Mountain Avenue following the fire.

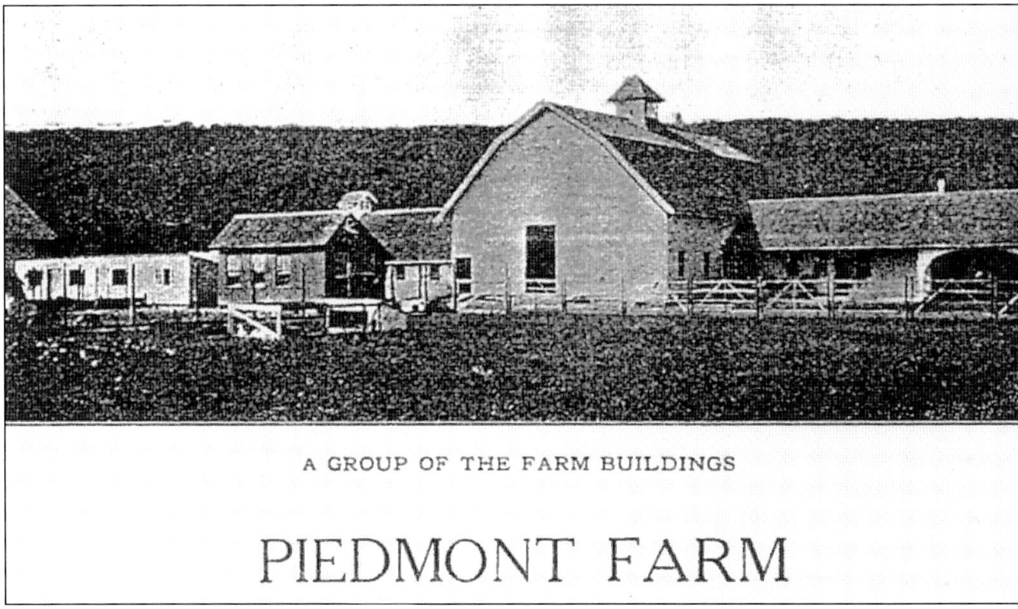

Piedmont Farm originally covered 70 acres. It was the working farm home of George M. LaMonte, who maintained a prized herd of Guernsey cows there and marketed dairy products. In 1950, the property was sold and developed into upscale housing.

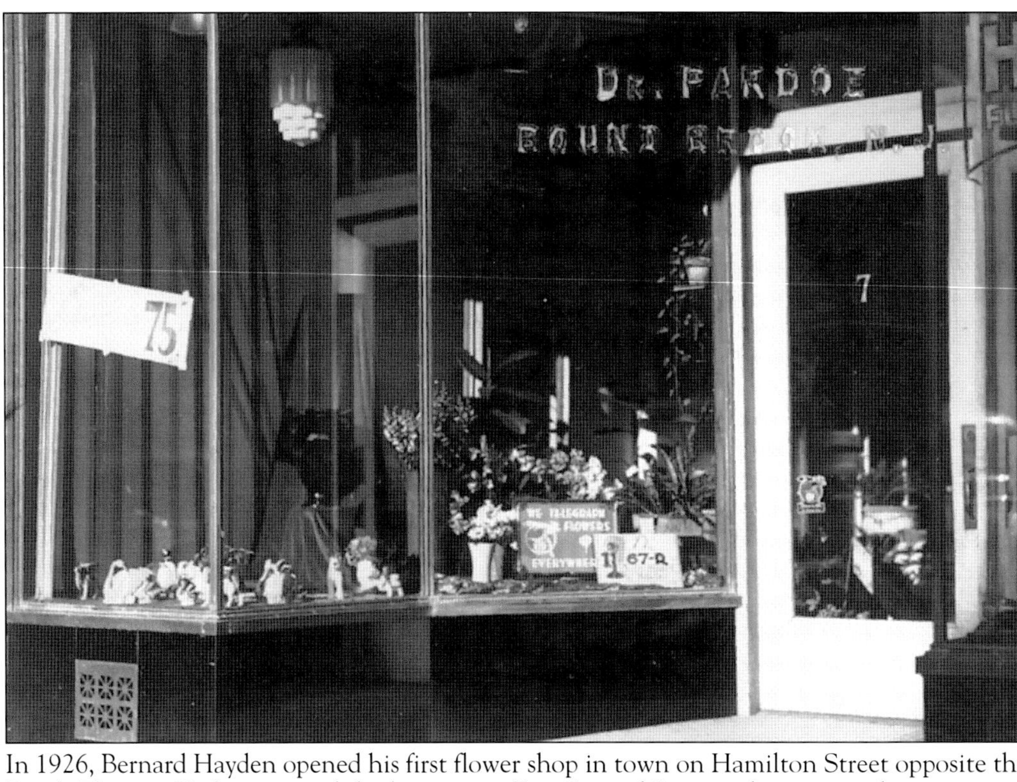

In 1926, Bernard Hayden opened his first flower shop in town on Hamilton Street opposite the Brook Theater. He later moved the business to East Second Street, where it is today.

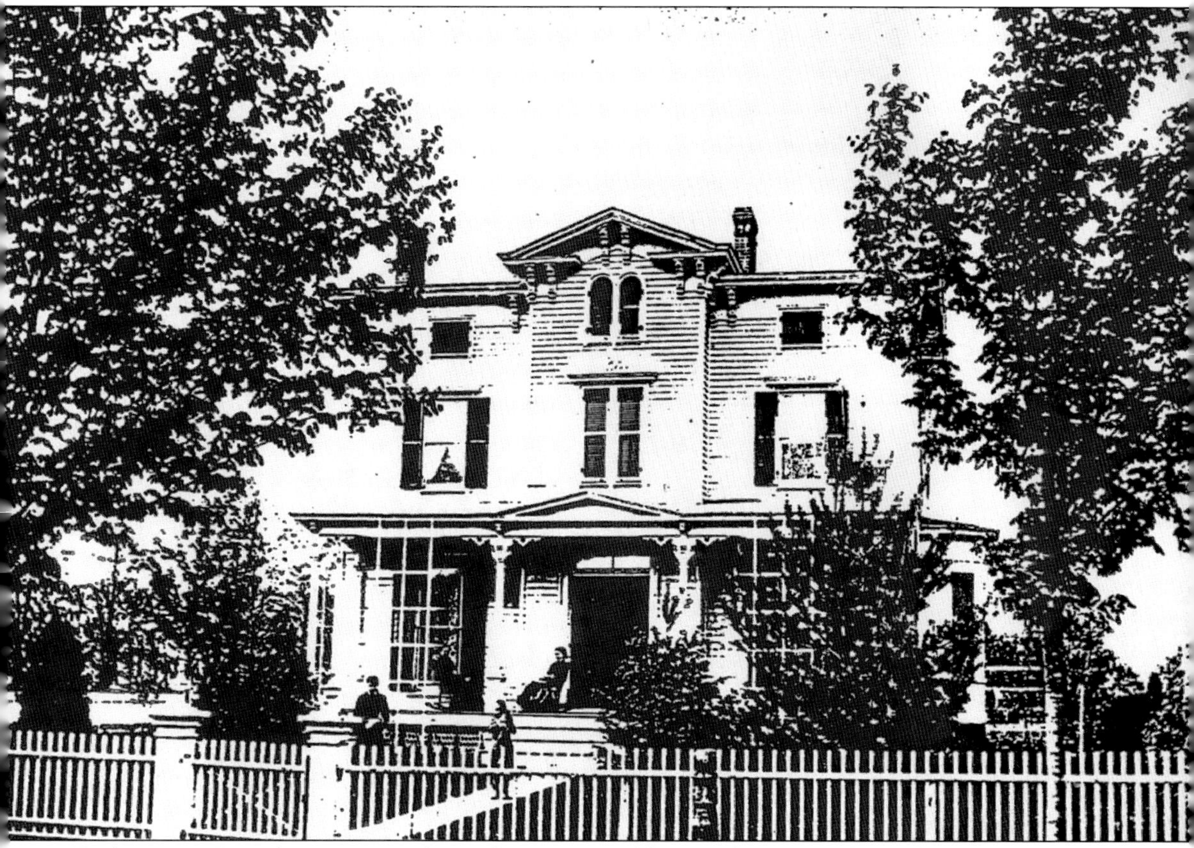

Built in 1875, and most recently used as Van Syckles' Real Estate Office, this home on the corner of Church Street and Union Avenue was built for the widow, Martha Ann Jelliffe Nevius. She married Peter Kenney, a widower, in 1876. At the time of their residence, there were four houses in that block, belonging to the Kenney, Whiting, Fisher, and Kingsbury families. North of Union Avenue, Church Street was known as Ross Lane.

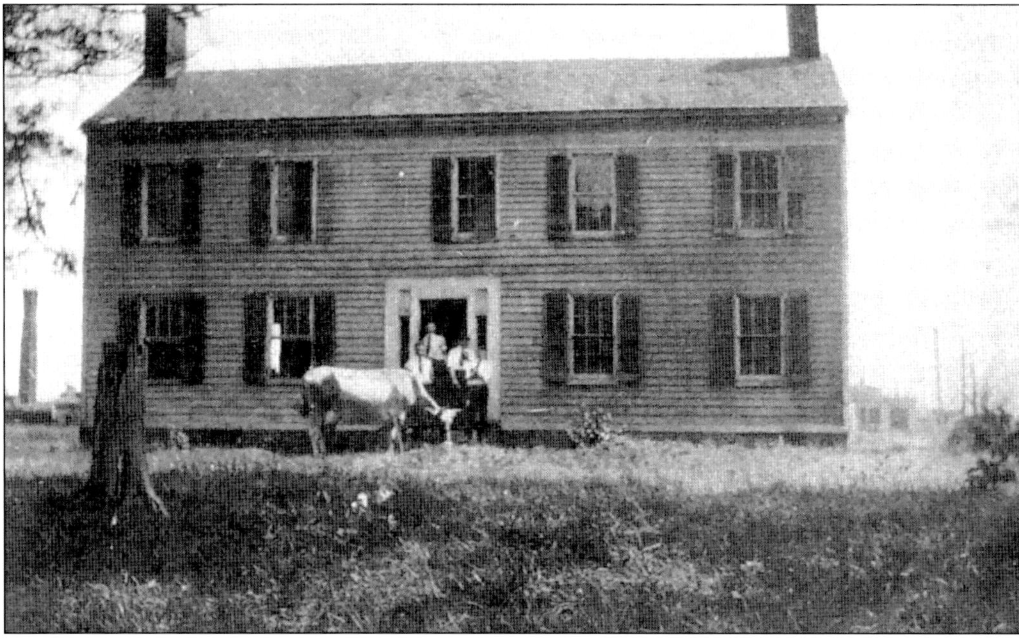

The early days of Calco Chemical Company (later American Cyanamid) is illustrated by this 1919 photograph of their original laboratory building, complete with visiting cow.

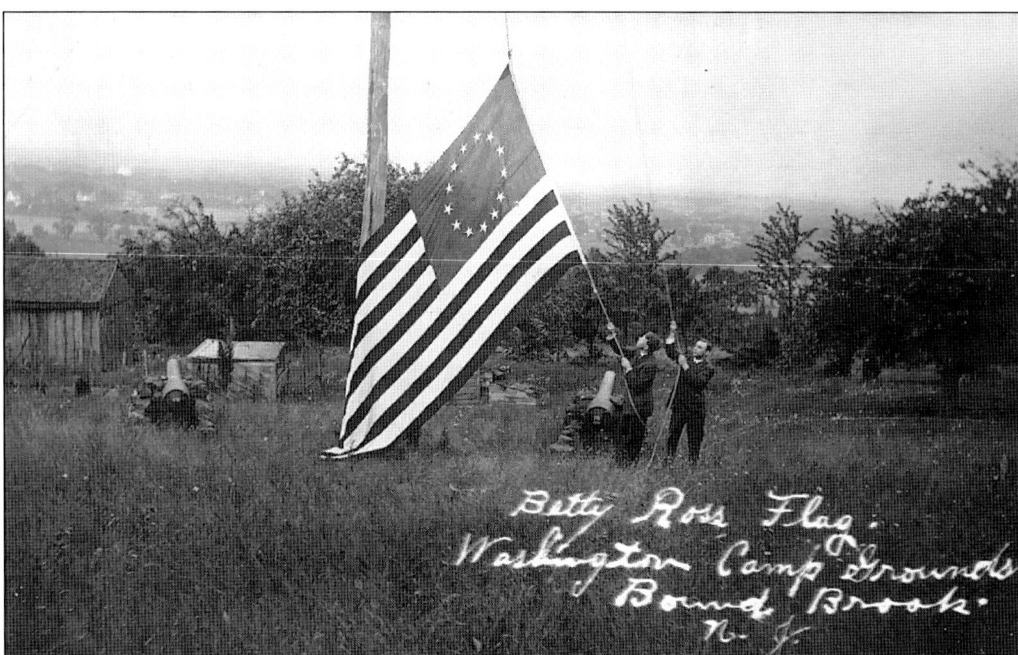

From its inception, the Washington Camp Ground Association was based in Bound Brook. In this view, we see the farm buildings formerly located on the site and the two cannons obtained as surplus from the federal government. The flagpole was made from a chestnut tree cut in Readington Township.

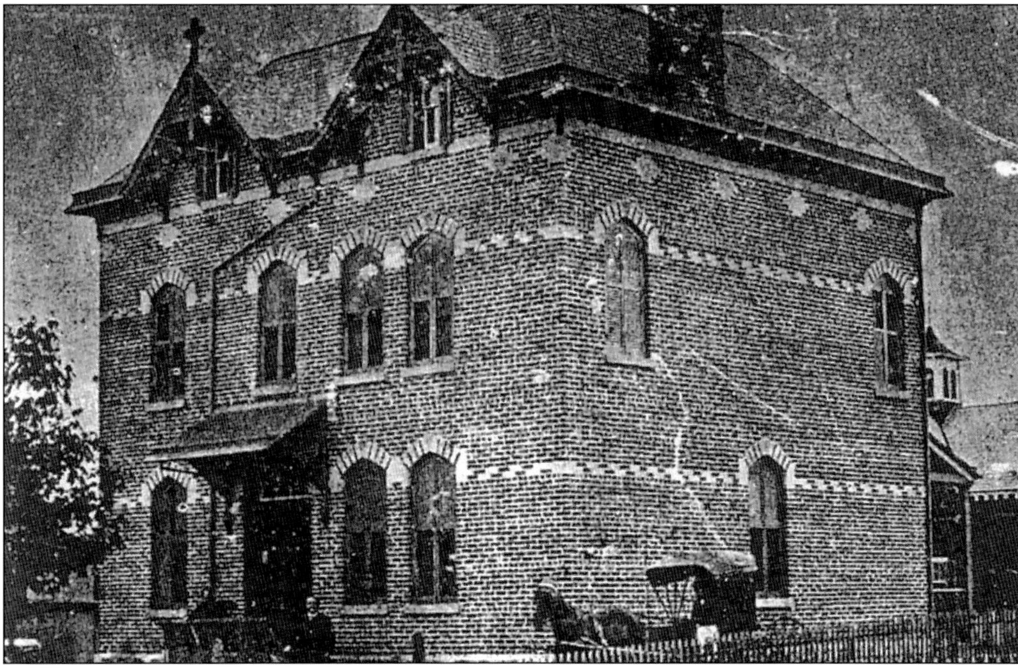

Saint Joseph Church Rectory was built on Mountain Avenue behind the church during the pastorate of Reverend Father Bogaard. Redesigned, it now serves as a residence for the nuns.

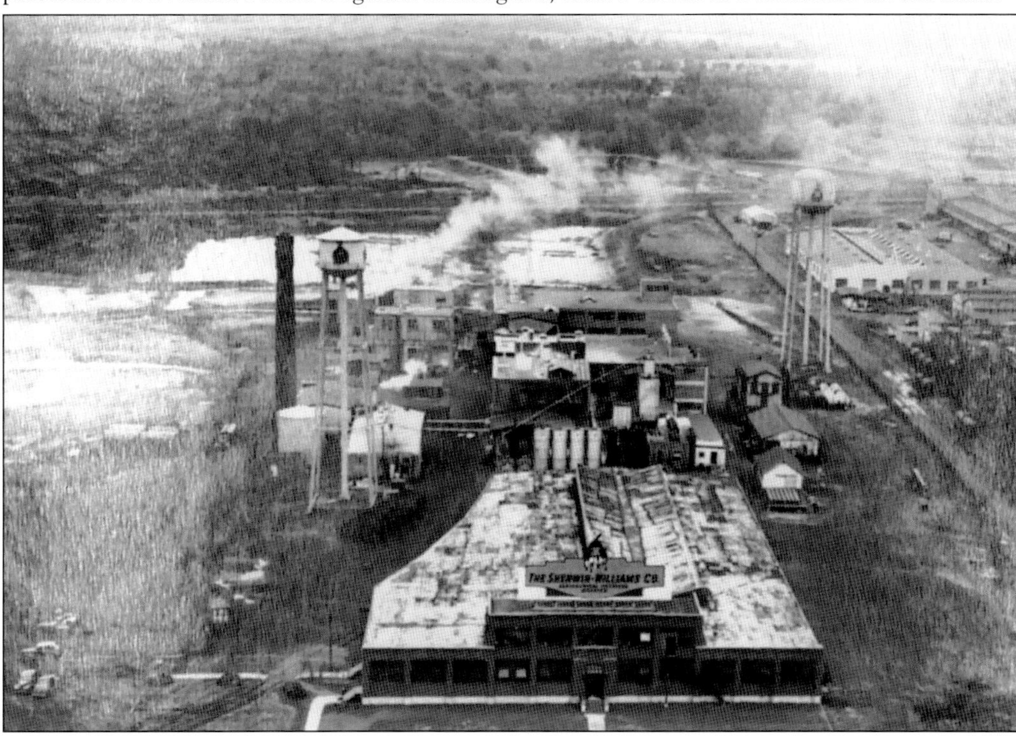

The Sherwin Williams plant was located west of the Middlebrook on farmland purchased from the Winsor and LaMonte estates. Paint and insecticides were manufactured there. Many employees were local residents.

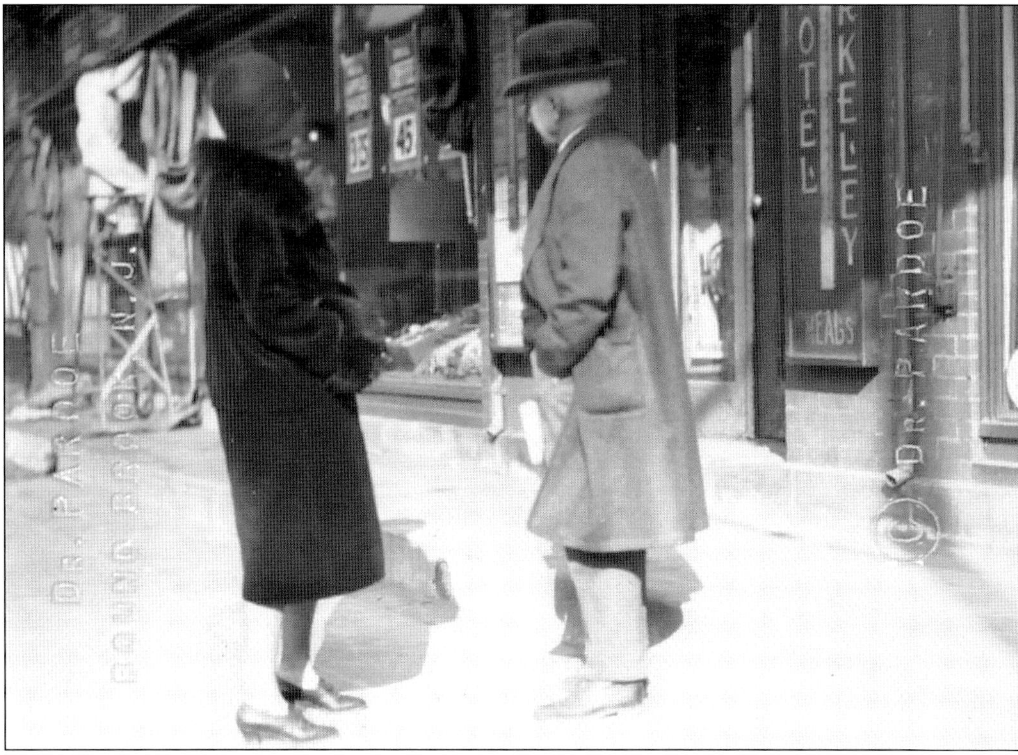

The Main Street scene has changed little in this 1920s photograph from its look in the 1890s. Some of these structures were razed to make way for more modern buildings.

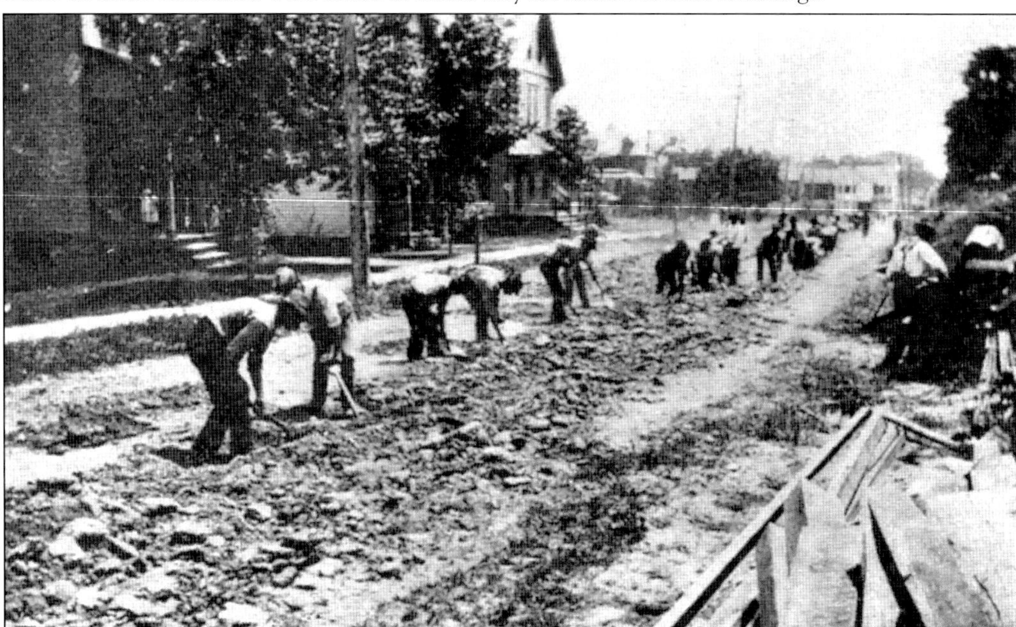

Before the advent of bulldozers and mechanized road equipment, this crew had to do the preliminary digging for laying the tracks for the trolley line. This is East Street, looking south toward Main Street.

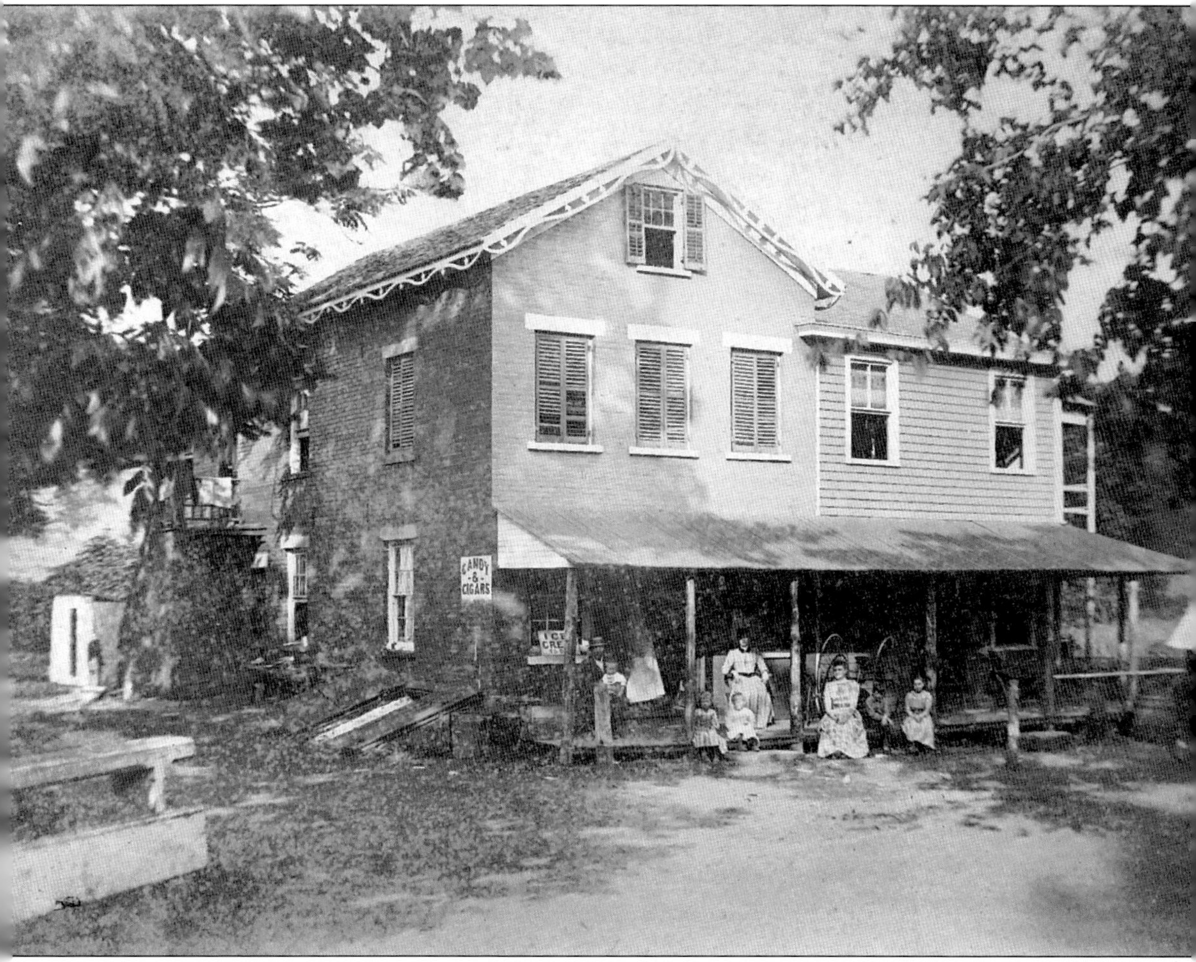

William Haelig bought Chimney Rock Hotel shortly after emigrating from Germany with his new bride in 1886. It was a popular site for church picnics and other outdoor events.

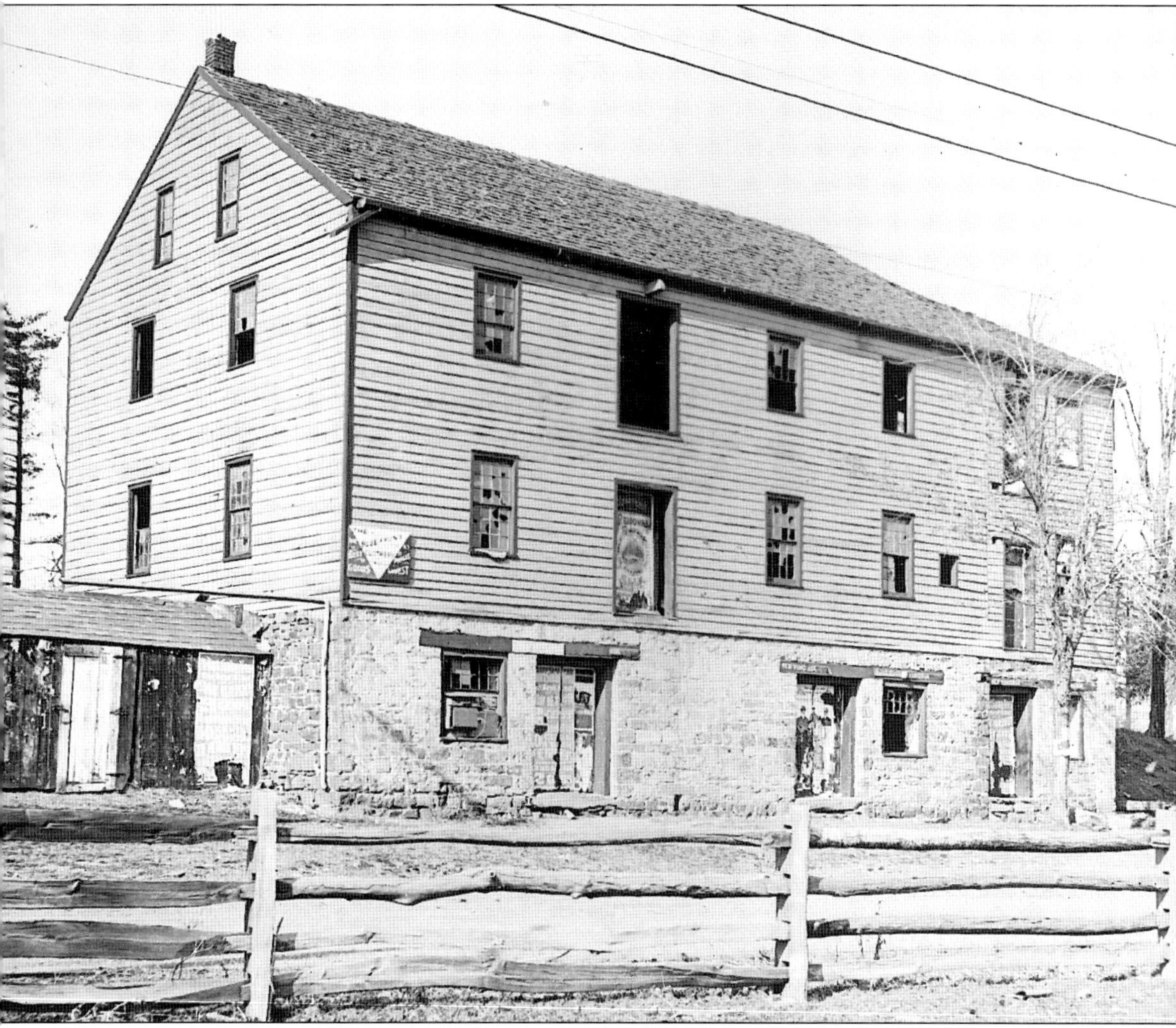

The Herbert Mill, built in 1835 on the site of an earlier structure, stood along the road west of the Middlebrook and served local farmers for many years. The millwheel constructed by John McNabb was made of oak and was assembled on the Van Horn House lawn, then erected on the mill site.

Bound Brook - About 1700-1779

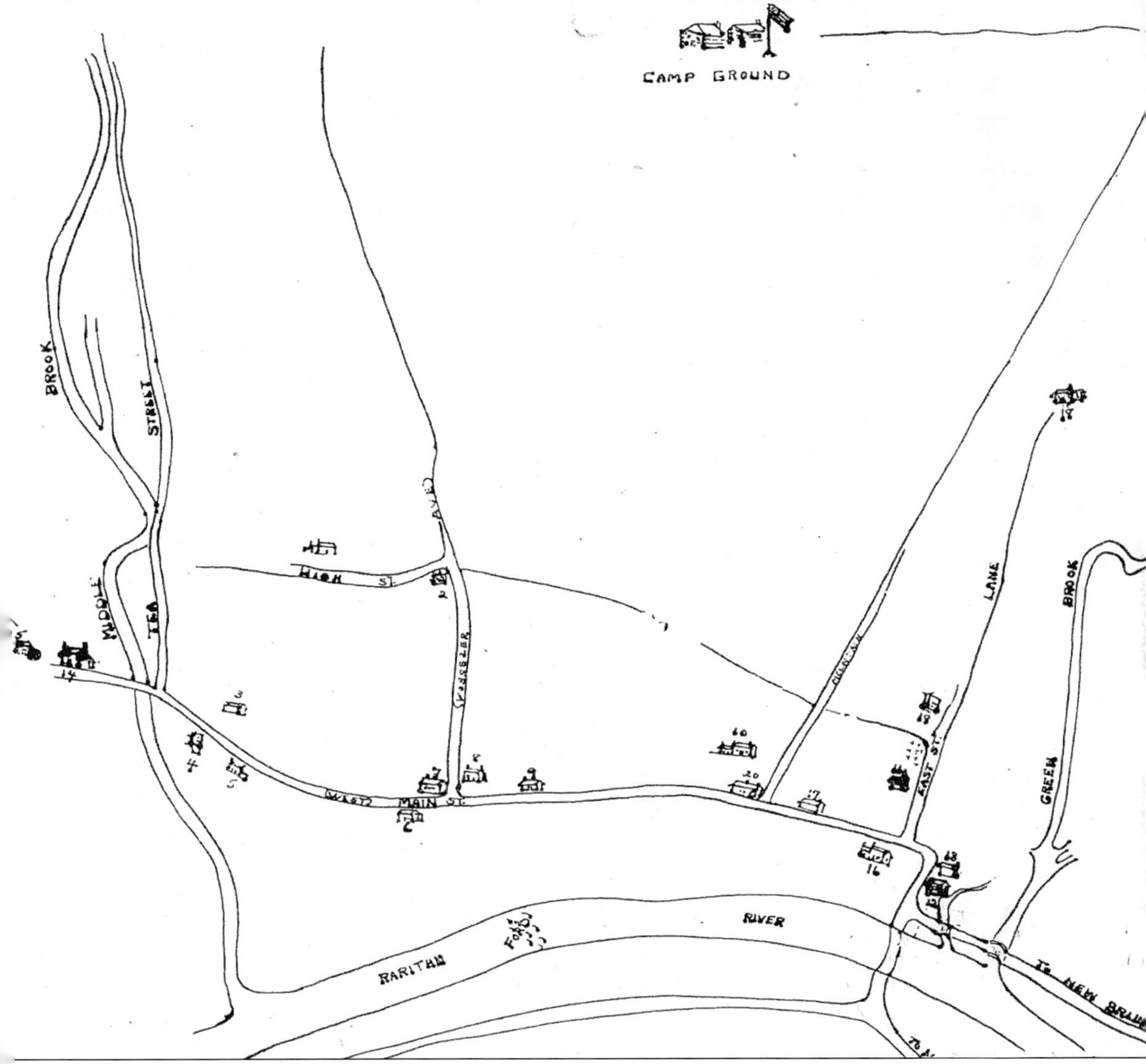

This map, created by Mrs. S. Aird Smith, was her conception of how Bound Brook looked in the 18th century. She prepared it with her review of the book *Lesser Crossroads*.

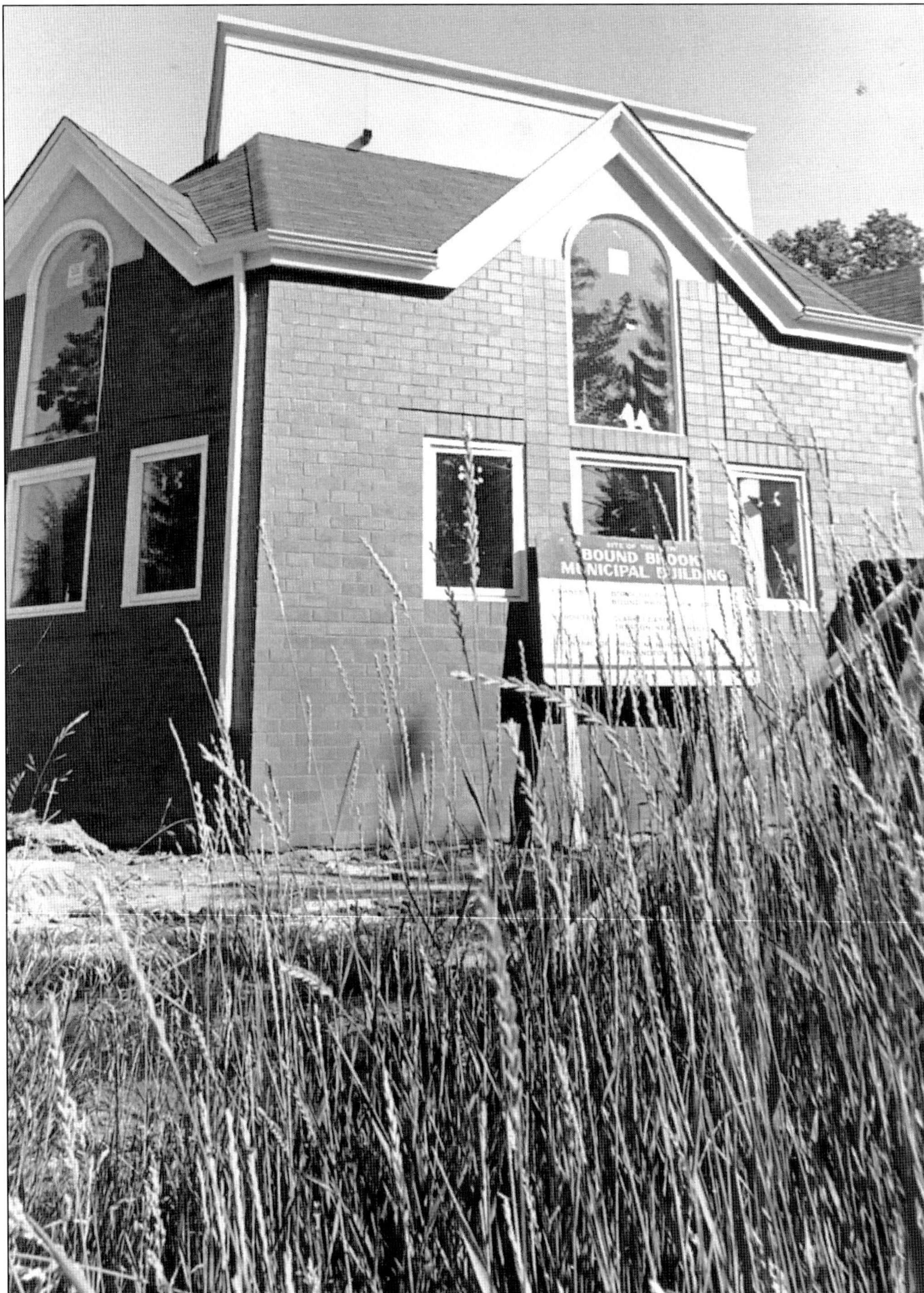

Present Borough Hall was constructed on the site of the Ransom Lamb house on the corner of Hamilton and Somerset Streets. During the prolonged construction period, the building looked as it does in this photograph.

Two

THE PEOPLE

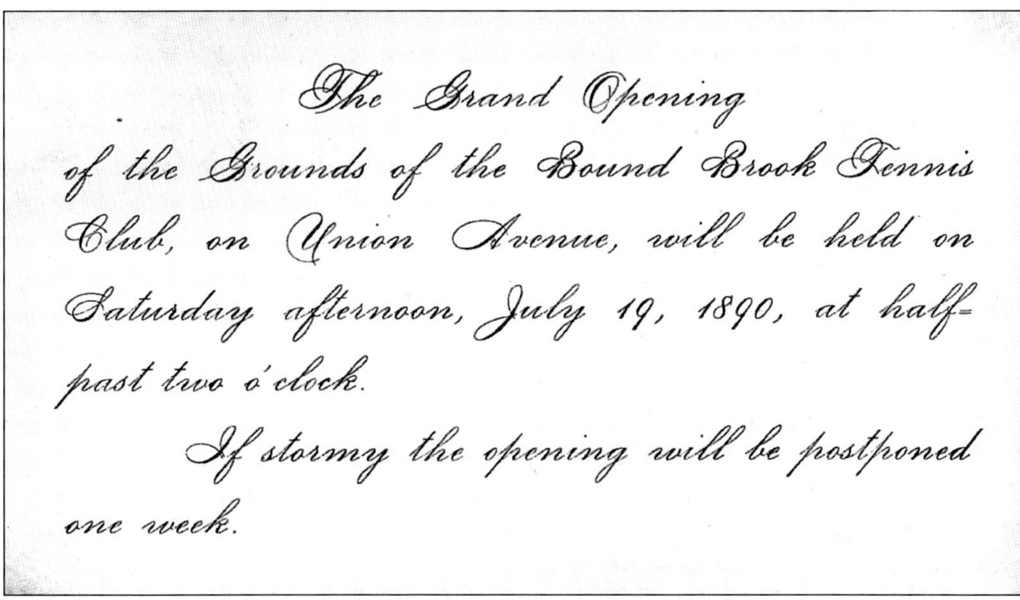

The Grand Opening
of the Grounds of the Bound Brook Tennis
Club, on Union Avenue, will be held on
Saturday afternoon, July 19, 1890, at half-
past two o'clock.

If stormy the opening will be postponed
one week.

Tennis, like bicycling, was a popular pastime in the 1890s. The town had its share of devotees, as this invitation illustrates. The Club Ball was a prominent social event held at the Voorhees Hall in 1892.

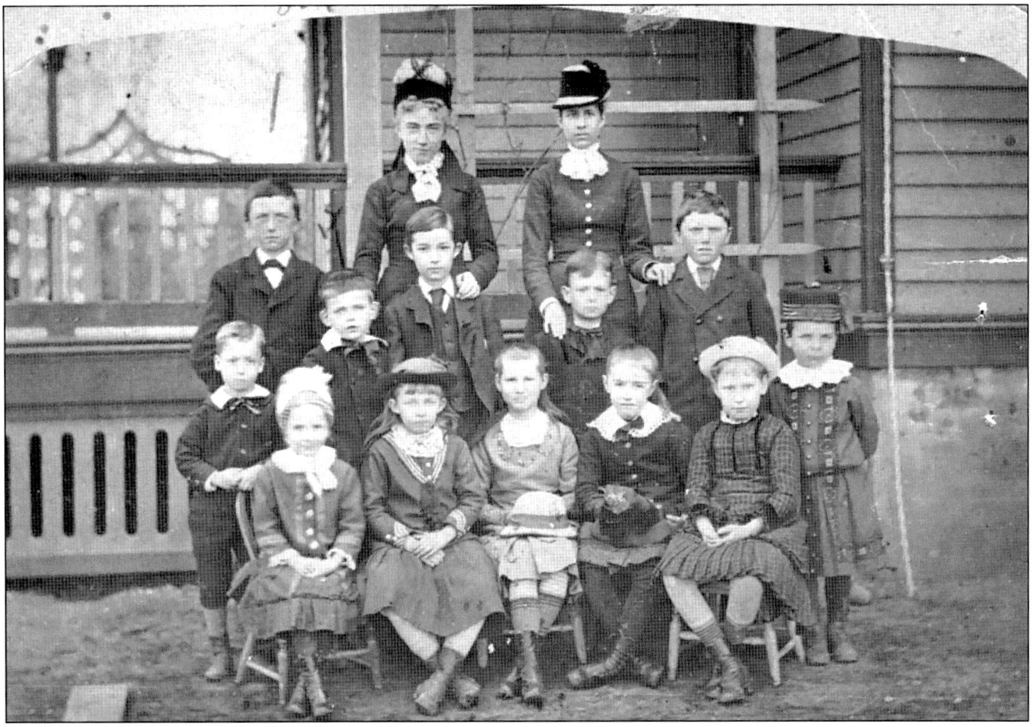

Miss Kate Coombs and her assistant, Miss Stryker, pose with her kindergarten class, c. 1878. The second child from the left is Emma Gillen, whose father had a store on the corner of Main Street and Mountain Avenue.

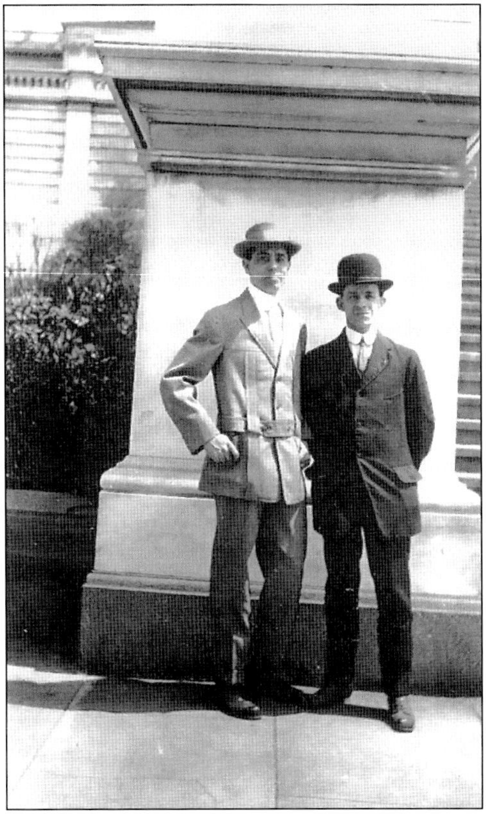

Elmer Schoonmaker, the dapper dandy in the derby hat, was the busy photographer in town for many years, with a studio in the Voorhees building.

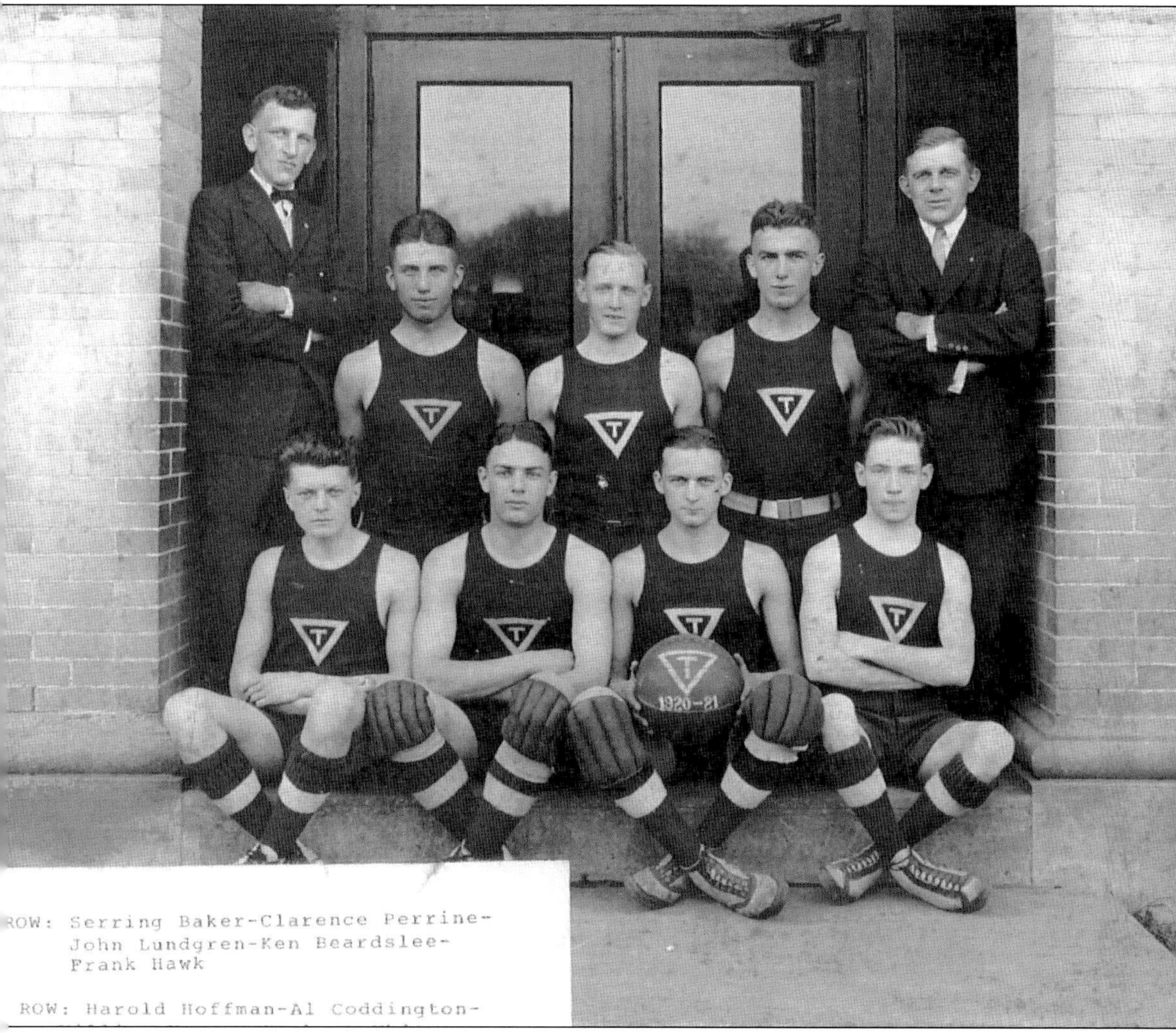

Representing their church in the local church basketball league, the Presbyterian team of 1920–1921 posed for their group photograph.

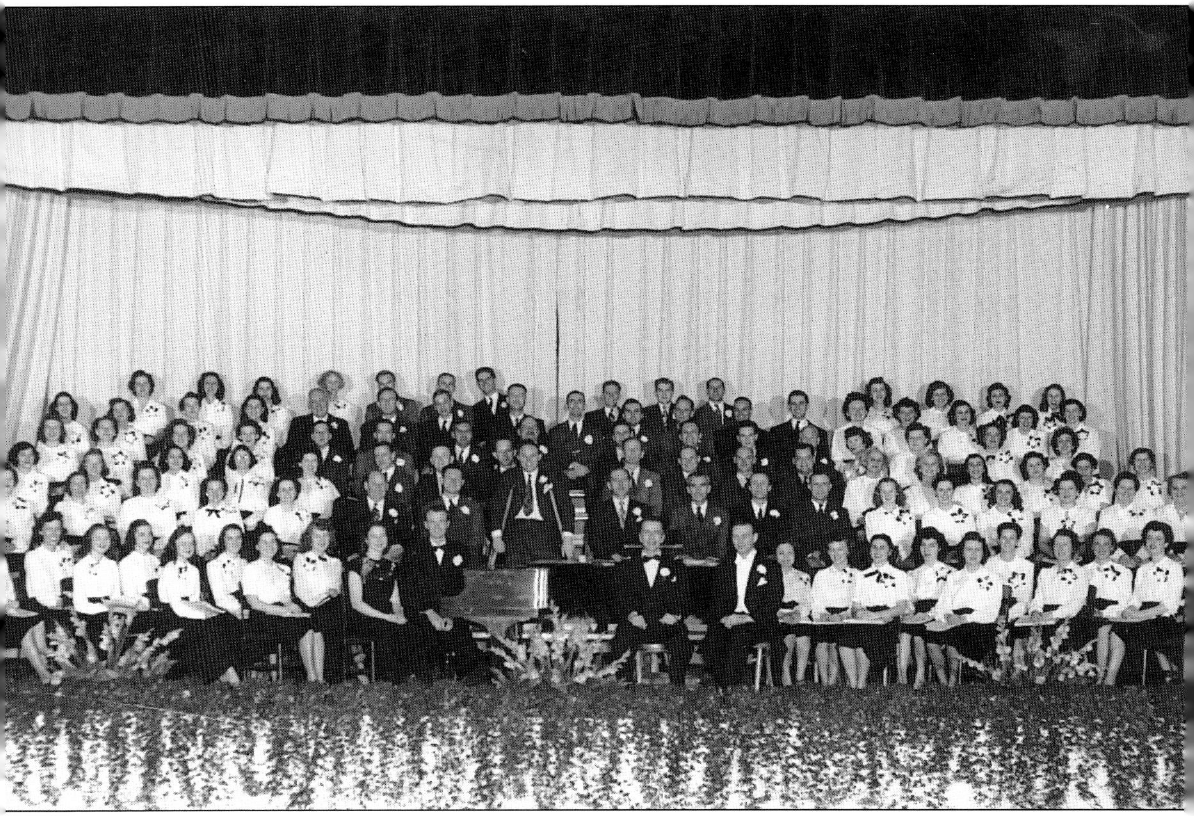

Founded in 1943, the Bound Brook Community Chorus brought enjoyment to local residents, as participants and listeners alike. The group was initially directed by Robert Shaw of the Fred Waring musical group.

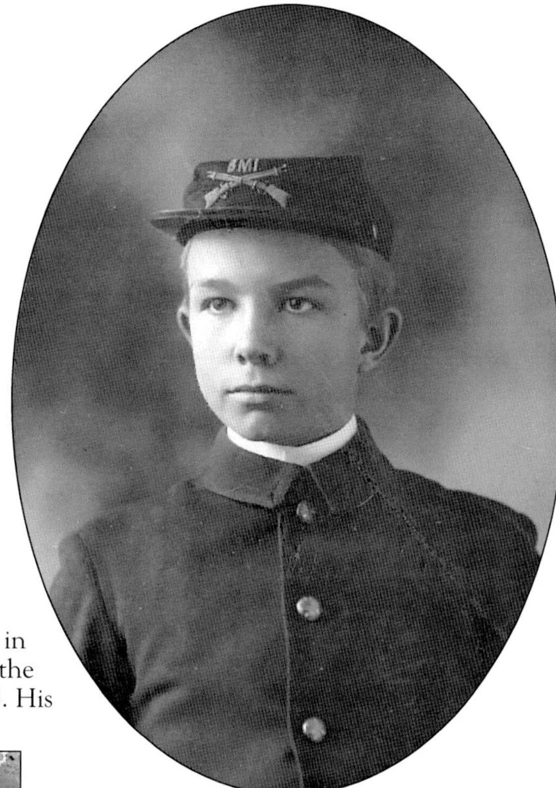

William Haelig is shown as a young boy in military school uniform in 1904 and as the Harley Davison Motorcycle dealer in 1915. His shop was located on East Main Street.

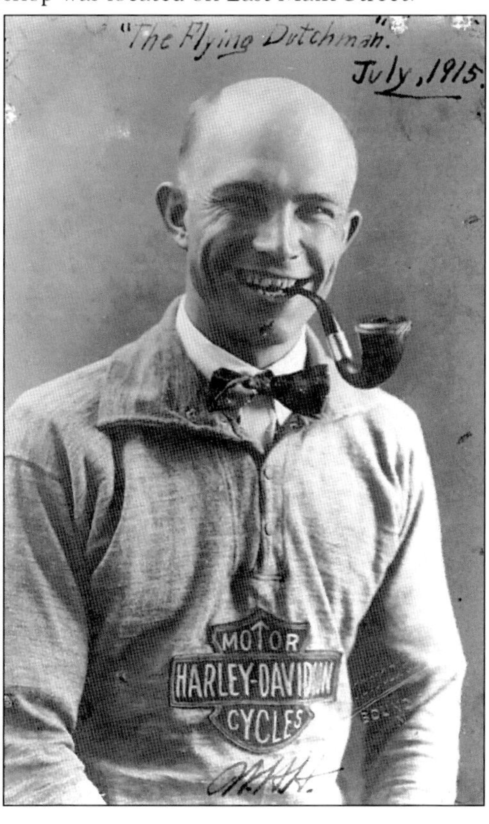

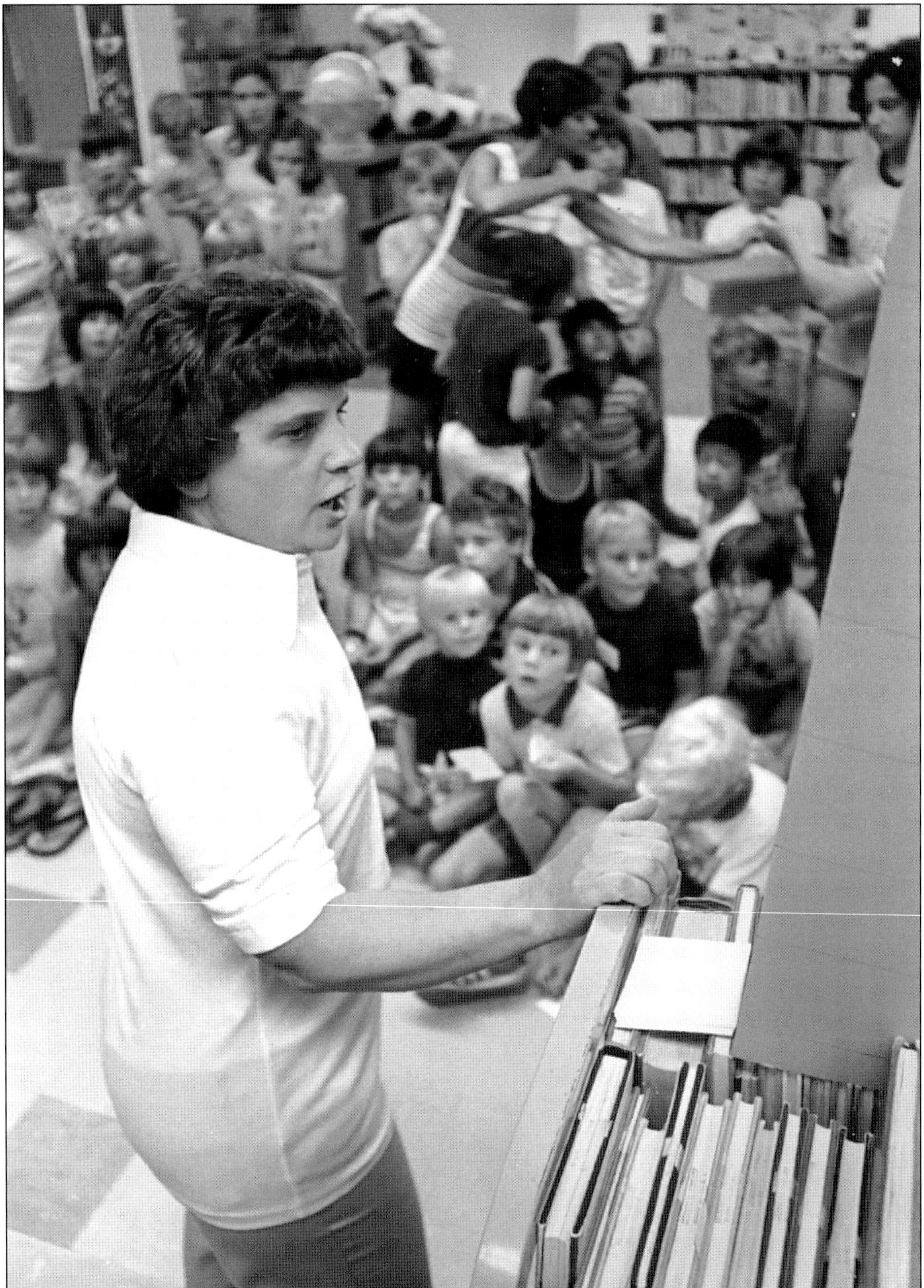

Dorothy Wisbeski, a popular children's librarian at the Bound Brook Memorial Library for more than 40 years, began working for the library as a page while still in school. She initiated many innovative activities to encourage child participation.

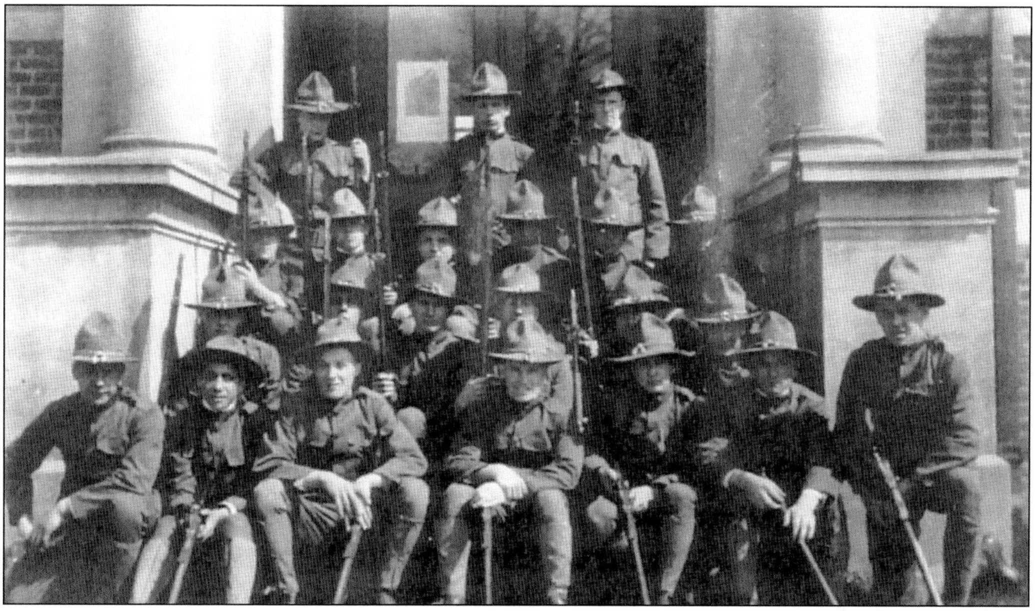

WW I saw the formation of the Home Guard with a unit at the high school. The young men posing on the school steps were part of the larger group in town.

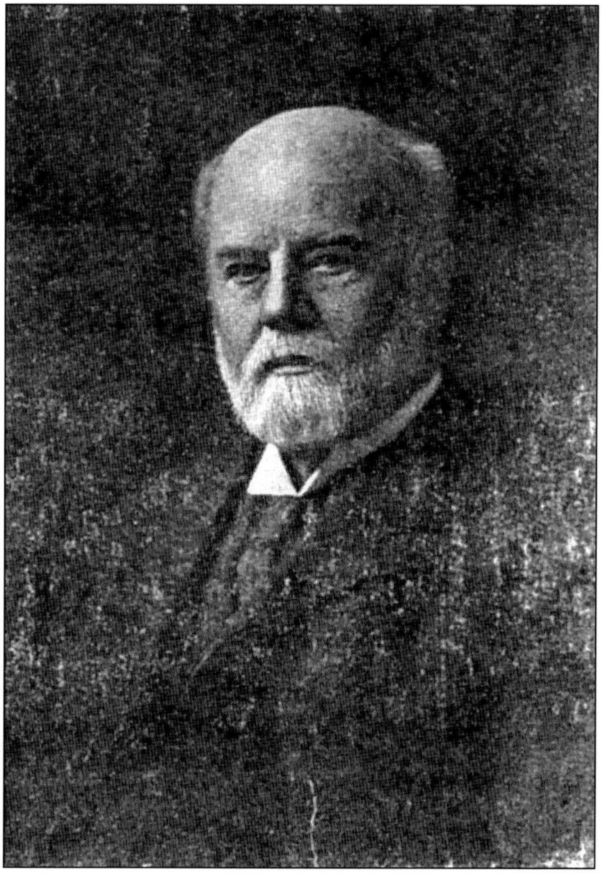

George LaMonte was born and educated in New York State. Before and during the Civil War, he taught in a female seminary in what is now West Virginia. Returning north, he first settled in New York City. In 1871, he bought a home in Bound Brook and became one of its prominent benefactors.

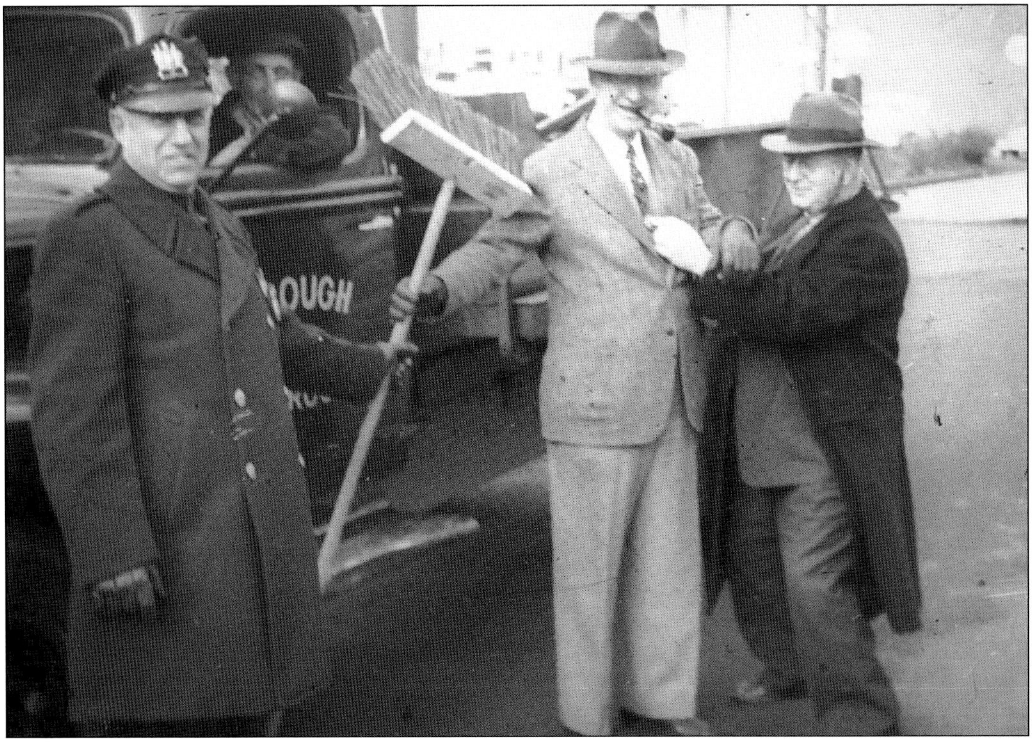

A 1944 clean-up drive brought out police officer Raymond Schure, jeweler William Fritts, and Dr. James Lovejoy to clown on Main Street for the camera.

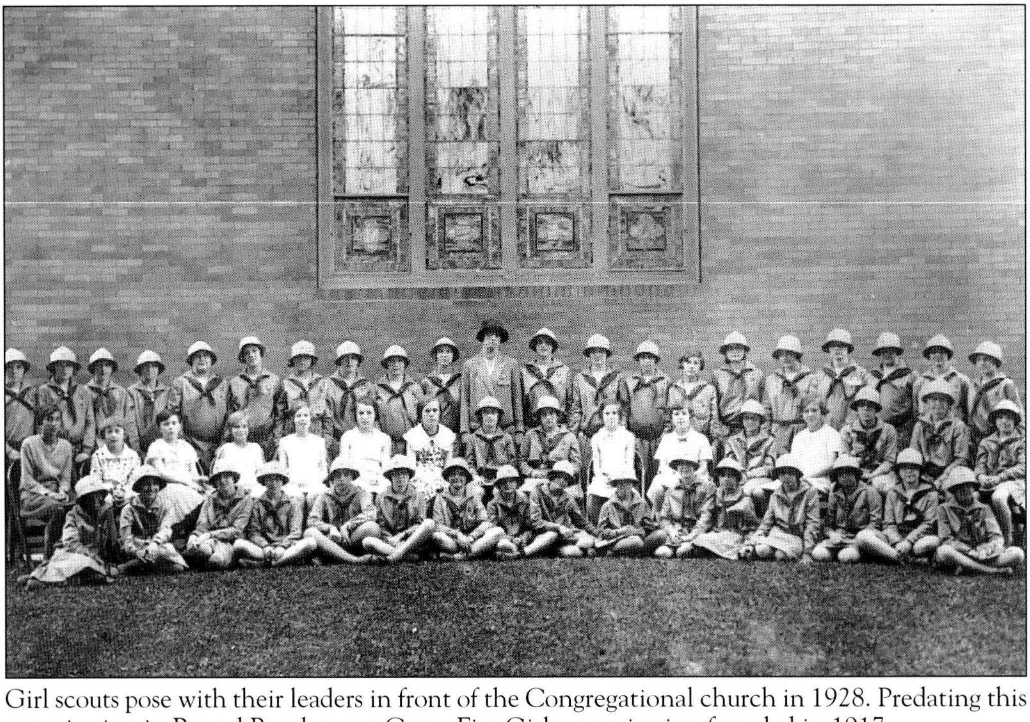

Girl scouts pose with their leaders in front of the Congregational church in 1928. Predating this organization in Bound Brook was a Camp Fire Girls organization founded in 1917.

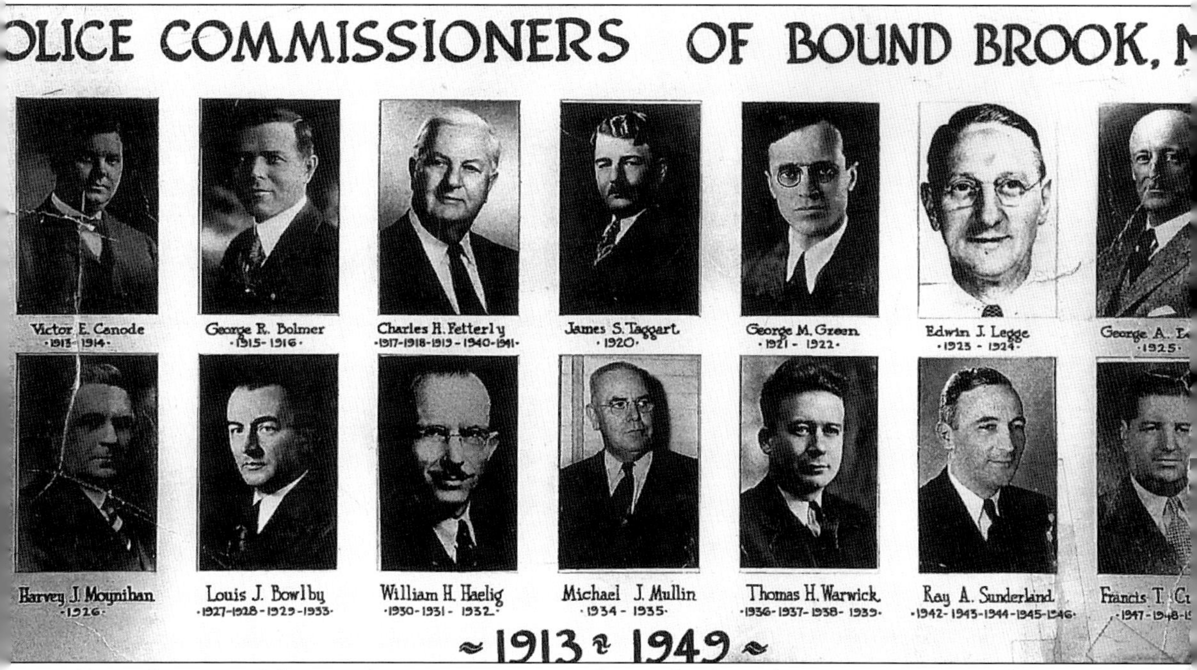

From the time of the town's incorporation as a borough, the police commissioner's job was an important one. This photograph shows the holders of the post from 1913 to 1949.

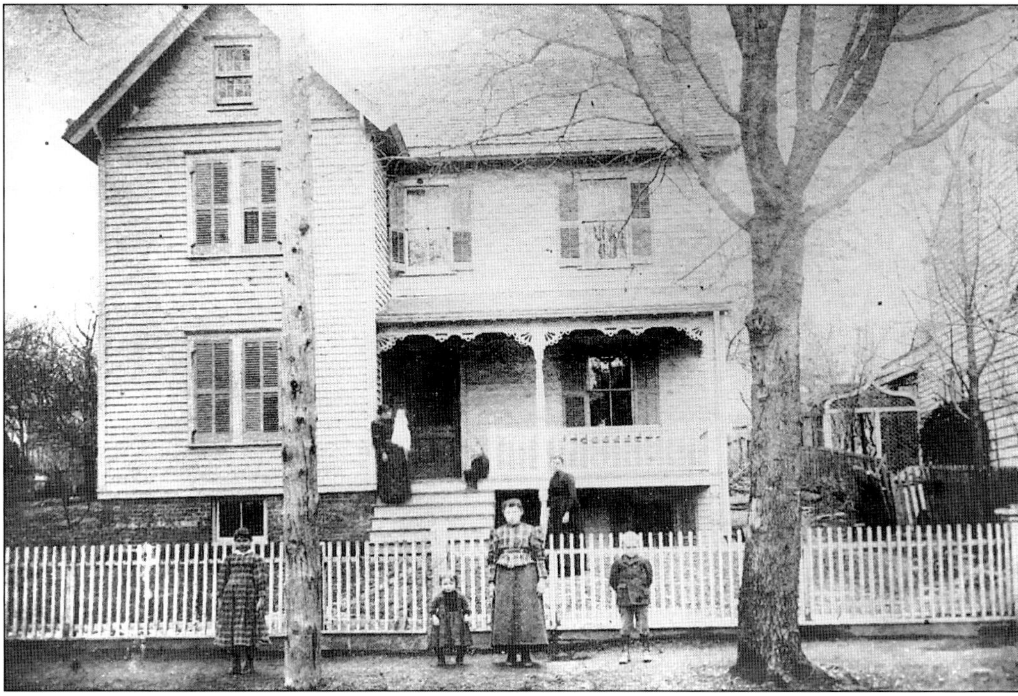

The Sutton family built this house on Second Street in 1892. Members of the family posed here for this 1893 photograph. Some of their descendants still occupy the building.

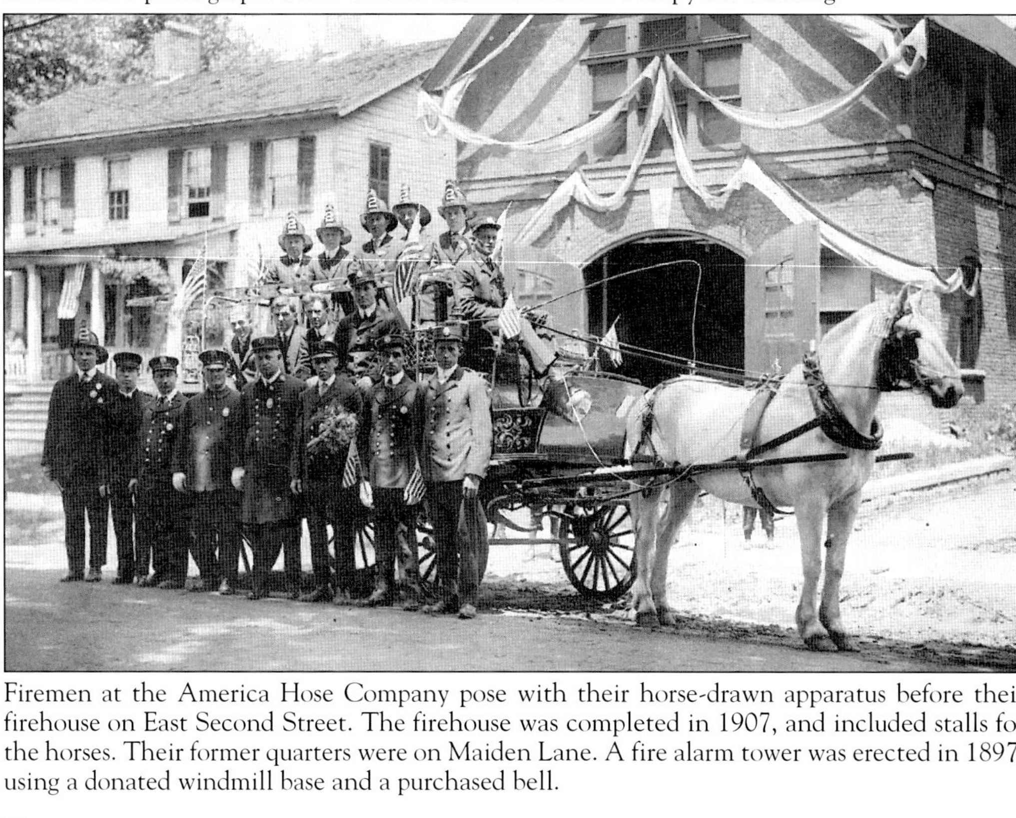

Firemen at the America Hose Company pose with their horse-drawn apparatus before their firehouse on East Second Street. The firehouse was completed in 1907, and included stalls for the horses. Their former quarters were on Maiden Lane. A fire alarm tower was erected in 1897, using a donated windmill base and a purchased bell.

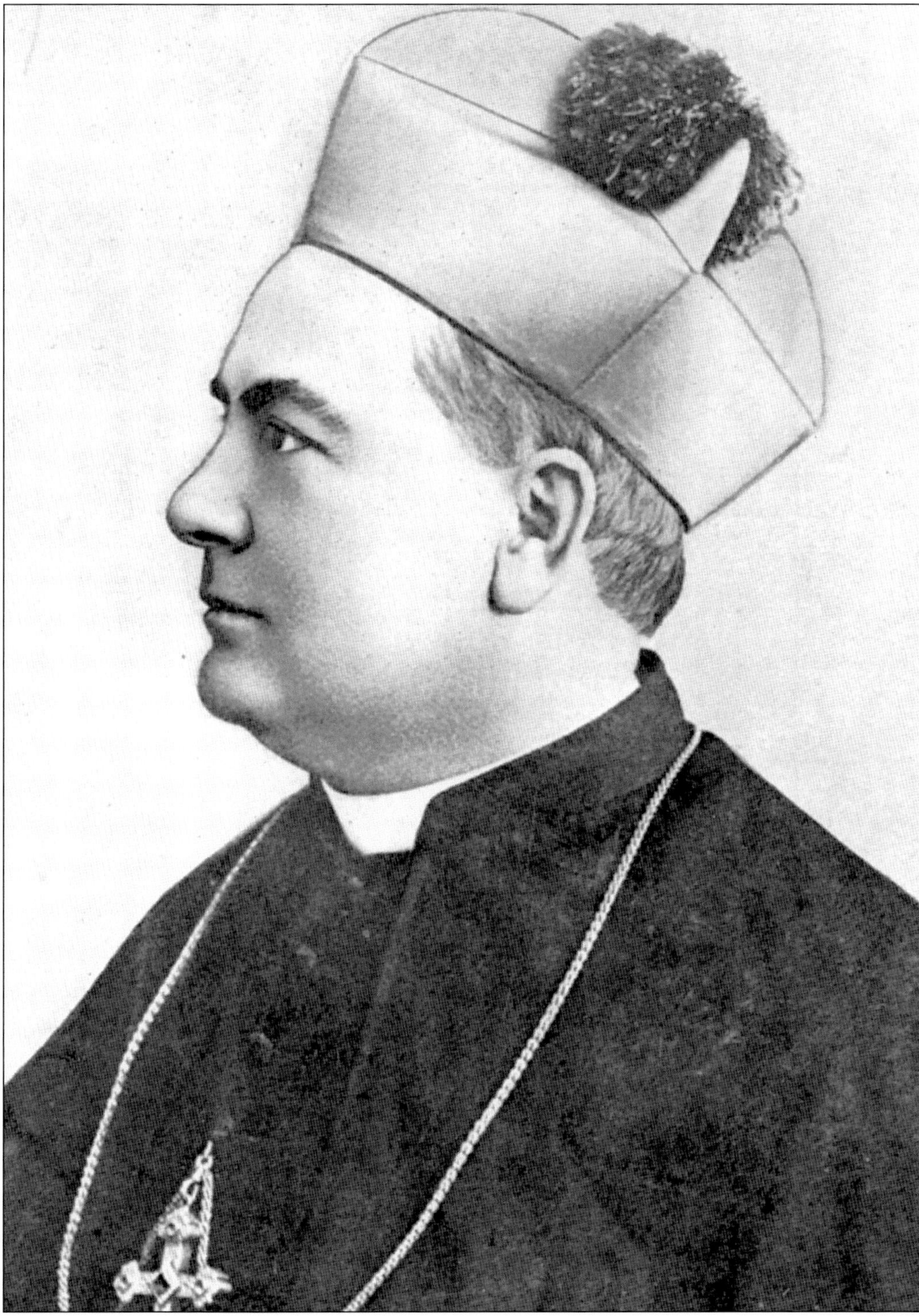
Bishop James McFaul was born in Ireland and came to the Bound Brook area with his parents when he was four years old. The family settled near Zarephath. He served as an altar boy in the old St. Joseph church building and said his first mass as an ordained priest in the same building.

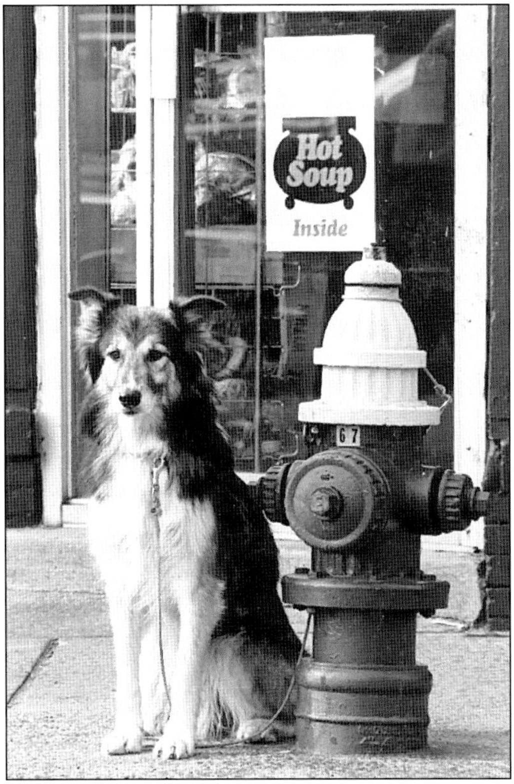

The House of Bread was a popular stop in the 1970s for baked goods, hot soup, and coffee. This patient canine awaits the exit of his owner from within.

Barbara Haelig and Mary Cook pose before the LaMonte Field scoreboard during the 1942 football season.

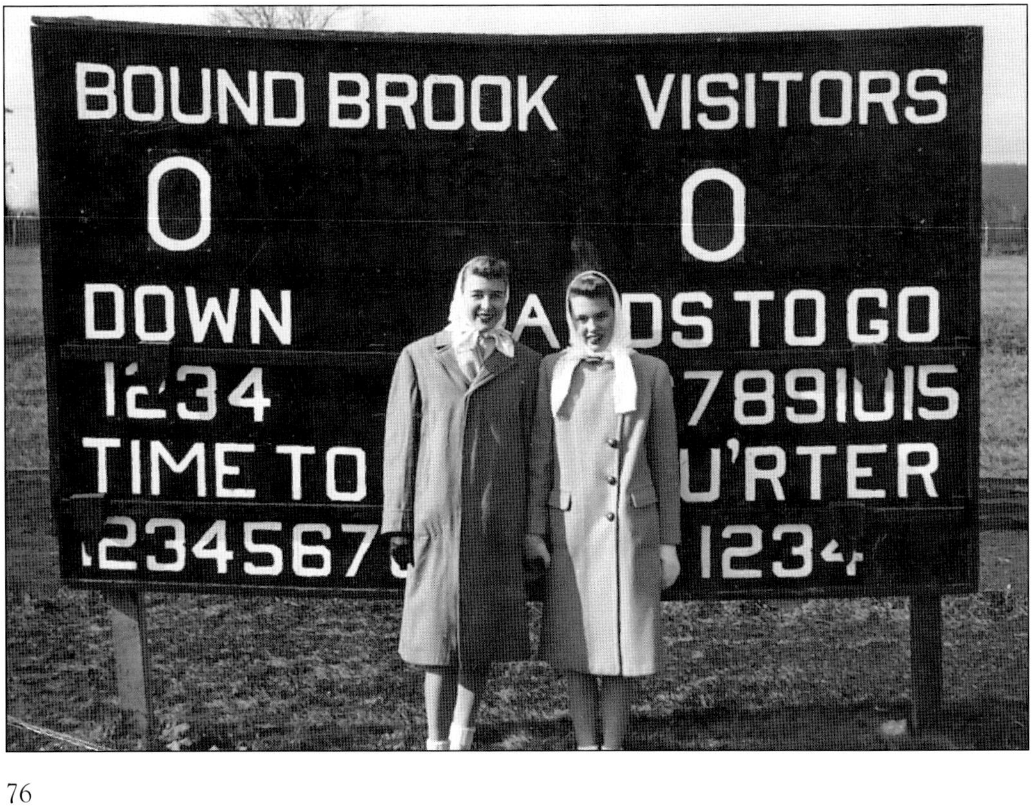

Malcolm Forbes and Elizabeth Taylor were among the motorcycle enthusiasts who gathered at Rick's Cycle Shop on Main Street.

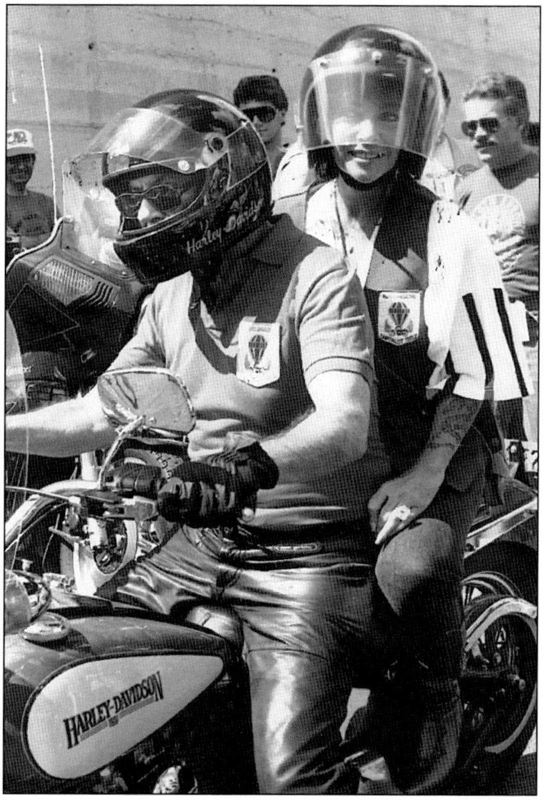

Folks in Bound Brook, like many others, always enjoyed an auction sale, hoping for a treasure or a bargain. The camera of F.N. Voorhees captured the event at the turn of the 19th century.

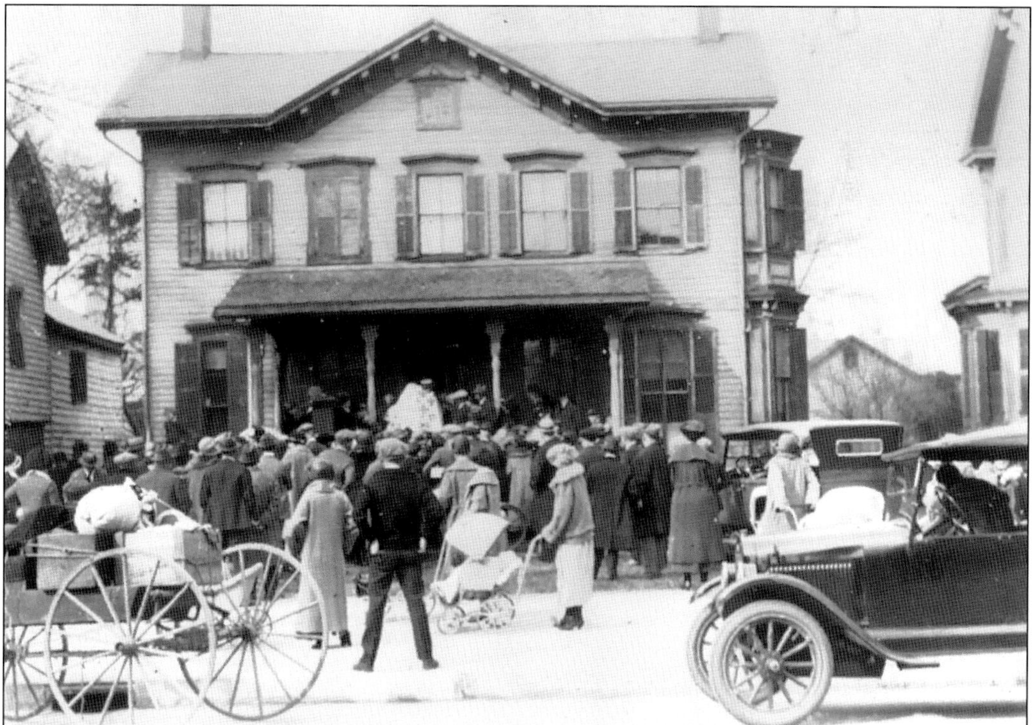

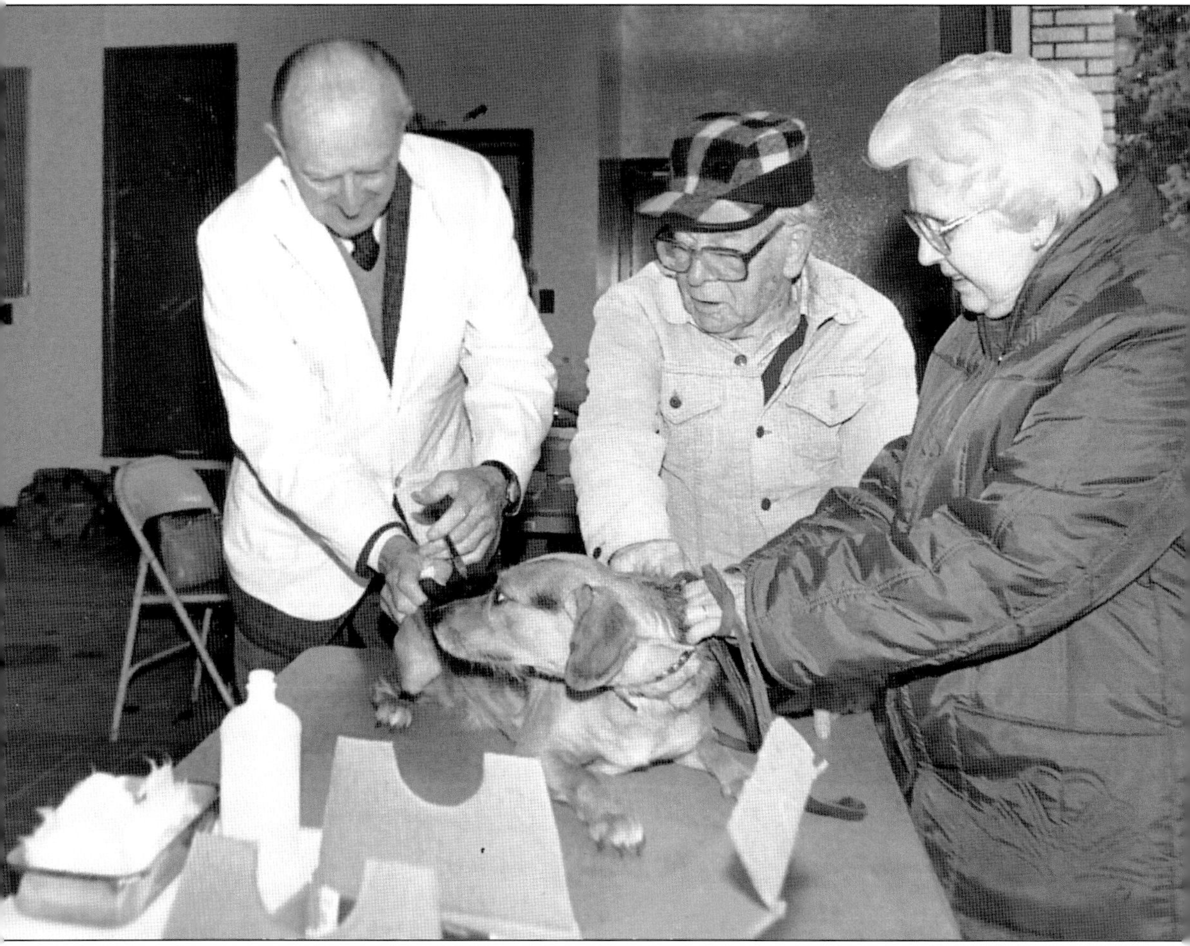

Dr. William B. Platt grew up on the Meyer's Farm in Finderne. He became a veterinarian with offices in Bound Brook and Middlesex Borough for nearly 50 years. He also manned local rabies clinics for nearly as long.

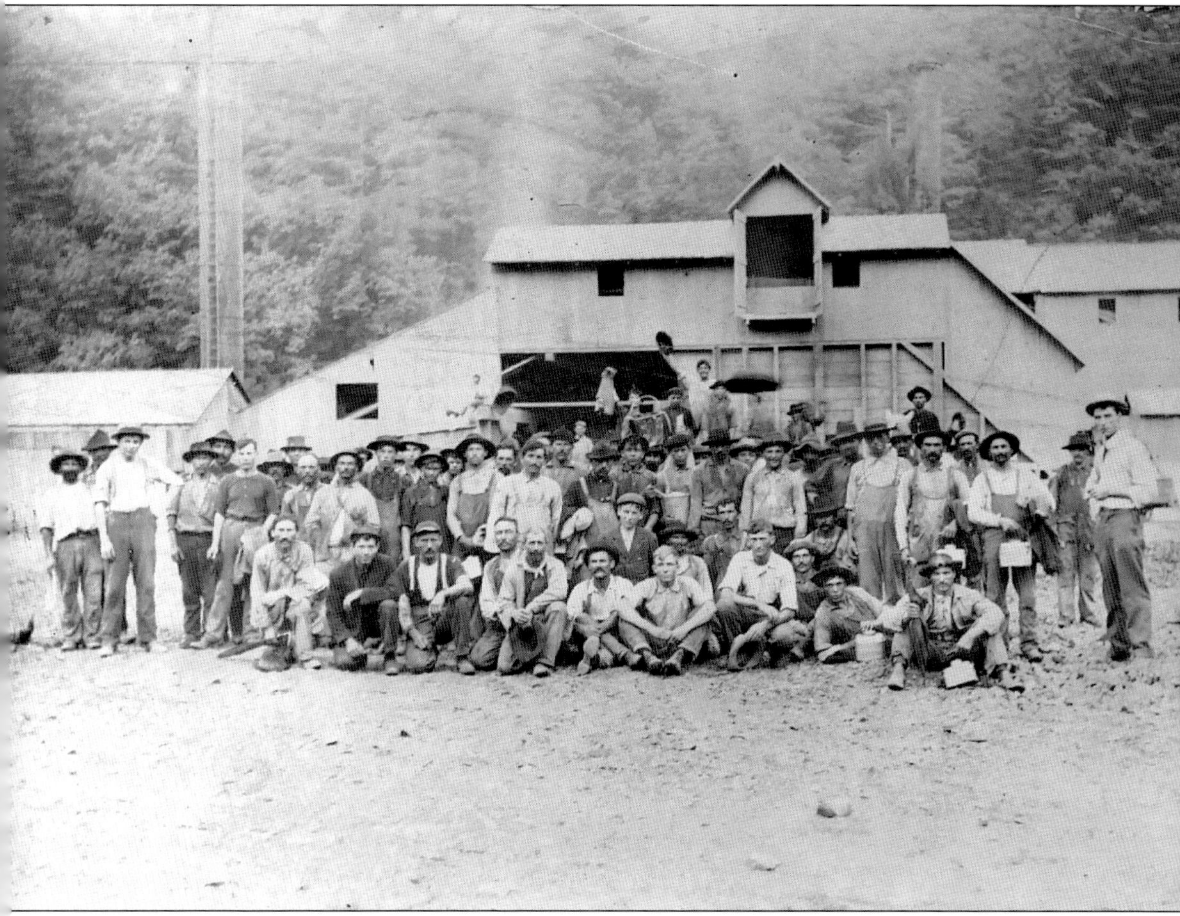

The Haeligs began to quarry stone not long after they purchased the Chimney Rock site. For many immigrants who arrived in Bound Brook in the early 1900s, the quarry gave them their first job.

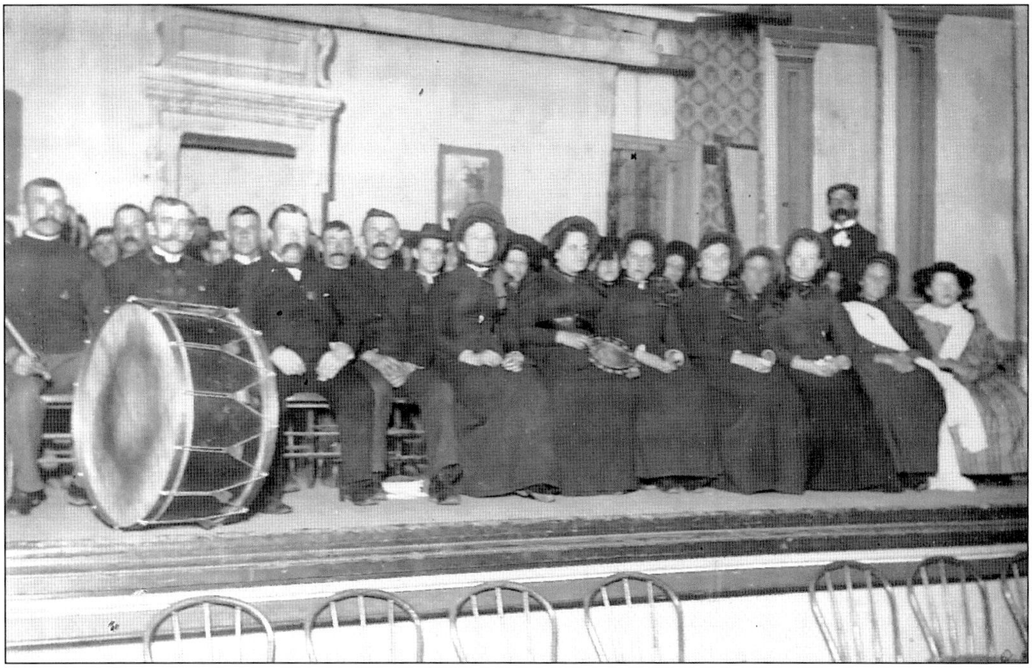

Salvation Army programs were crowd-pleasers at the close of the 19th century, when attendance was counted in the thousands at some of the outdoor programs. Here, the band performs indoors at either the Voorhees building or Bound Brook Hall.

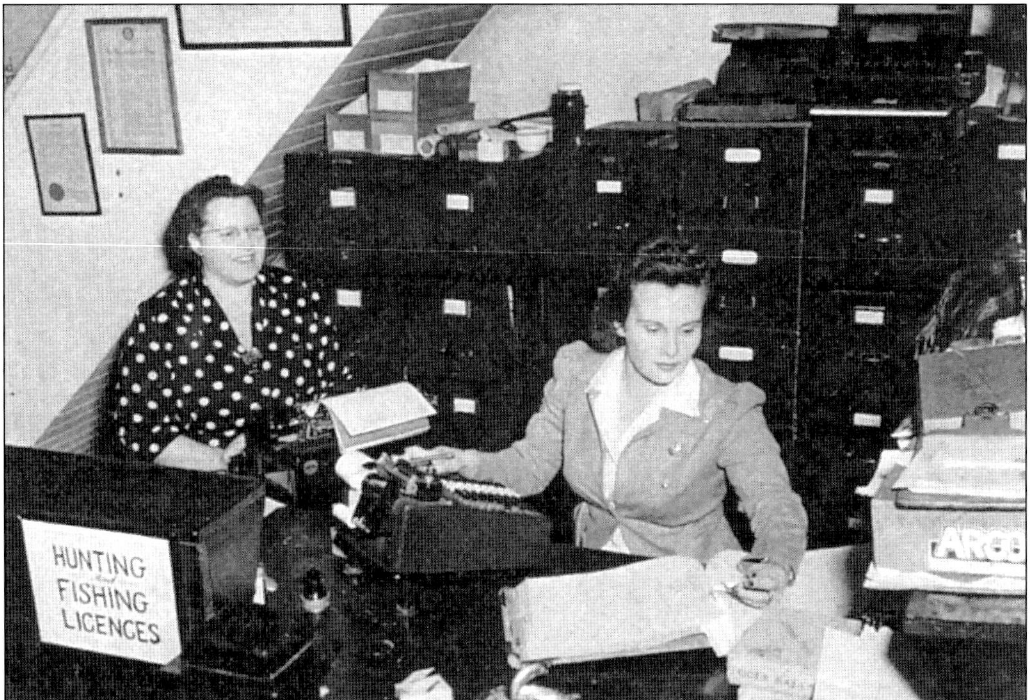

Effinger's Sporting Goods occupied a building on East Main Street for many years. Store clerks dispensed fishing and hunting licenses, as shown in this 1940s photograph.

The charming little girl in this 1918 photograph is Adeline Sofferin, age four. Her father, Jacob, was one of the founders of the Jacob Schiff Congregation. He and his wife kept a dry goods store on Main Street.

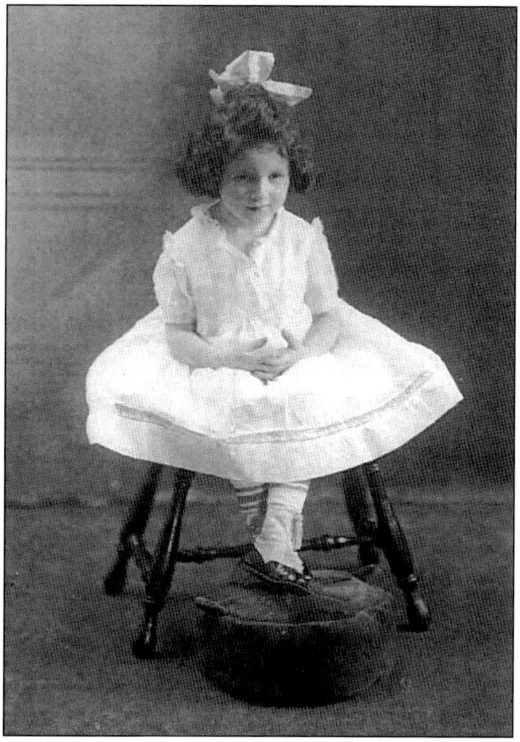

The Malloy family posed for this group photograph in the 1920s. The picture was taken at their home in Middlebrook, where James Malloy ran a well-known dairy farm.

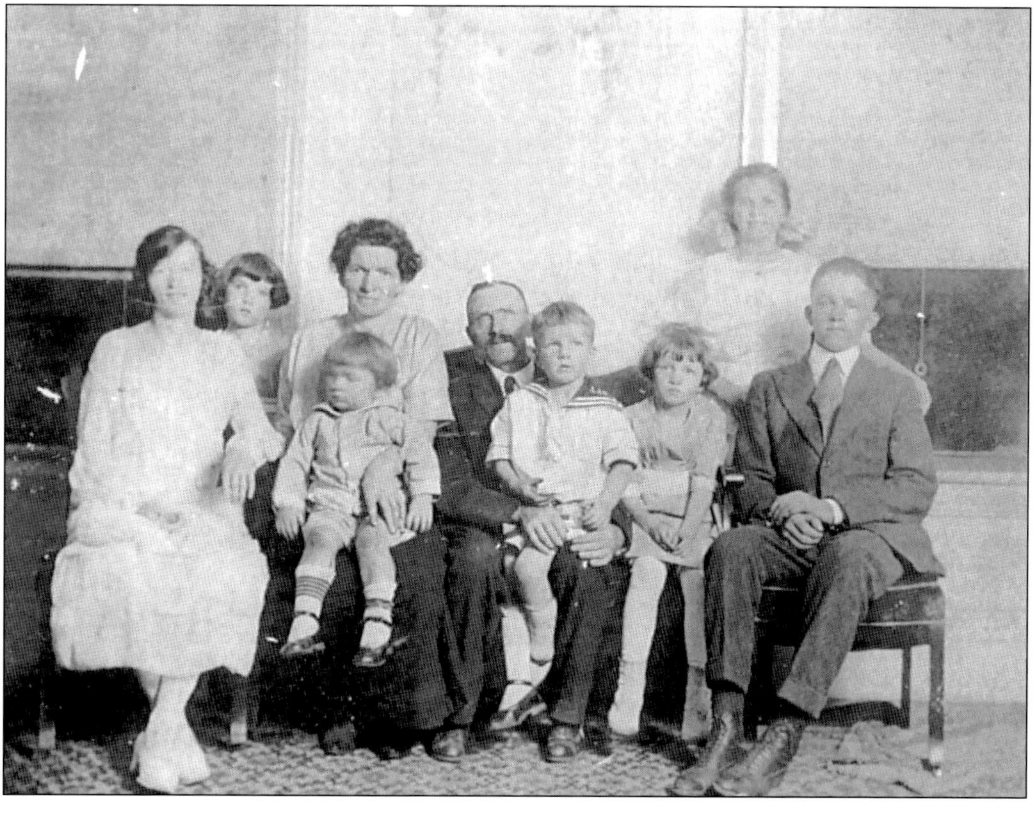

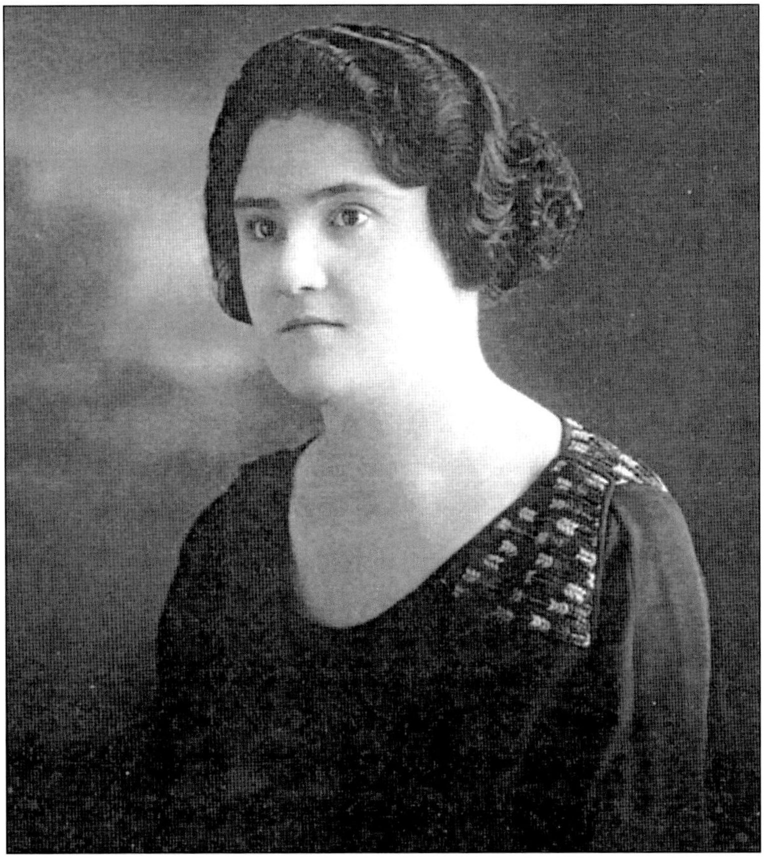

Vivian David came here from Snowshoe, Pennsylvania, and began a teaching career in the Bound Brook school system. During her 41-year career, she served as principal of all three elementary schools. She is shown (left) in 1924 and (bottom) with Neil Mackenzie shortly before her death on December 14, 1996.

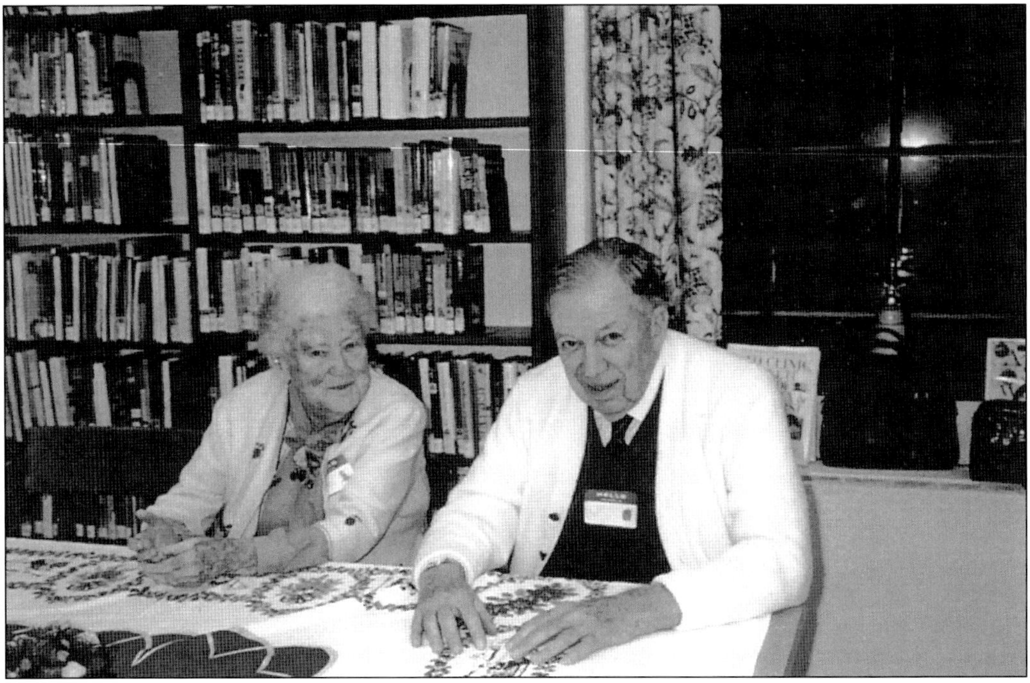

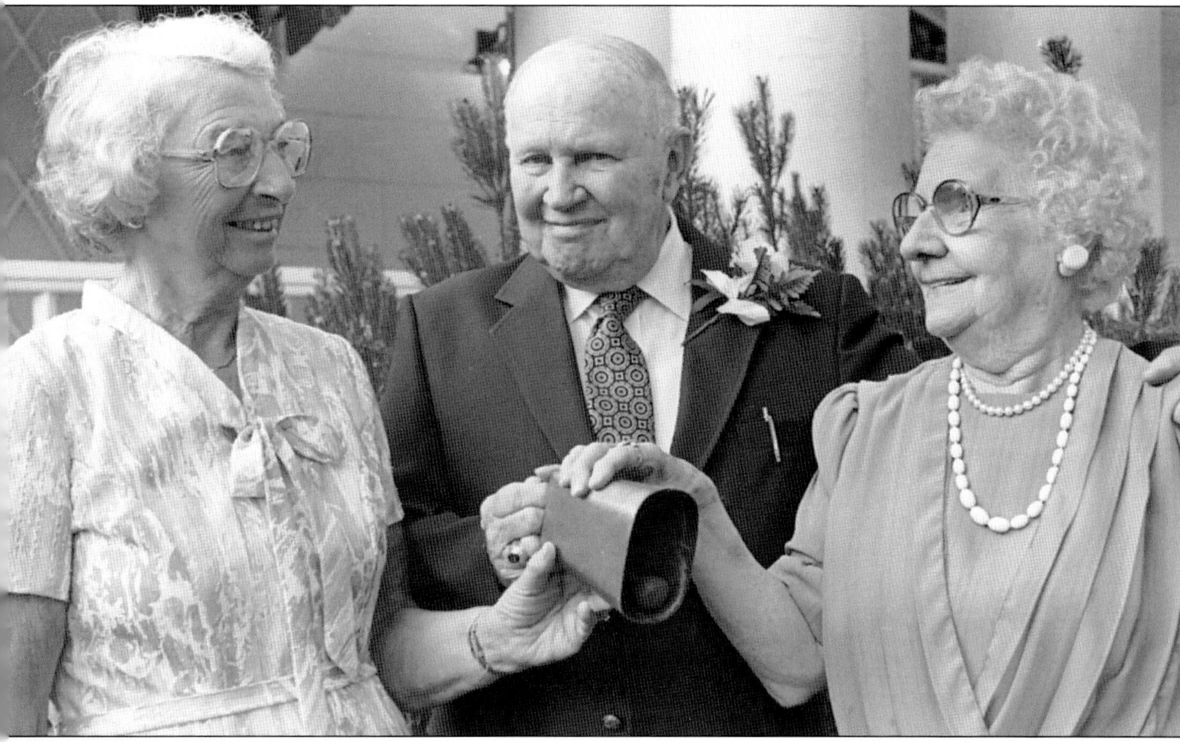

Marjorie Allaire Gould, Firman Loree, and Marian Johnson were among the attendees of the 60th reunion of the Bound Brook High School class of 1926.

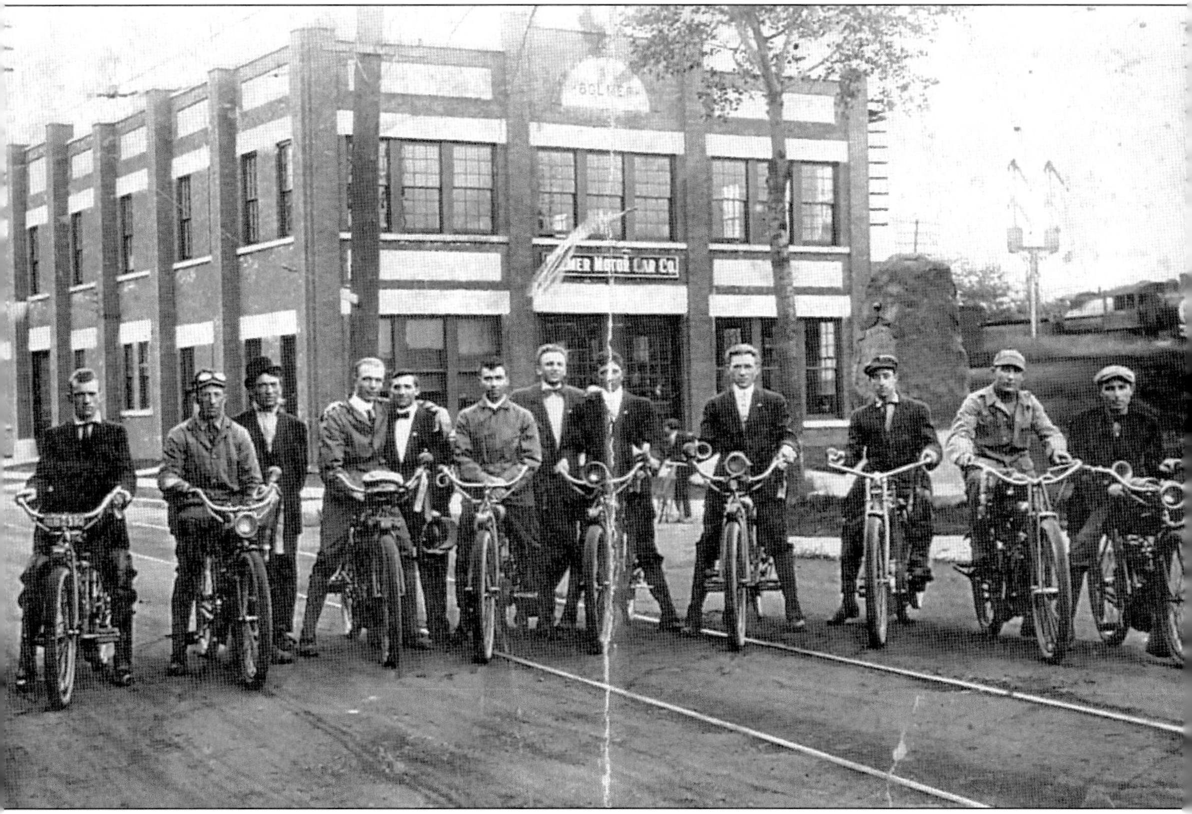

The bicycle captured America's fancy in the late 1880s, and Bound Brook was no exception. The pastime later evolved to include the motorcycle when this group posed in the 1920s.

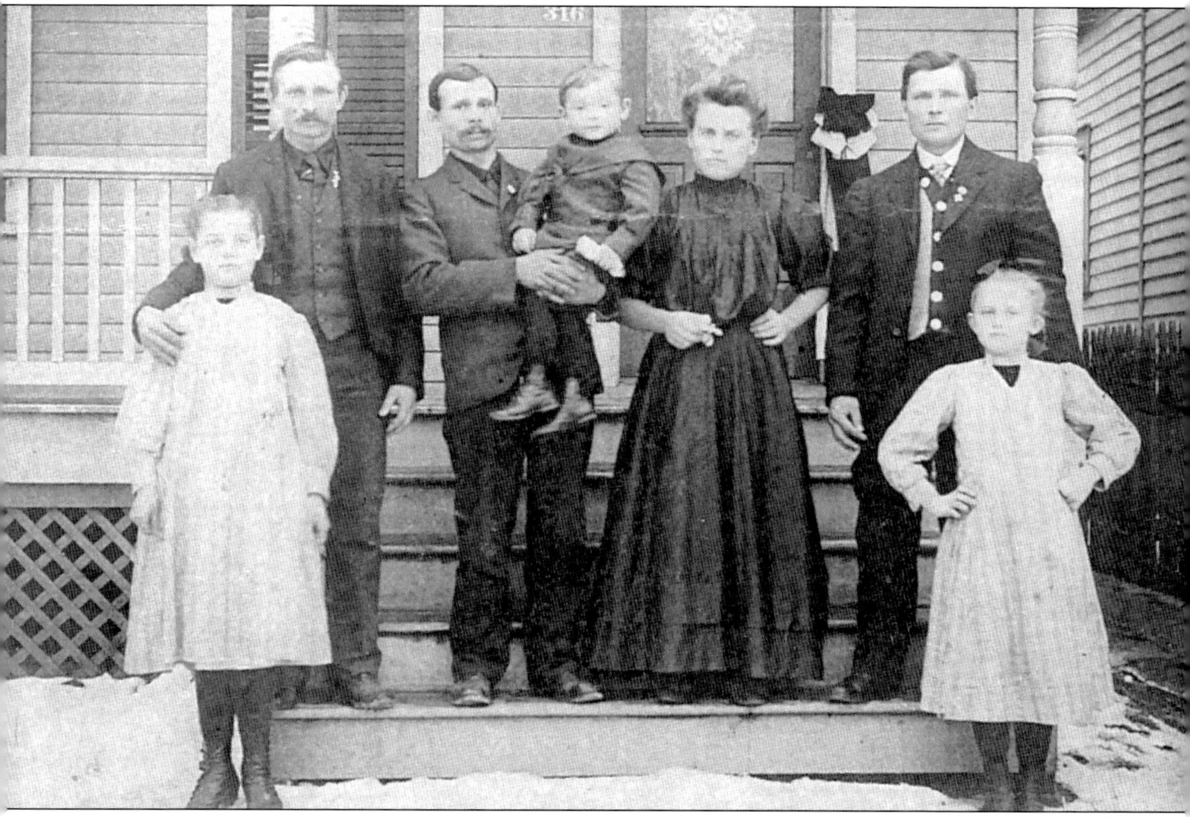

Posing in front of their home in Middlebrook in 1910 are members of the Zavacky family, who came to Bound Brook from Osturna in Slovakia. They, along with other families from the same region of Slovakia, found ready employment in the Woolen Mill.

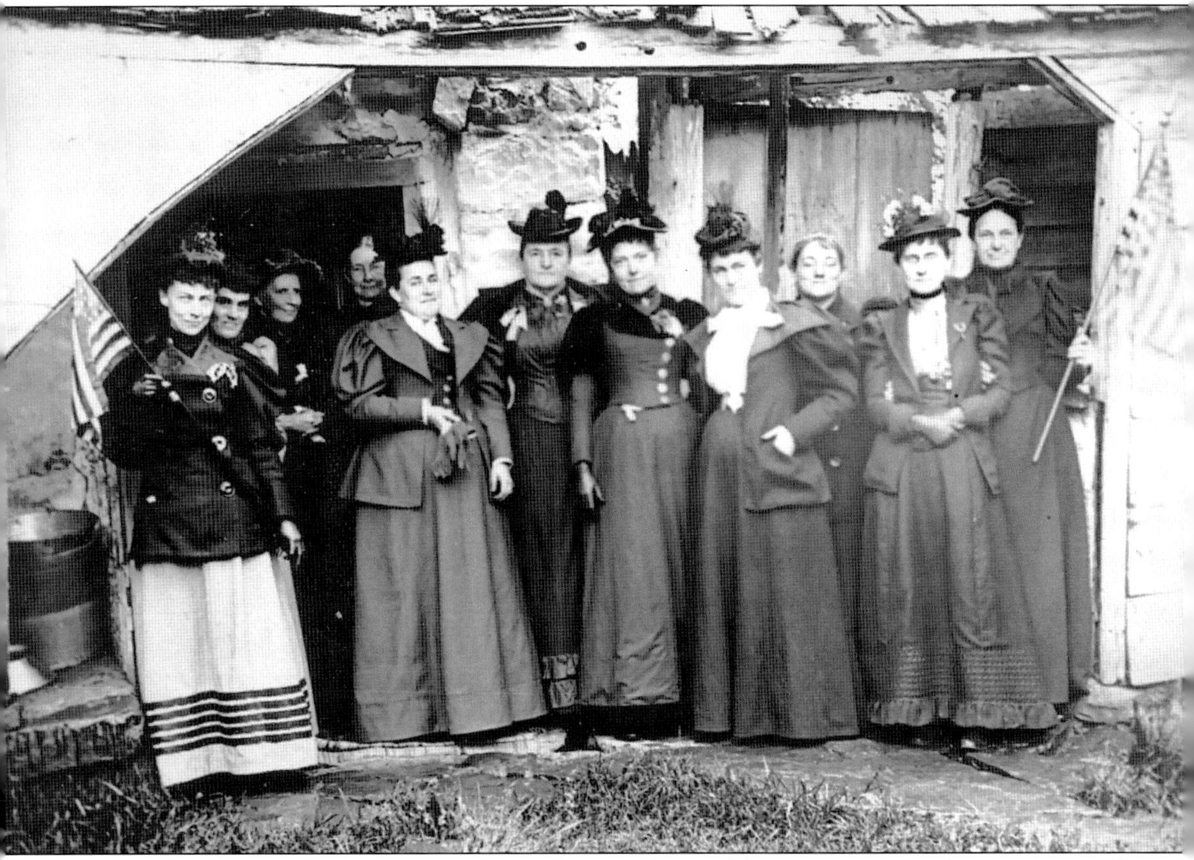

Members of Camp Middlebrook chapter of the Daughters of the American Revolution journeyed to Bedminster in 1895 via spring wagon to visit the historic "old farm" property made popular in Andrew Mellick's book *Story of An Old Farm*.

James P. Malloy and Frank Kolbek were two of the town's prominent businessmen in the early 20th century. Kolbek first ran a bottling and beer distribution business, and Malloy's horse-drawn milk wagon was a familiar sight around town.

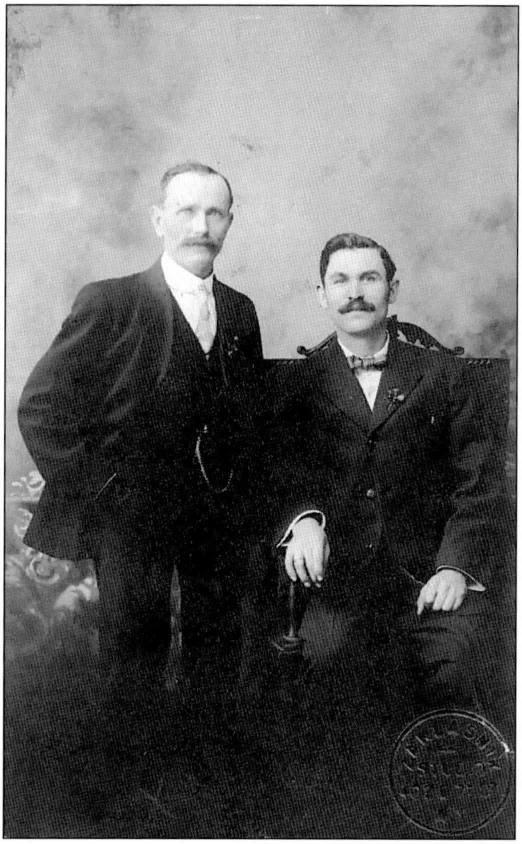

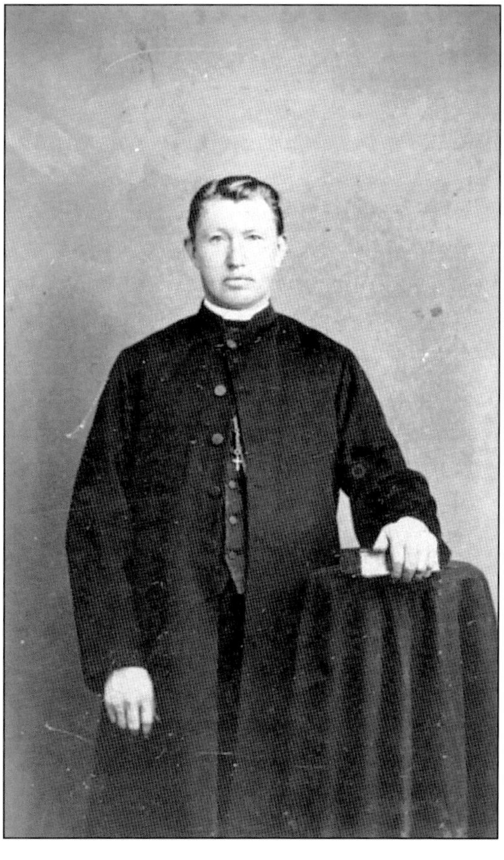

Father Martin Van den Bogaard was born and educated in Holland. He was the first resident pastor of St. Joseph Church beginning in 1877. He also served the mission church at East Millstone at the same time. In 1882, he was transferred to Somerville. Returning to Holland, he died in 1915.

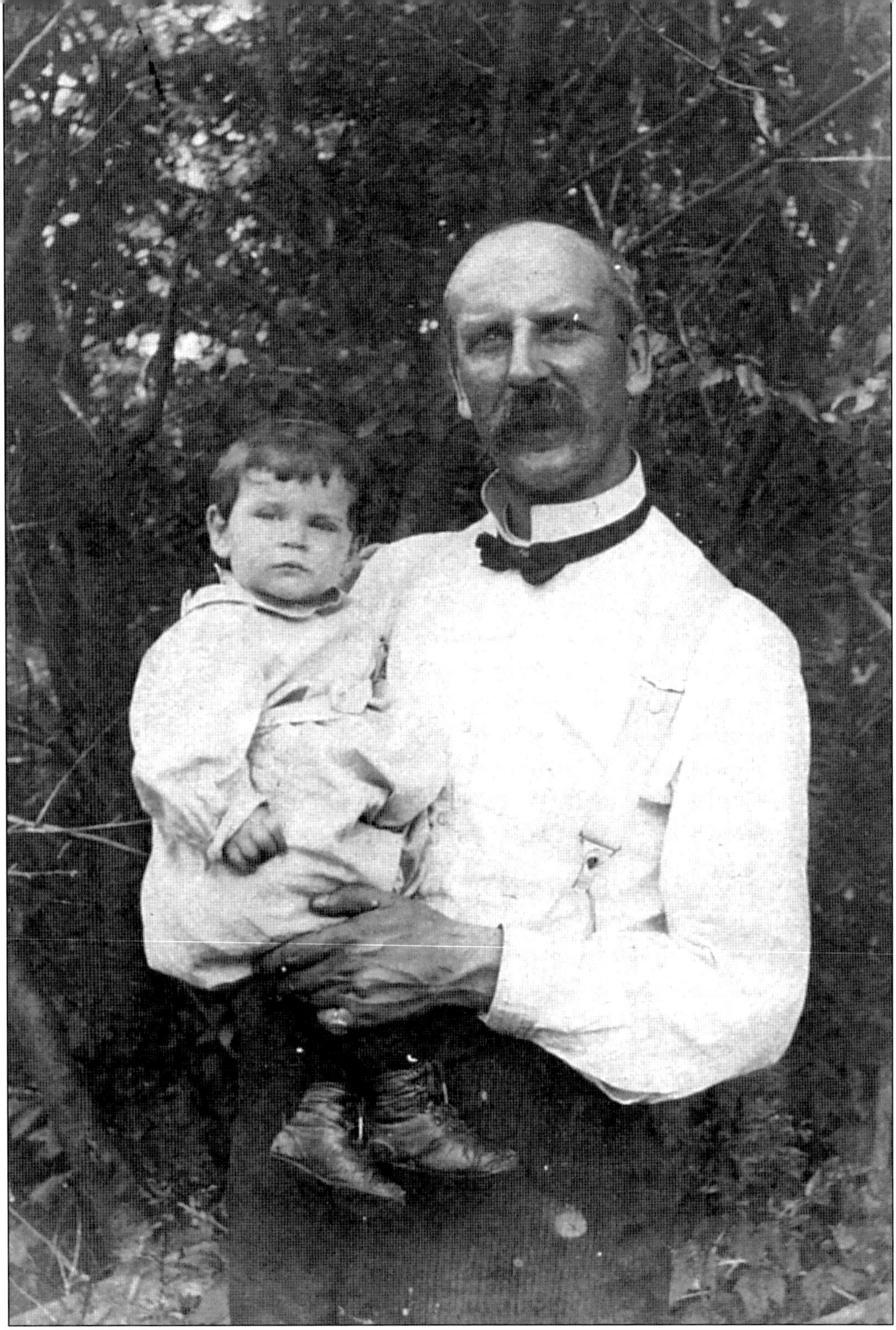

David Hastings came from Belfast, Ireland, to accept a job at the Woolen Mill. During his lifetime, he served the town in many capacities, including postmaster.

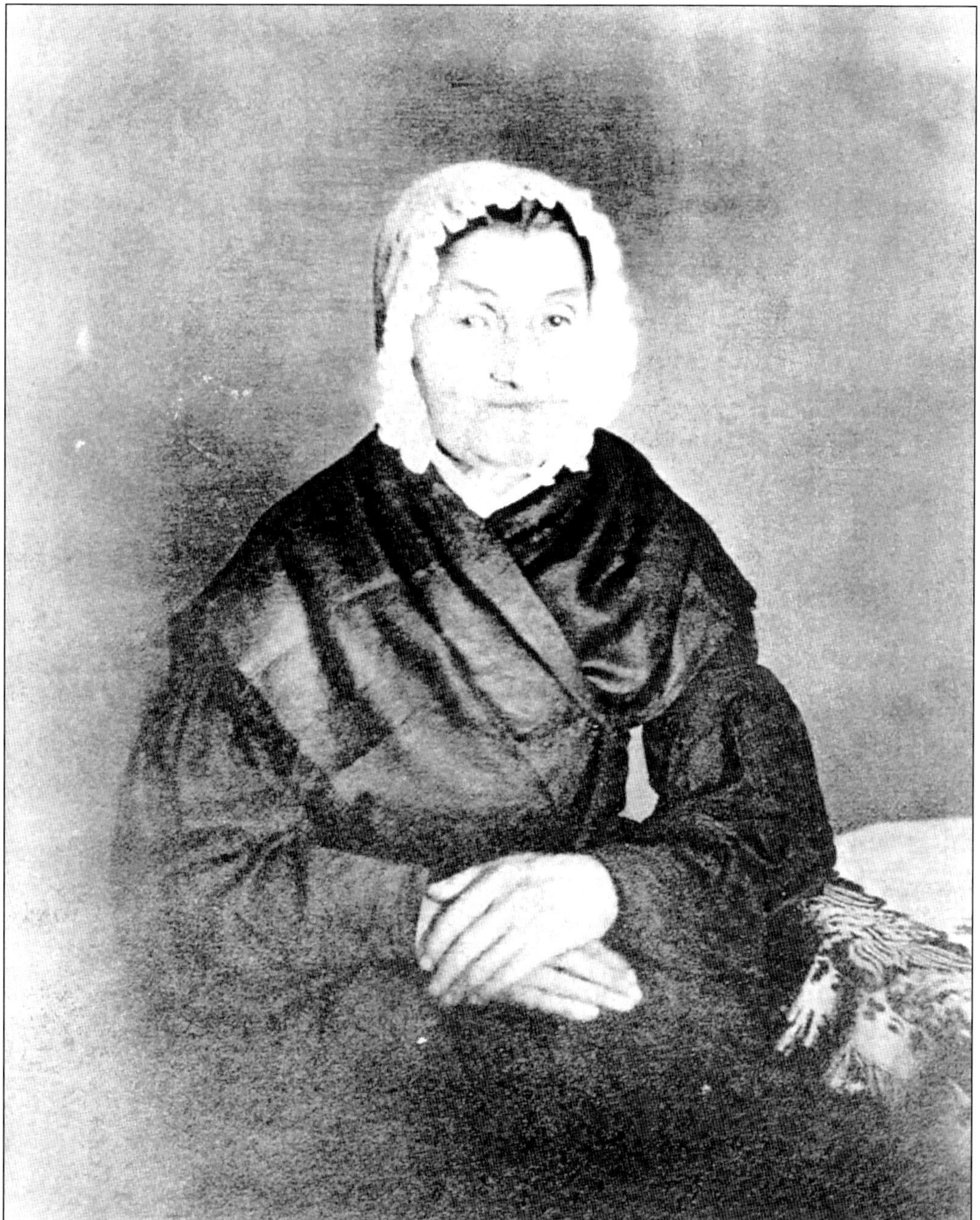

Mary Faville, wife of Jonathan Smith and daughter of Thomas and Mary Faville, was born on the family farm on Tea Street. As a child during the Revolutionary War, she remembered George Washington's army encamped along the Middlebrook and British raiding parties that threatened her family.

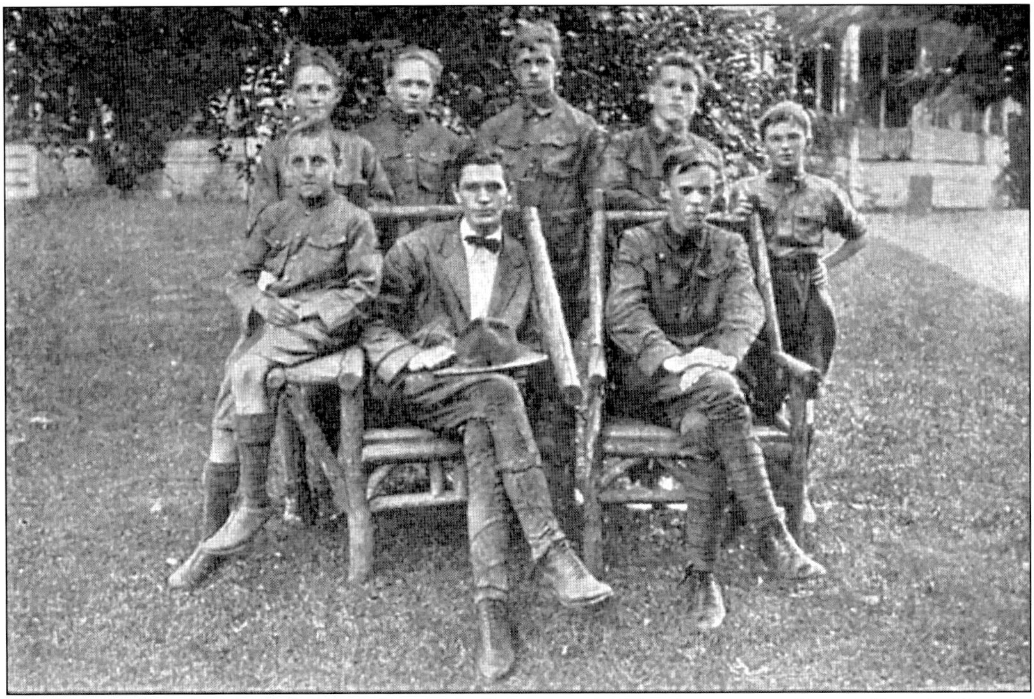

In 1917, when this photograph was taken, there were 60 boy scouts in Bound Brook. During WWI, they were trained to serve the community, working with the Red Cross and running a large garden patch.

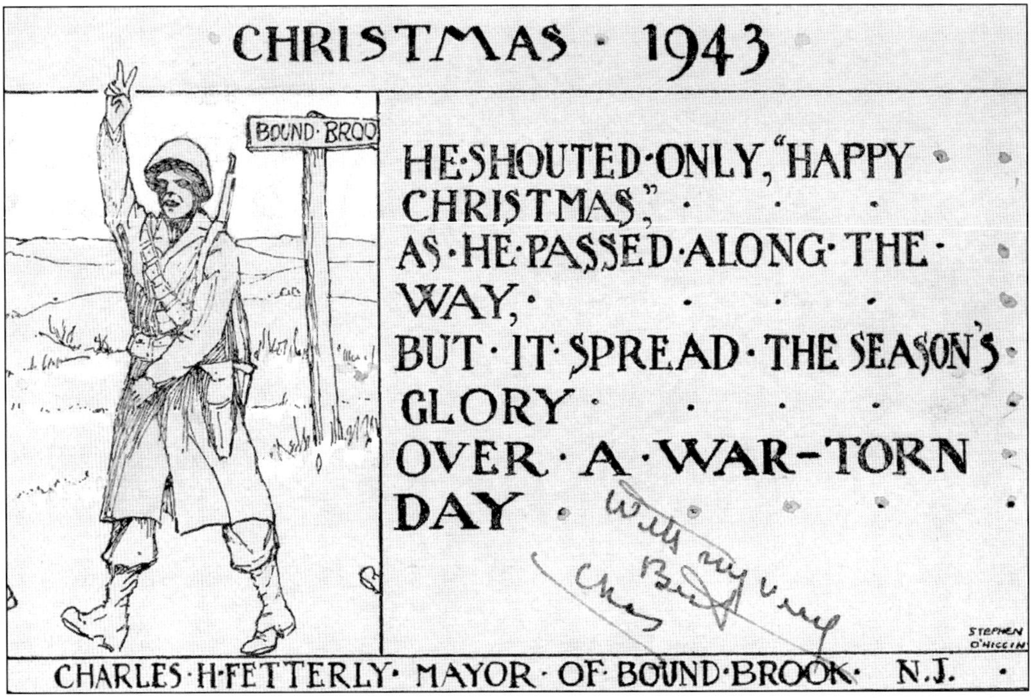

Charles Fetterly, local druggist, served as mayor during the Great Depression and WWII, when he sent out these Christmas cards to all local men and women in the armed services.

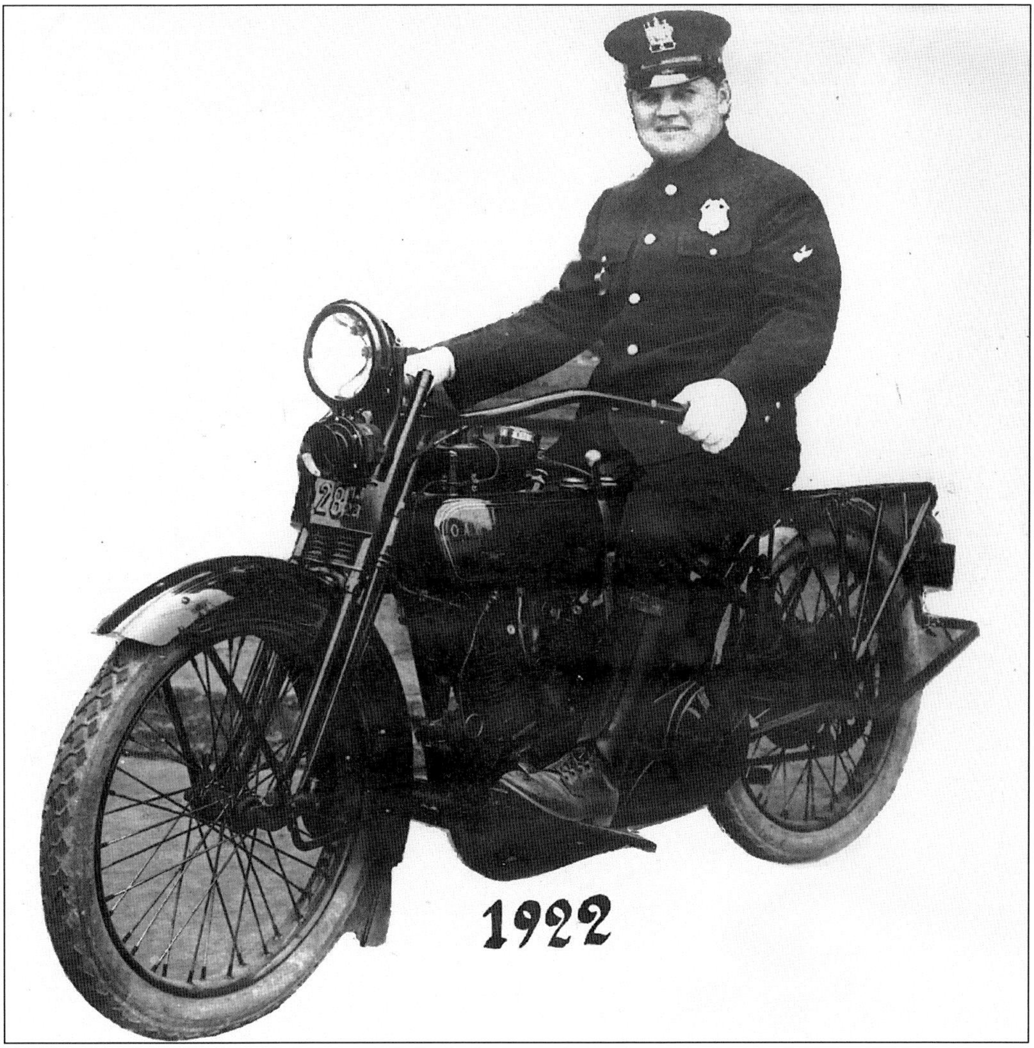

Otto Williams was appointed to the Bound Brook police force in 1922. He was the town's first motorcycle patrolman. In 1940, he was appointed chief to replace William Nash.

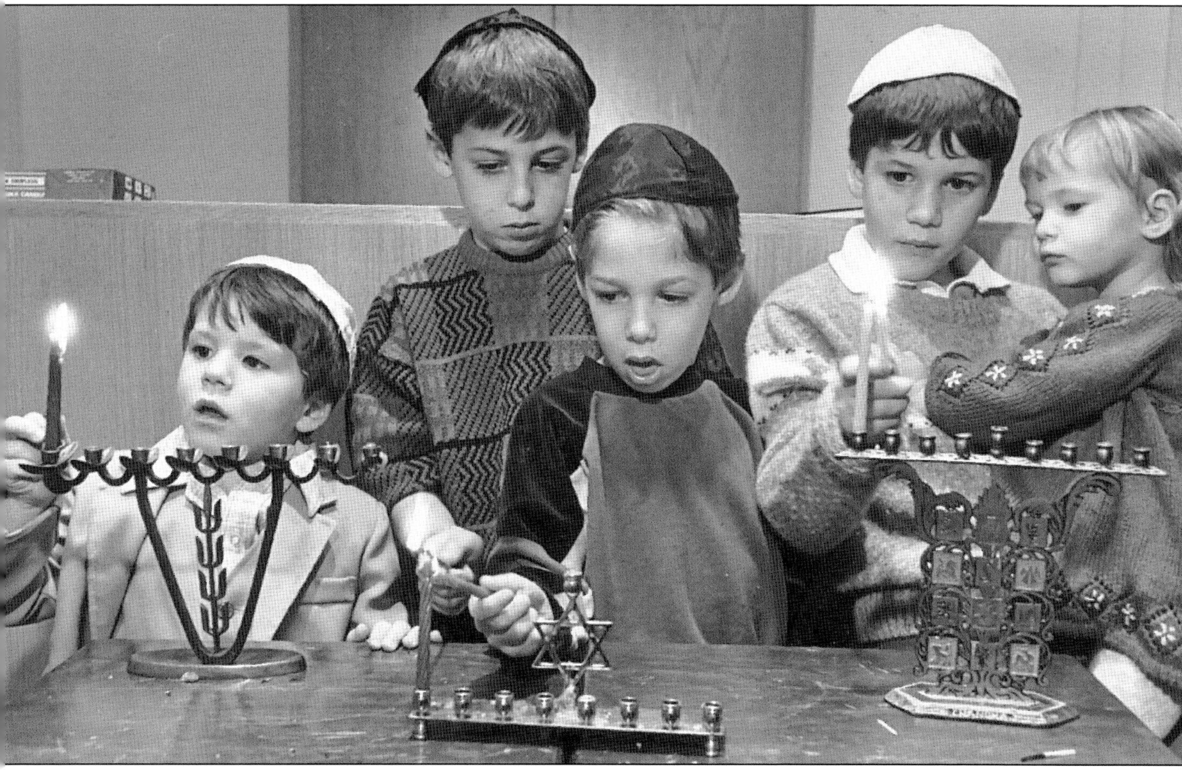

Lighting the first day's candles of the Hanukkah on their menorahs are children of Congregation Knesseth Israel.

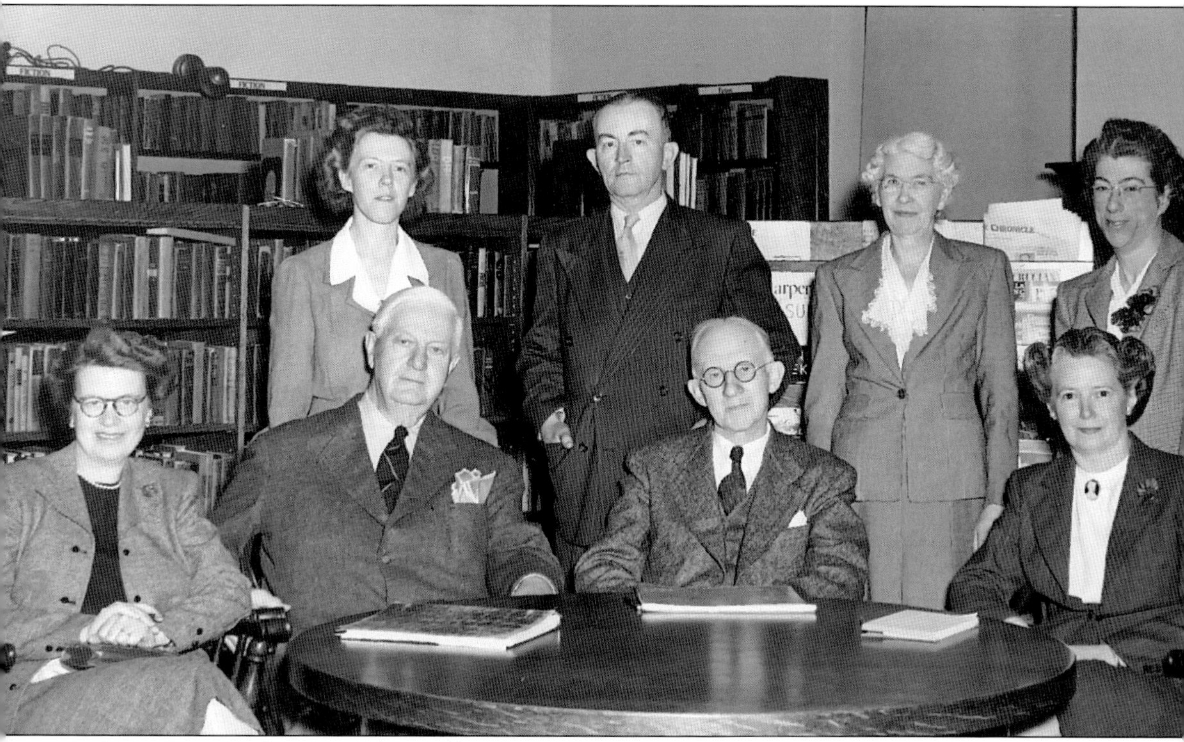

Roberta Doxsee, the town's first college-trained librarian, was hired in 1925. She is shown here in 1947 with trustees and other library staff shortly before retirement.

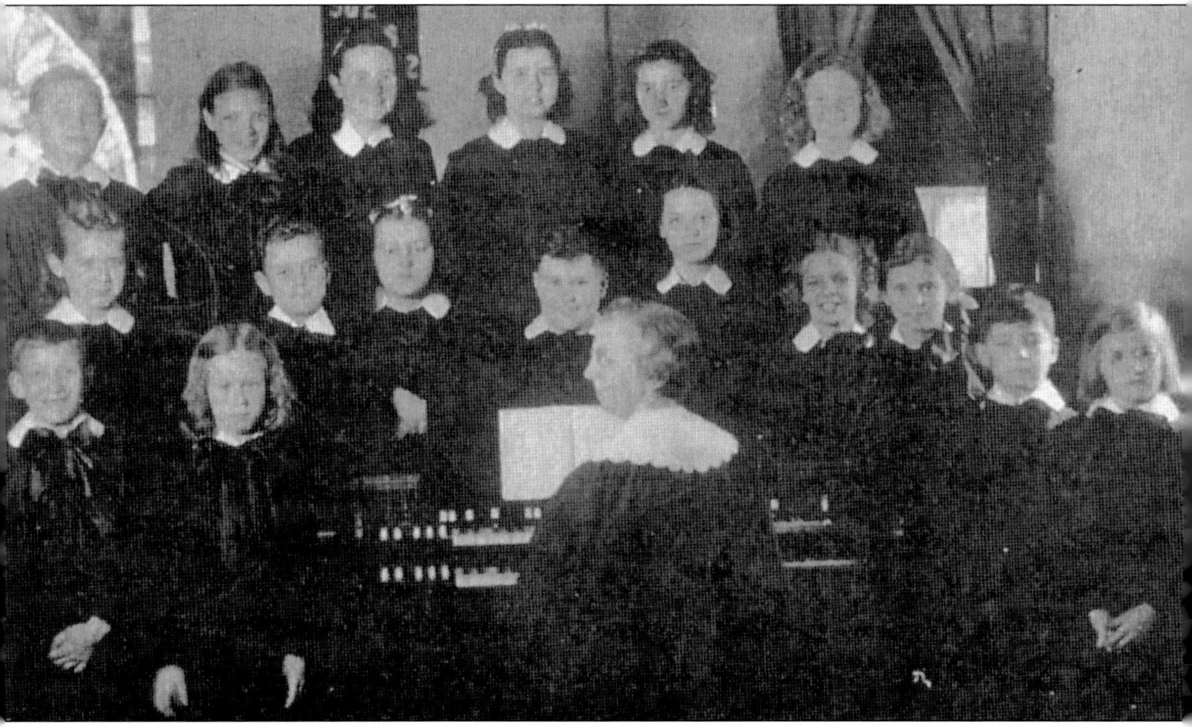

Miss Adela LaRue, a busy local piano teacher, also served as director of music for the Methodist Church for many years. She is shown here with the junior choir in 1938.

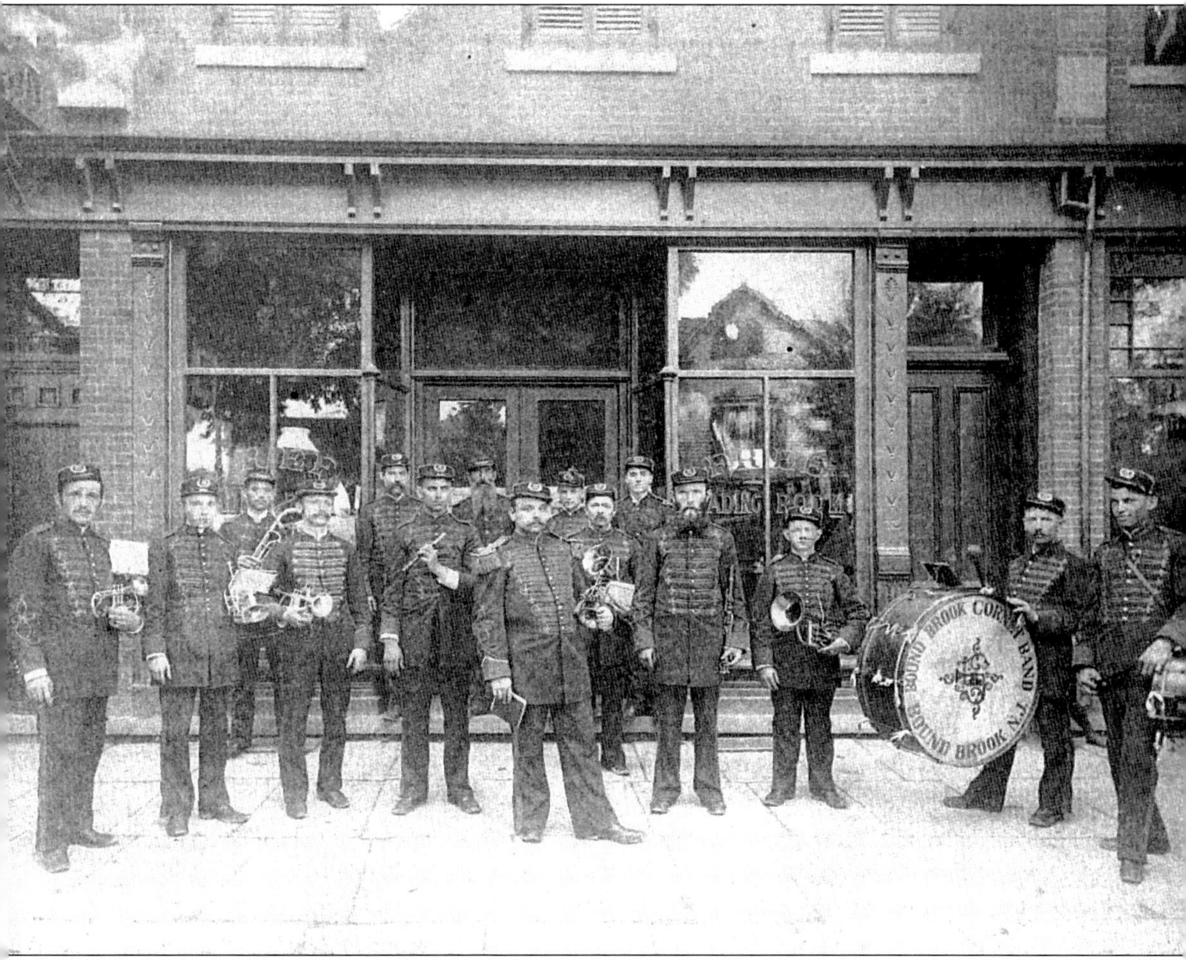

At the end of the 19th century, every town had at least one cornet band. Bound Brook was no exception. The group poses here on Main Street in front of the building housing the Free Reading Room, the forerunner of the public library.

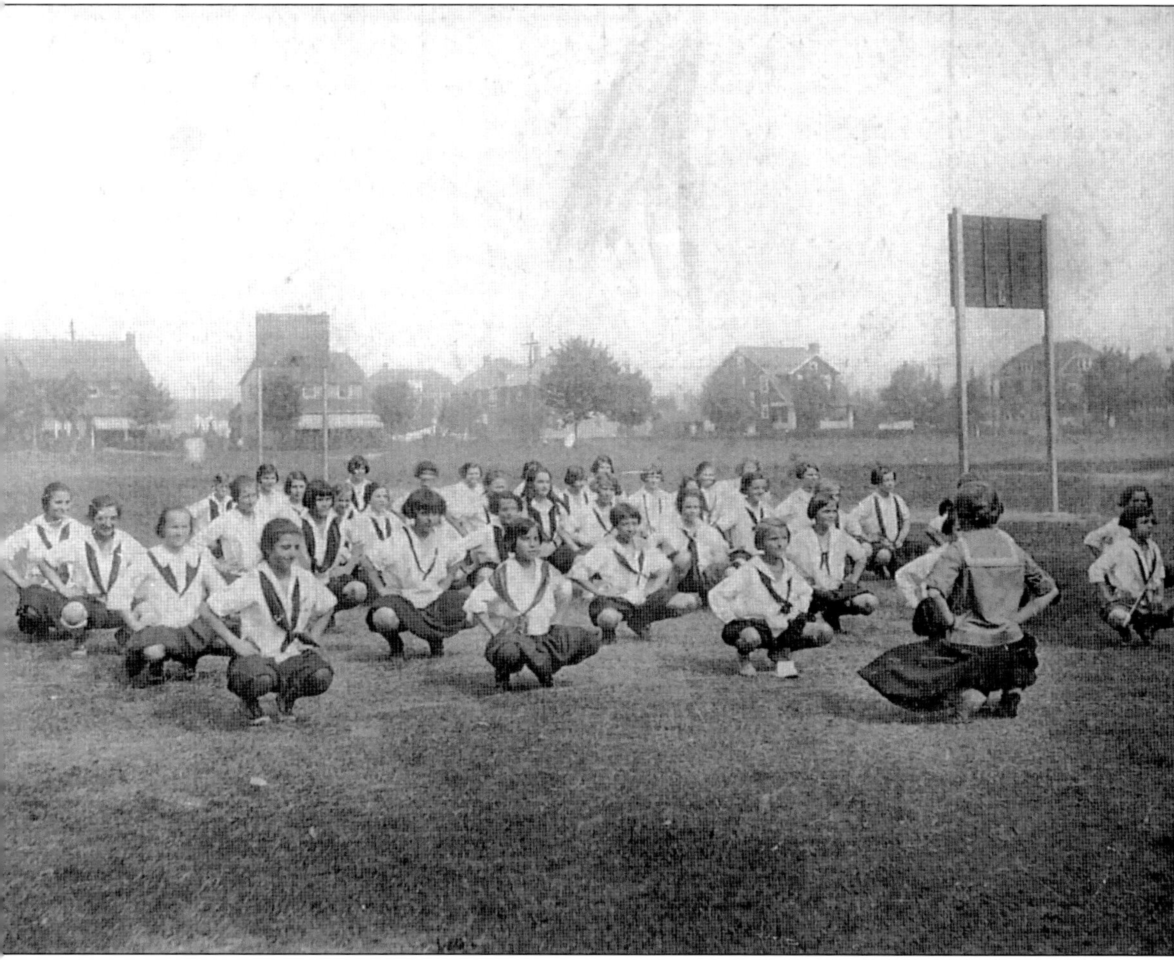

In 1926, the girl's gym class at Washington School went through exercises behind the school building. Note the houses on West Maple Avenue in the background. Anna David Reading is the girls' instructor.

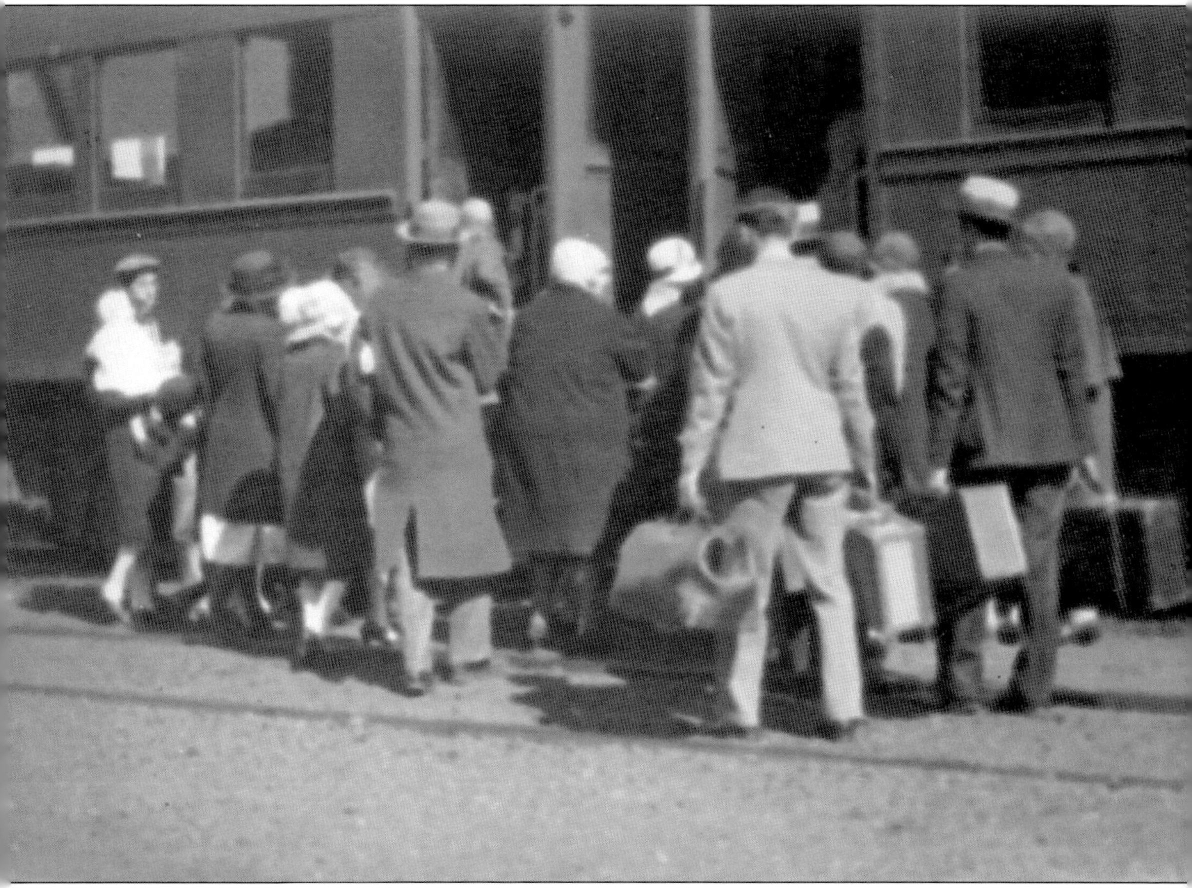

Good railroad service was one of the attractions that brought many new residents to town and provided commuter service to those who worked in New York City.

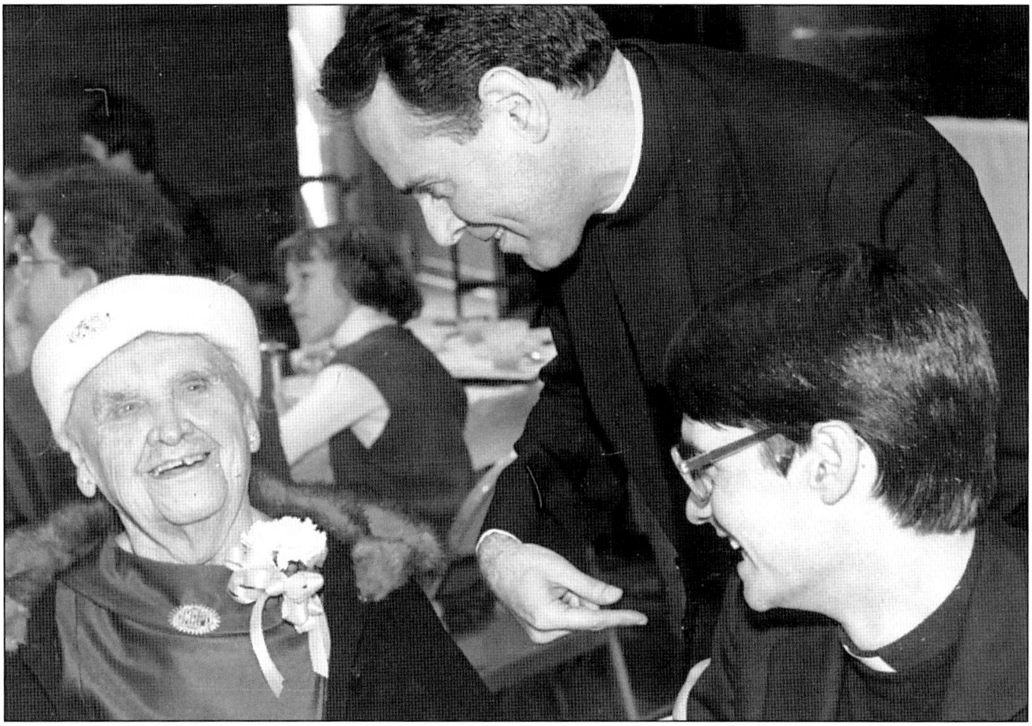

Fr. Michael Alliegro and Fr. Octavio Carpenta congratulate Mary Pfister, age 94, as one of St. Joseph Church's oldest parishioners.

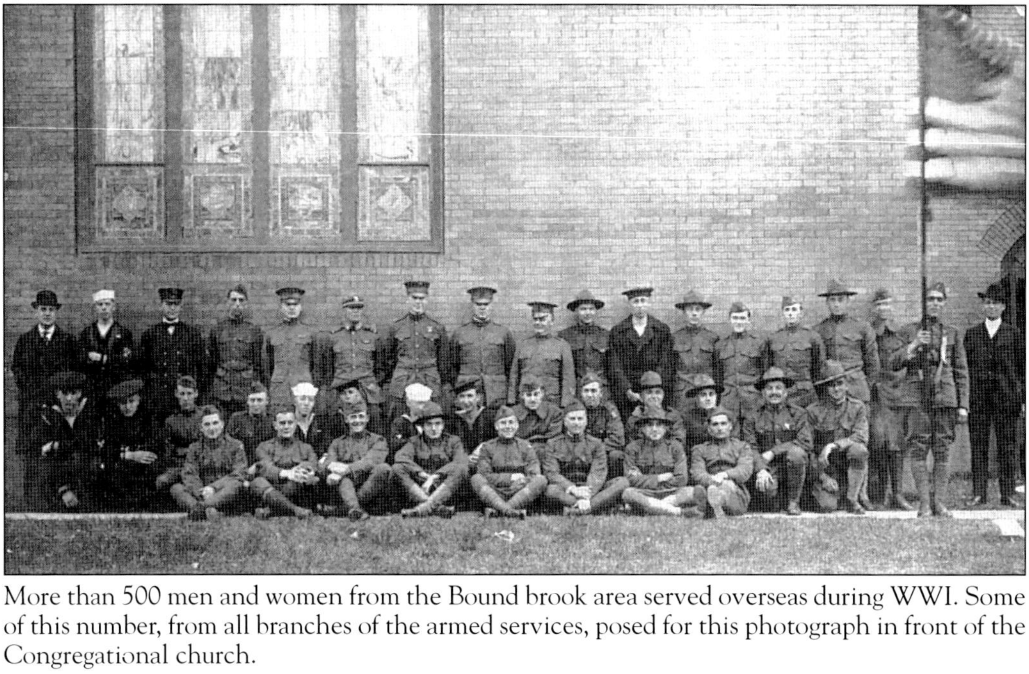

More than 500 men and women from the Bound brook area served overseas during WWI. Some of this number, from all branches of the armed services, posed for this photograph in front of the Congregational church.

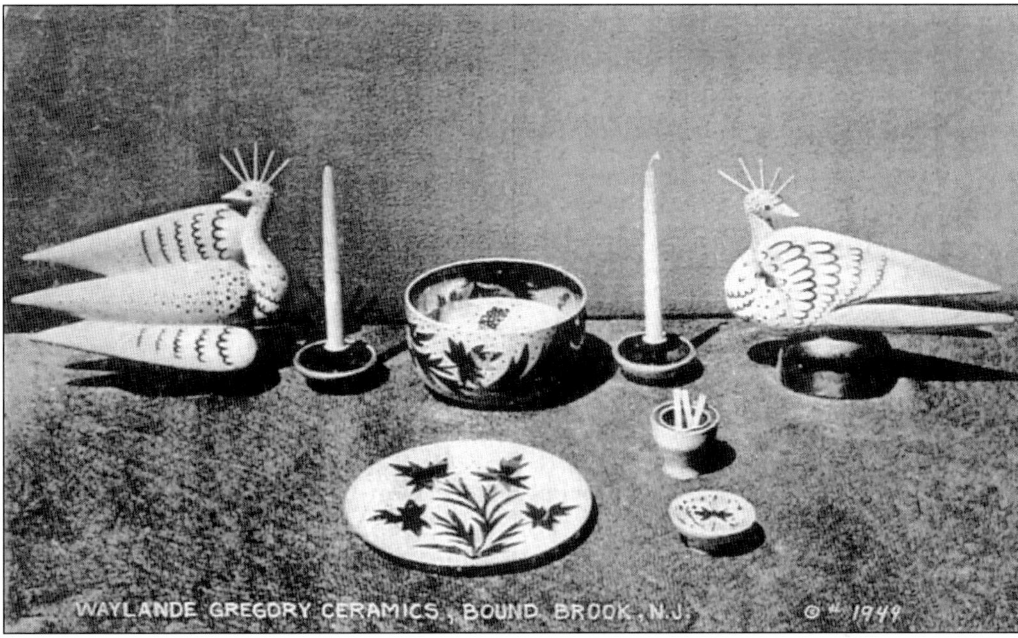

Waylande Gregory lived in Warren Township but called his residence Bound Brook. He was a prominent artist and sculptor displaying his work at the 1939 World's Fair. There is a large piece of his sculpting work in Roosevelt Park in Edison.

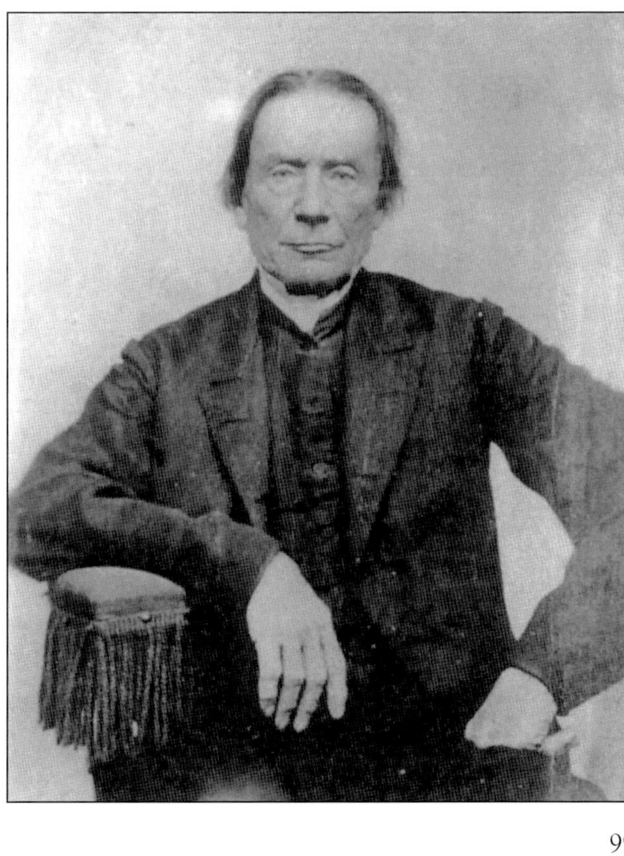

Rev. Ravaud Rogers, a Princeton graduate, served as pastor of the Bound brook Presbyterian Church for 44 years, from 1830 to 1874. A dispute with the church elders forced him from its pulpit. He retired to Georgia.

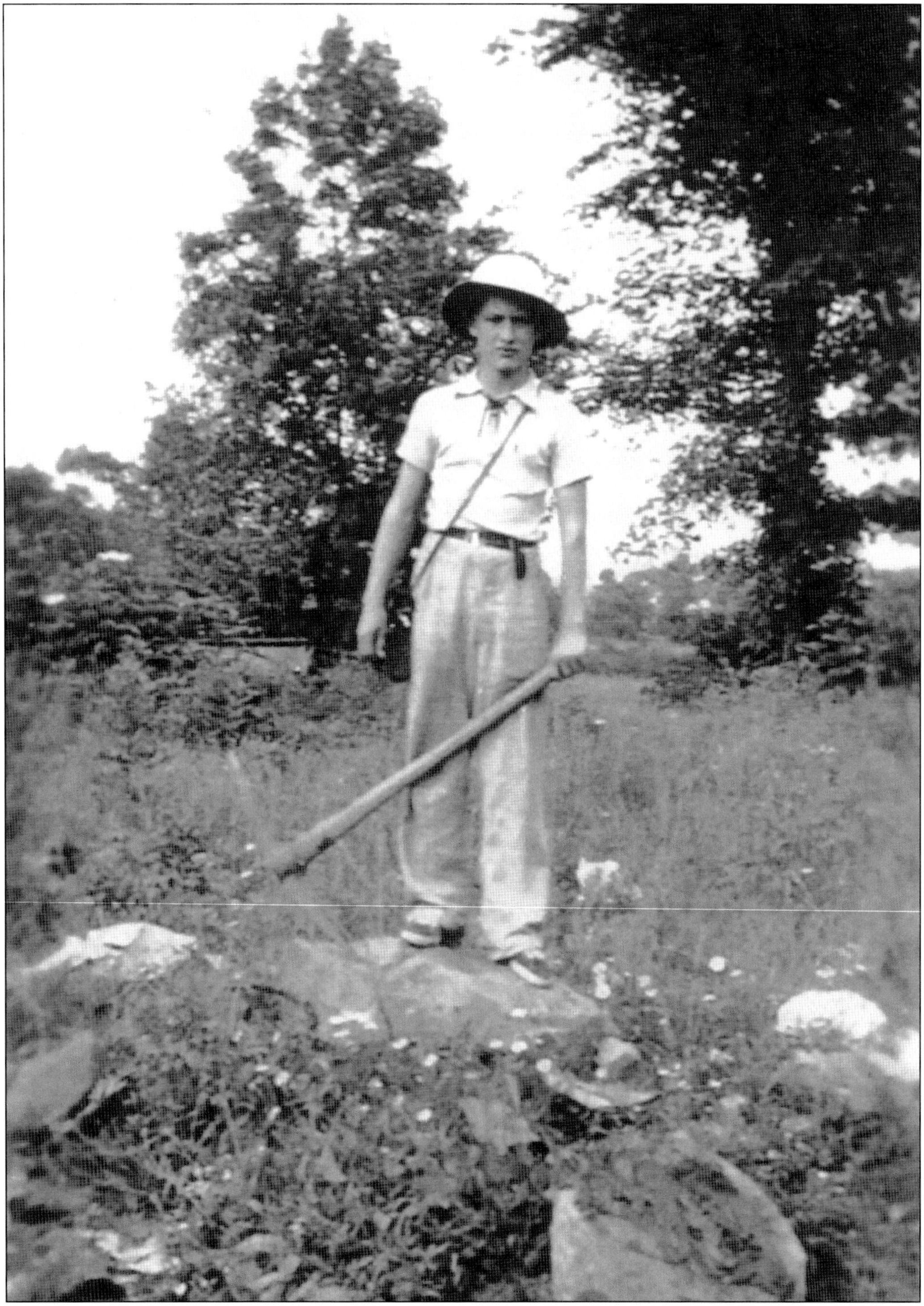

Charles Miller, a Bridgewater native who moved to Ames, Iowa, regularly came east to attempt to locate the remains of his ancestors' home on Tea Street. His son Charles Jr. is shown here among the identified foundation stones.

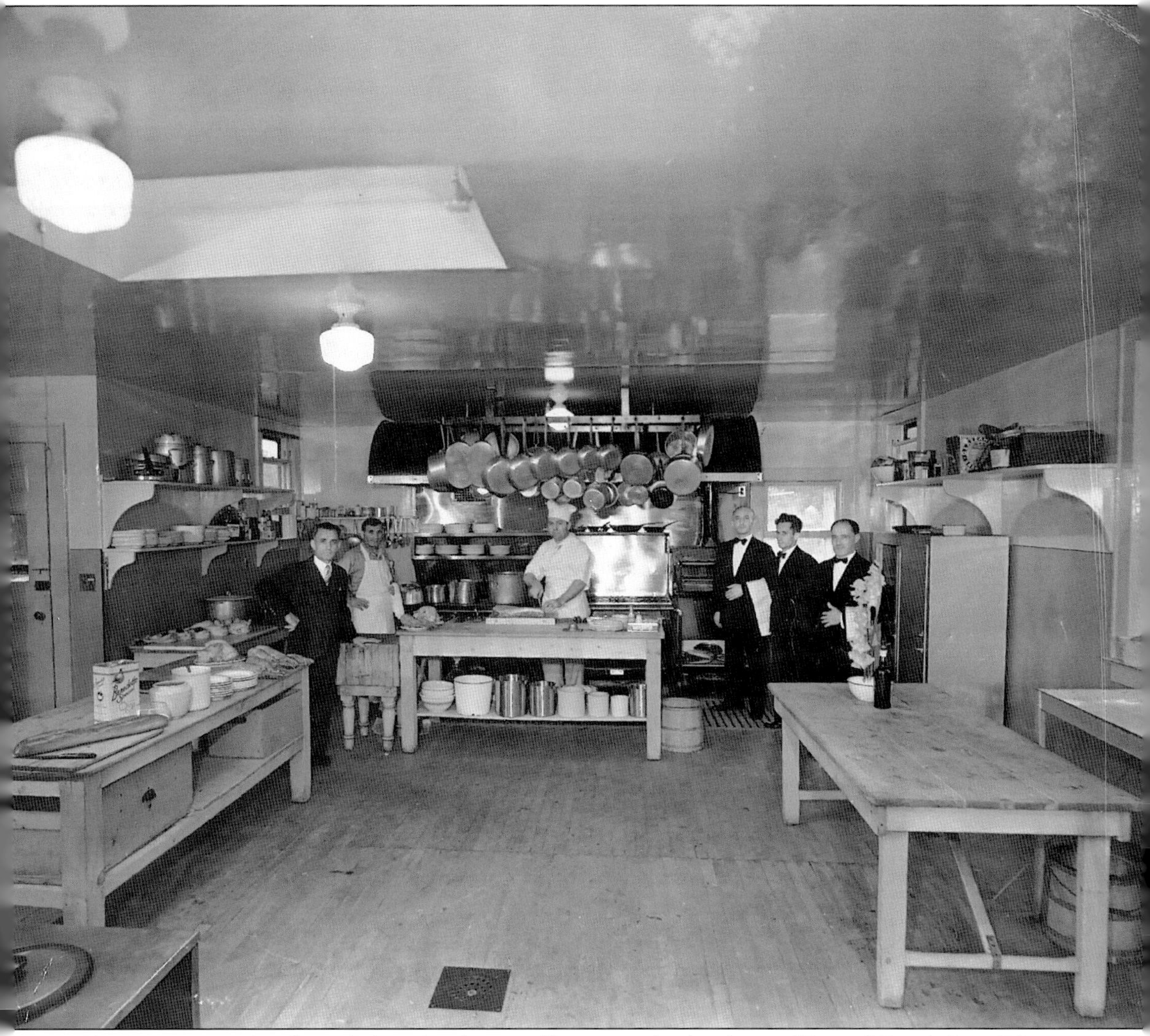

The Nangeroni family and their kitchen staff pose in the kitchen of Bound Brook Inn. Their culinary expertise kept several generations of residents well fed.

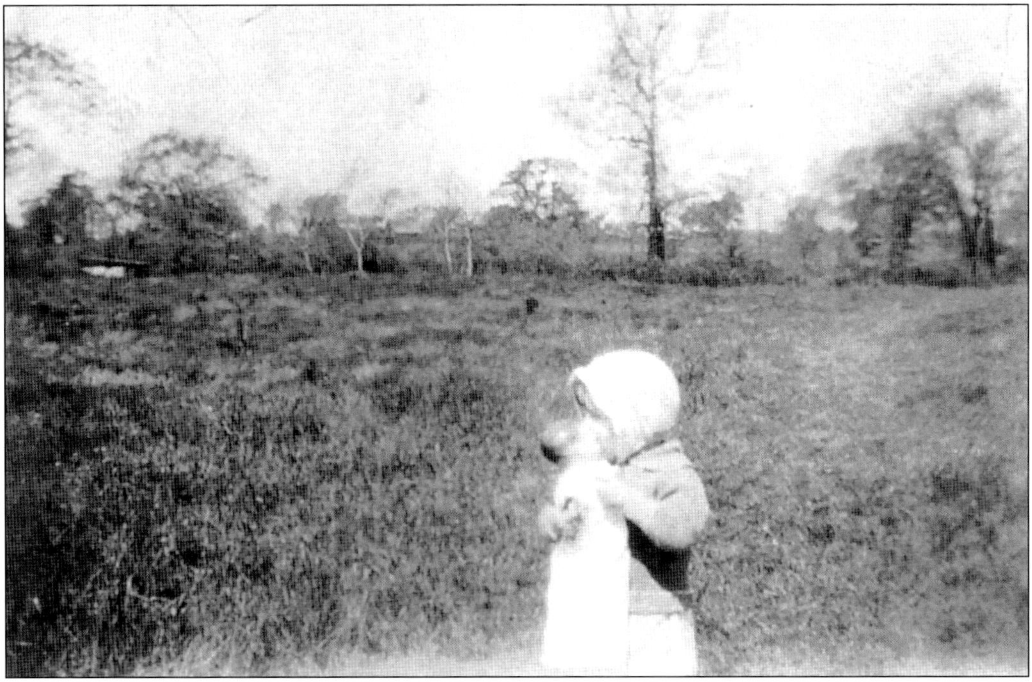

Wheatland Avenue appears to be rural in this 1927 view. The little girl with her doll is Dorothy Agans.

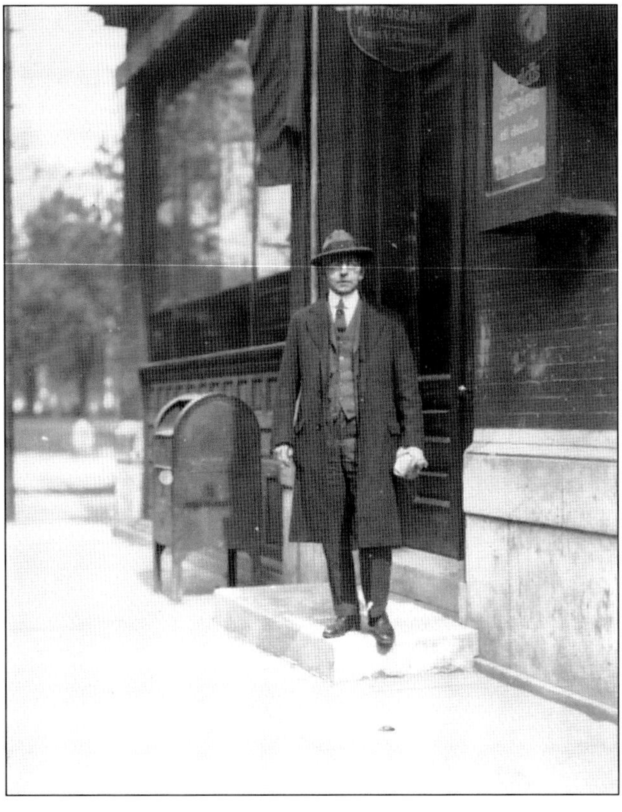

Dr. Jonathan Pardoe was a graduate of the University of Pennsylvania Dental School. Following graduation, he opened an office in the Voorhees building. His greater claim to fame was his photography, for which he won many awards.

Randolph Mason was born at high noon on July 4, 1895. The local Daughters of the American Revolution chapter presented him with a gold souvenir spoon. His parents were W.B.R. and Rachel Manning Mason.

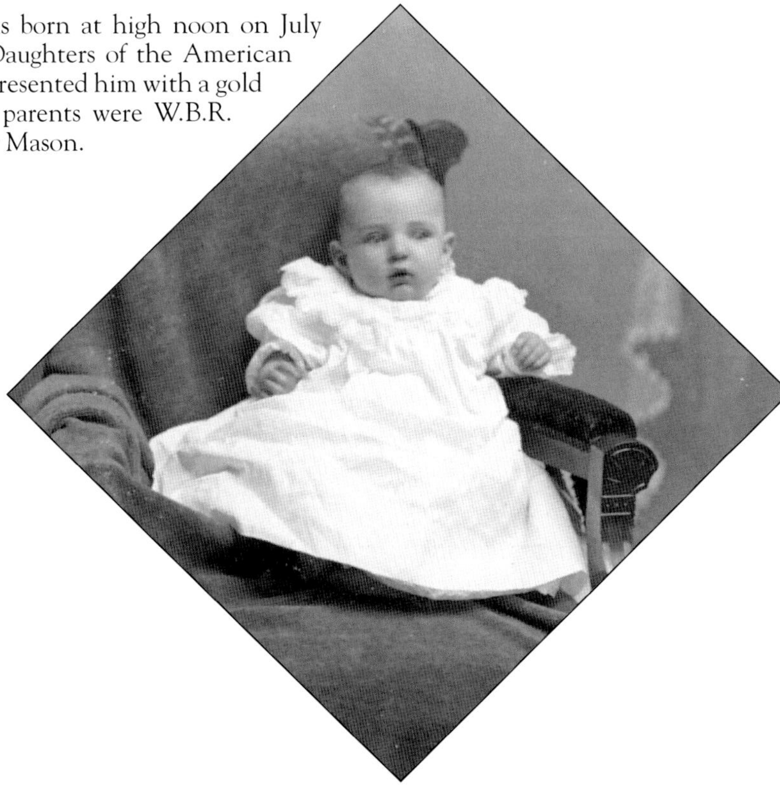

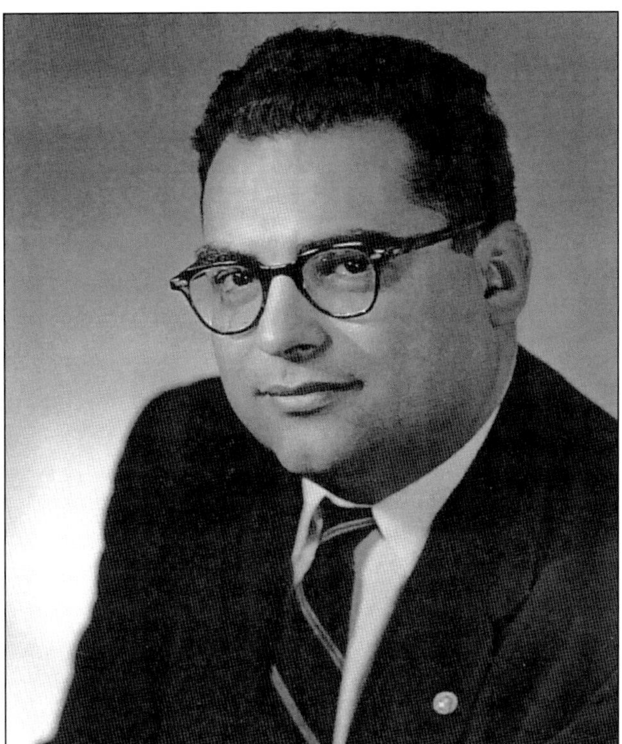

Eli Barbati, the son of Italian immigrant parents, played the violin in the orchestra and was a member of the debating team in high school. He served in the armed forces in WWII and went on to become a busy local attorney, serving for a time as the borough attorney.

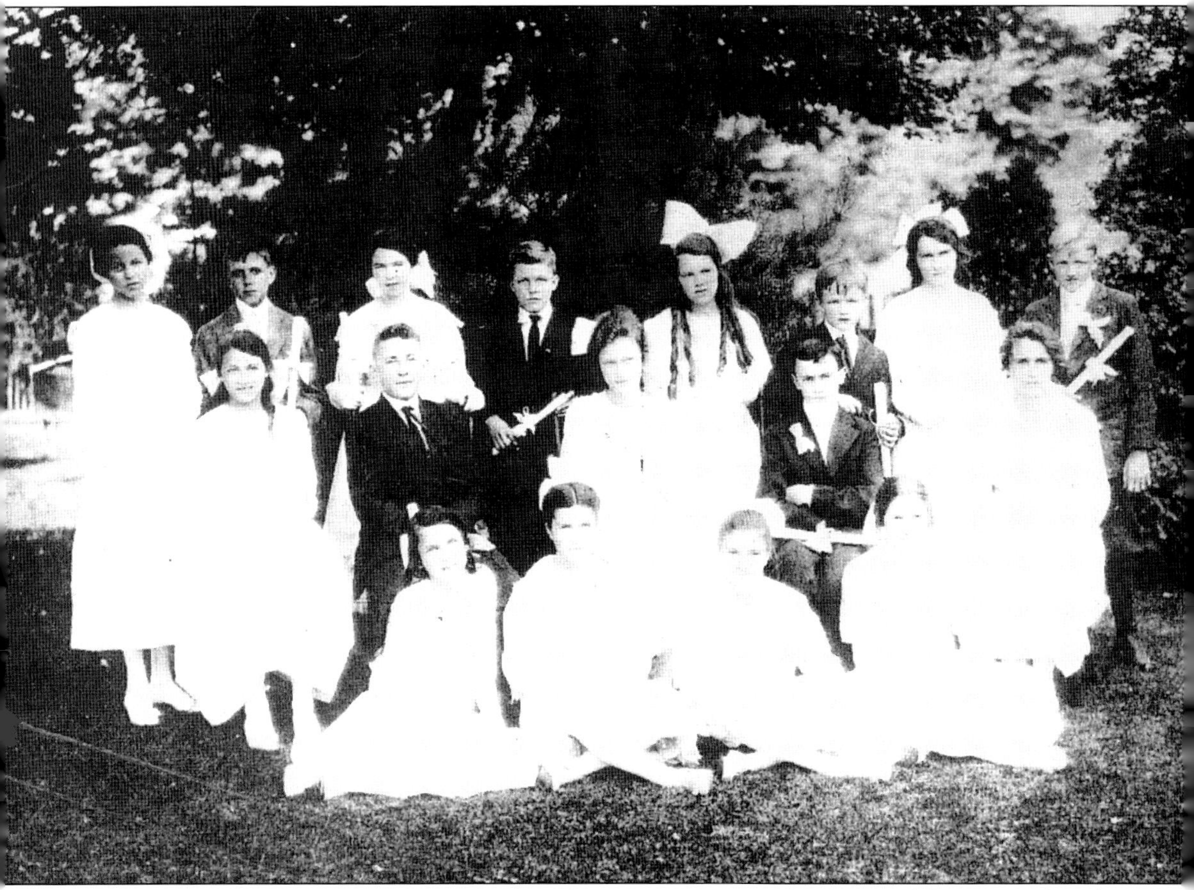

In June 1917, the eighth grade graduating class at Watchung School in Middlesex posed at the home of their teacher, Miss Clementine Petit. Among the graduates were Margaret Bourke-White, first on the left, and Bernard Hayden, a longtime local florist, standing last on right.

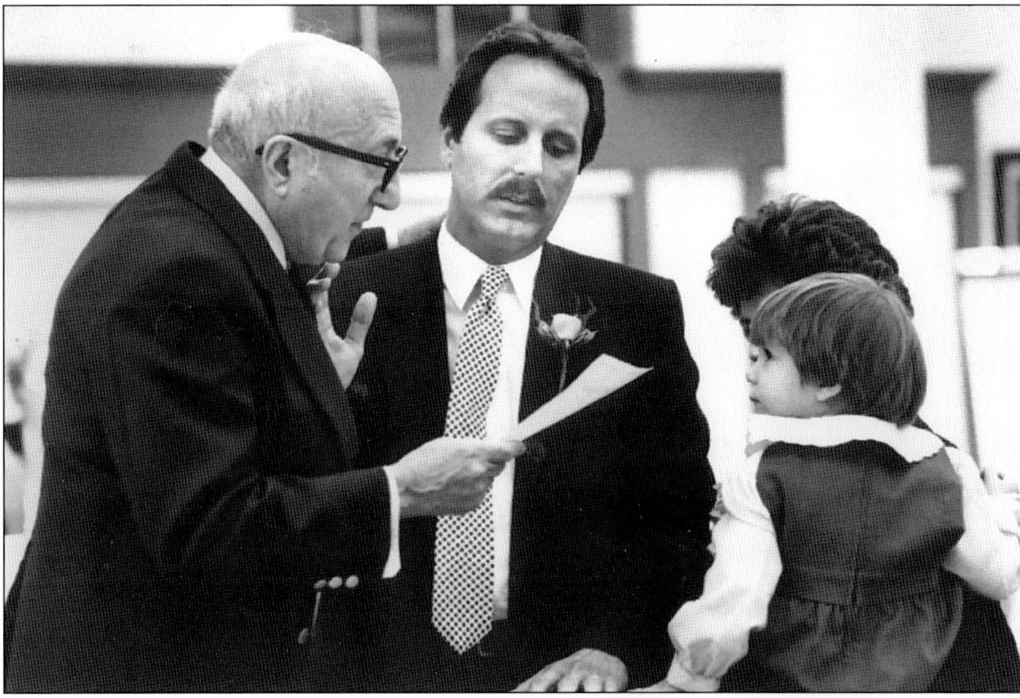

Samuel Chiaravalli, longtime local resident, graduated from Fordham Law School in 1934 and began his law practice here. Sixty-five years later, he is still at his desk in his law office every day. He is noted for his expertise in criminal law. Shown here, he swears in Peter Angelokas as mayor of Bound Brook in 1987.

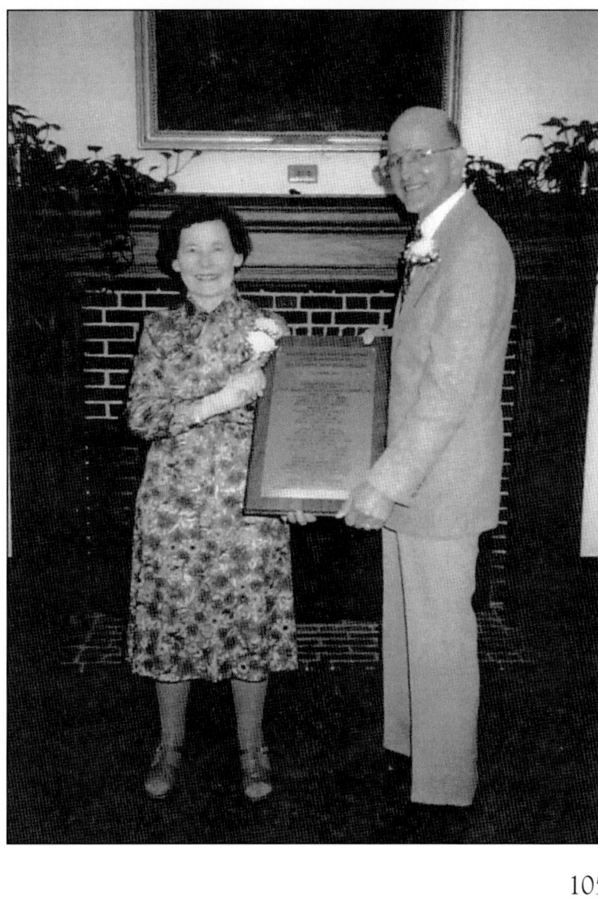

Two of the most constant benefactors of the Bound Brook Memorial Library are Mrs. Shirley Klompus and Mr. John Haelig. Their gifts have made many amenities possible over the years.

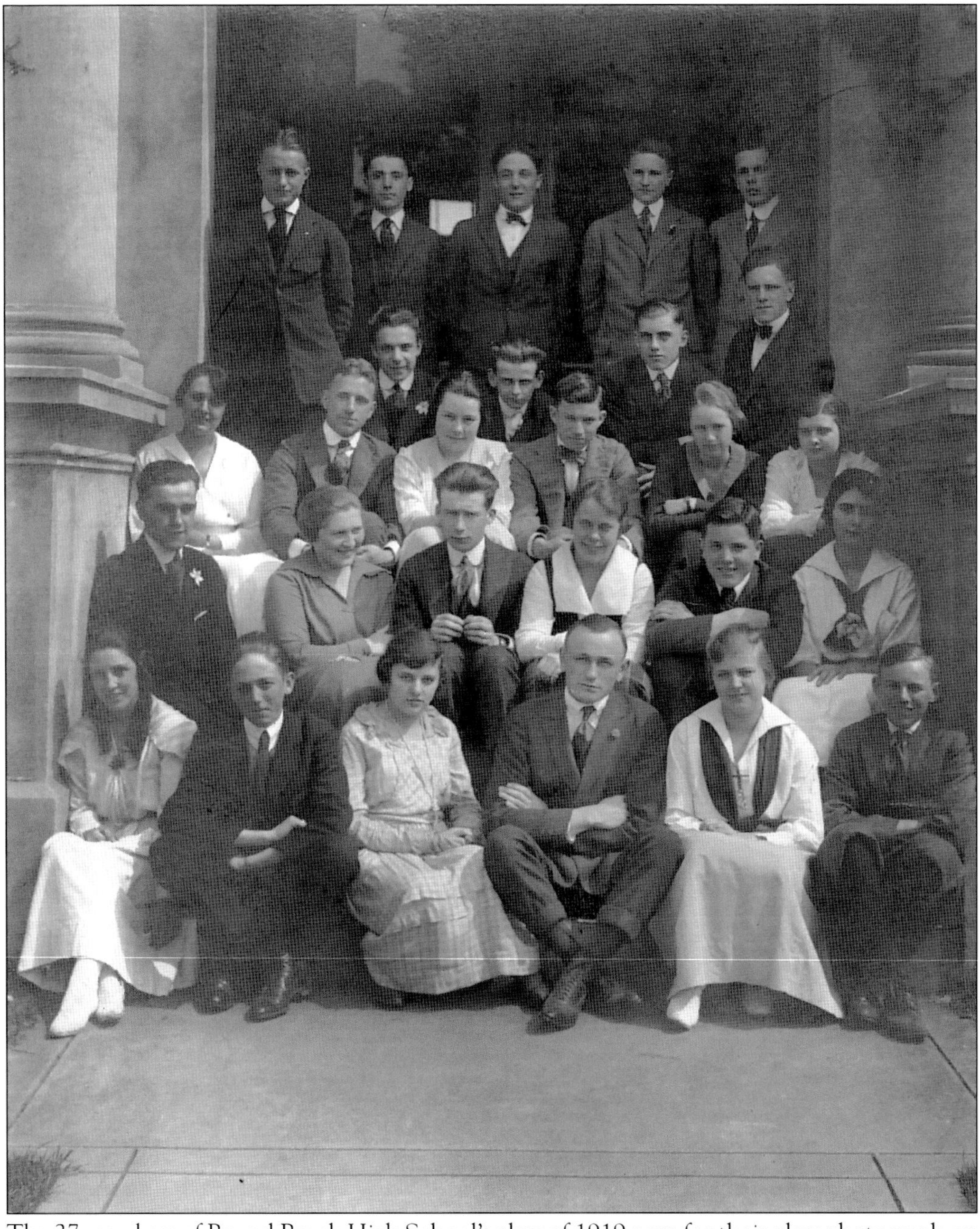

The 27 members of Bound Brook High School's class of 1919 pose for their class photograph on the steps of the school building.

This well-dressed little girl in the stylish cloche hat is Ann Dickenson, the daughter of Mr. and Mrs. Quinton Dickenson. The picture represents the early 1930s.

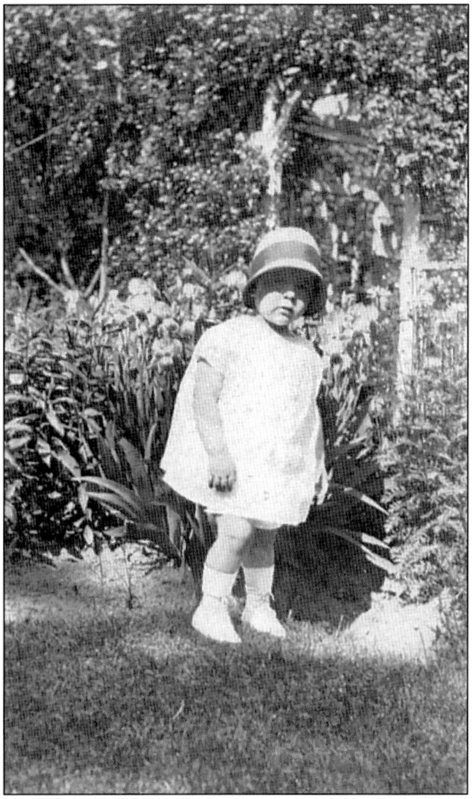

The Methodist congregation literally turned their church around in 1898. They moved their building from Main Street to a new foundation on Second Street.

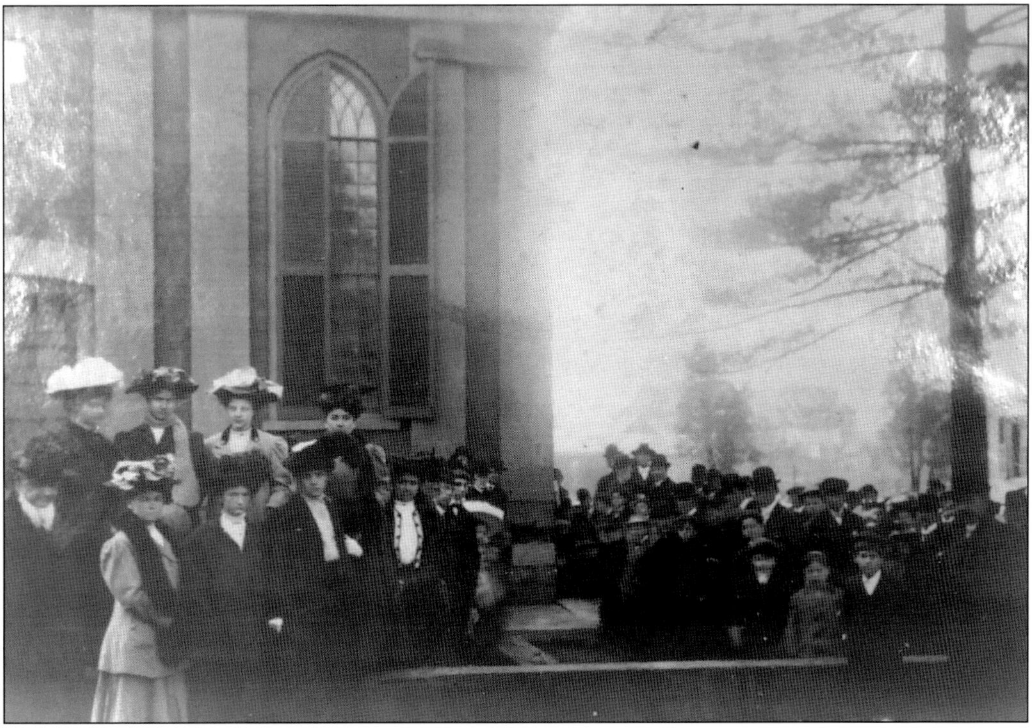

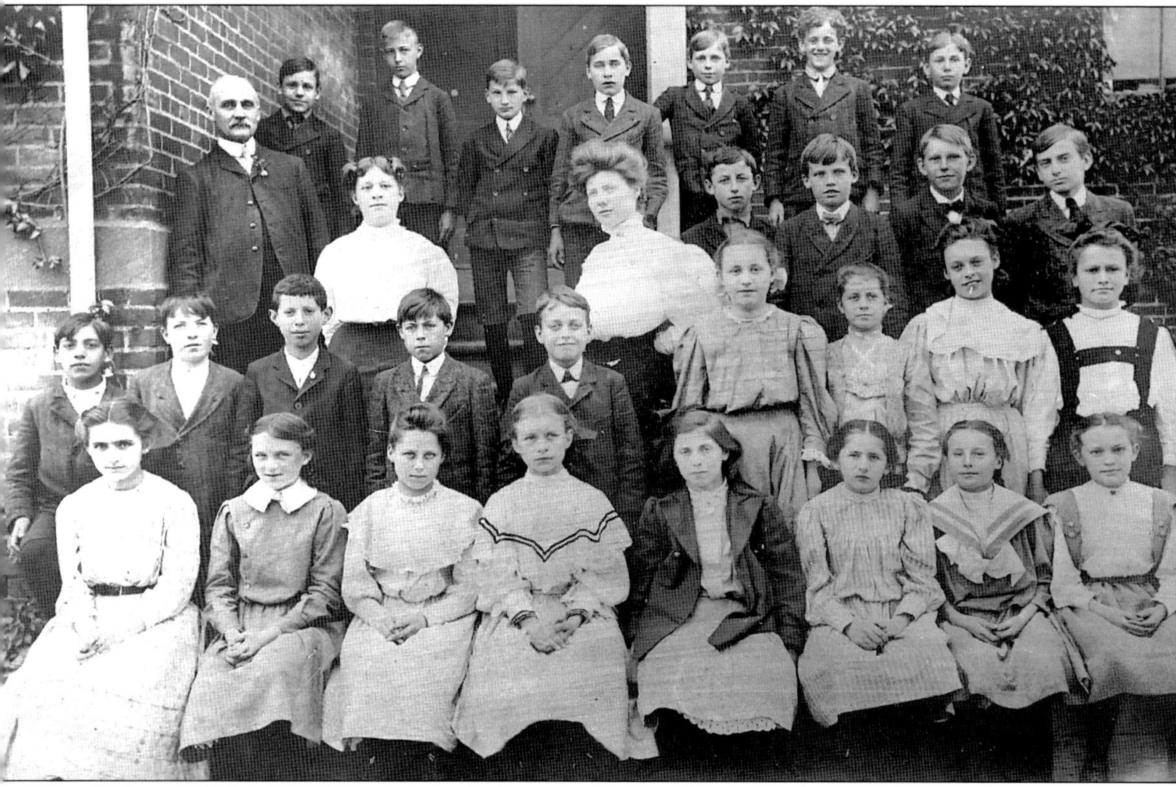

Lafayette School students pose with their teachers in this 1908 photograph. Students attended classes there through the sixth grade and then moved on to Washington Grammar School.

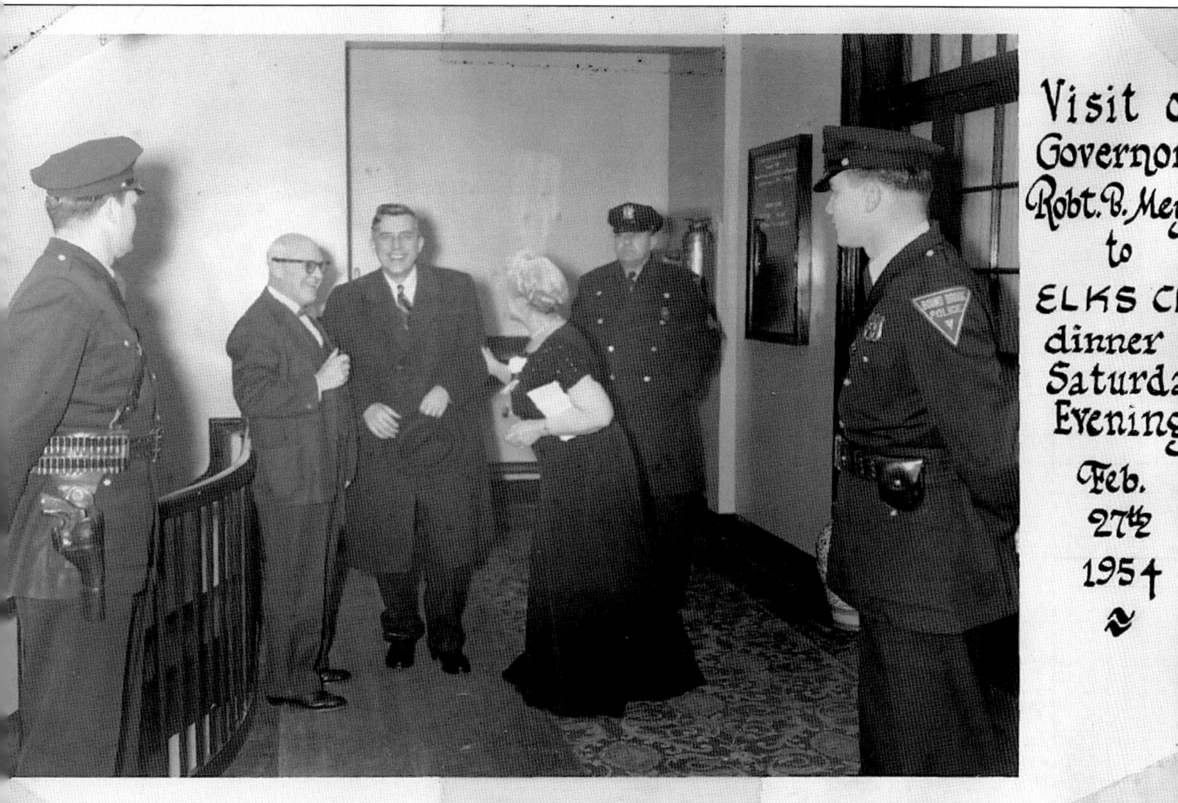

The Elks Ball, held annually, is one of the town's social highlights, especially in 1954, when then governor, Robert Meyner, was one of the guests.

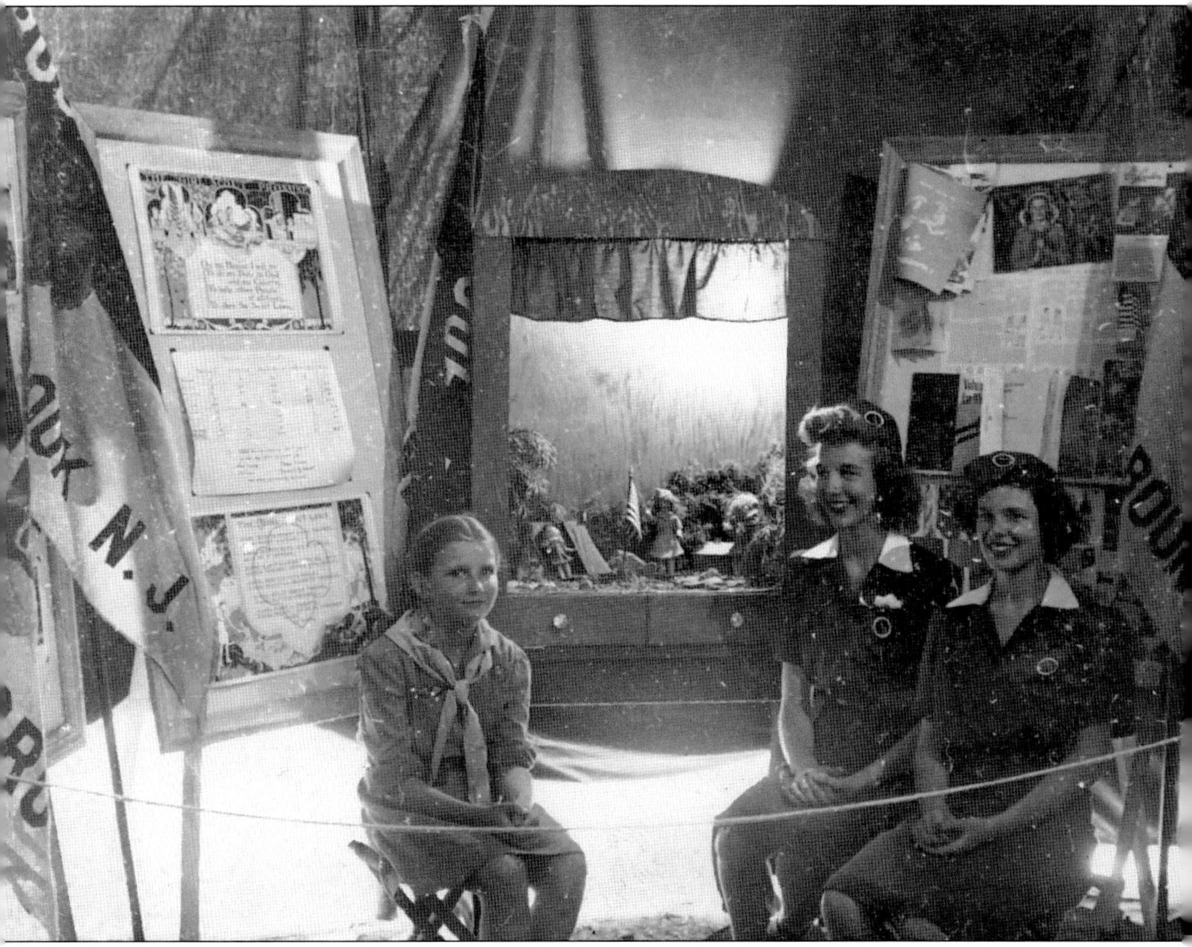

The greater Bound Brook Exposition, held in 1944 during WWII, featured a variety of displays, one of which was this one by the local Girl Scout troops. Posing for the camera are, from left to right, Kathy Dykes, Barbara Haelig, and Cecily King.

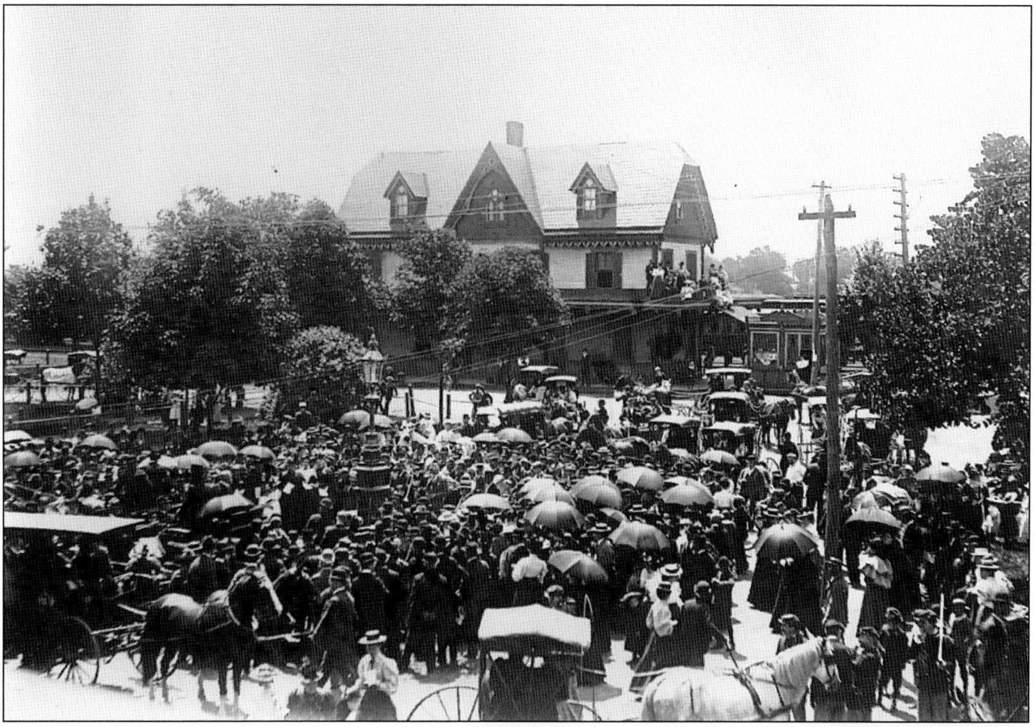

A large crowd gathered on Memorial Day 1896 for the dedication of the fountain in the train station plaza. George LaMonte's horse was the first equine to use the fountain; Mrs. Titus Davis, the Presbyterian minister's wife, was the first human to use it.

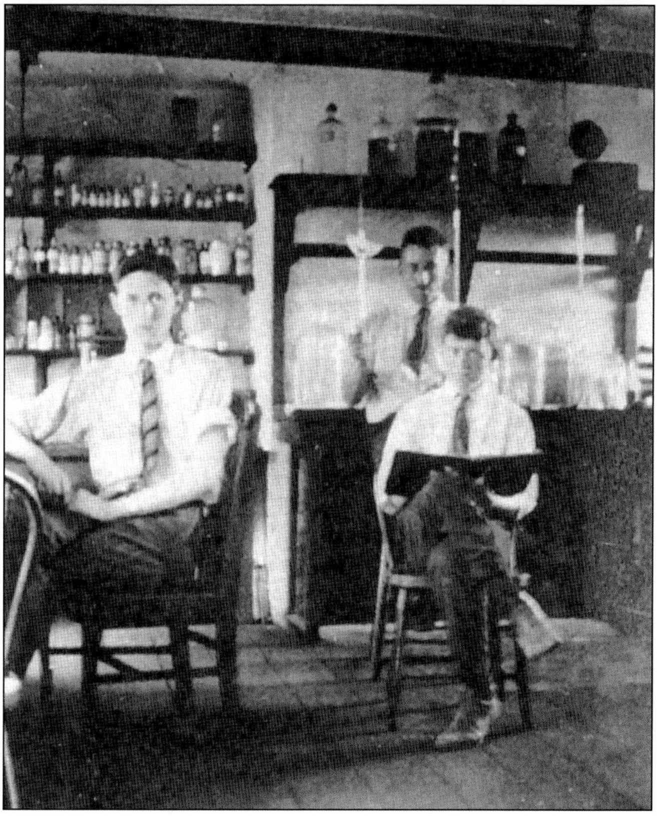

Henry Johnson, left, and Ervin Kelsey pose in the early lab of Calco Chemical Company in the summer of 1919. Kelsey went on to become a professor at Harvard.

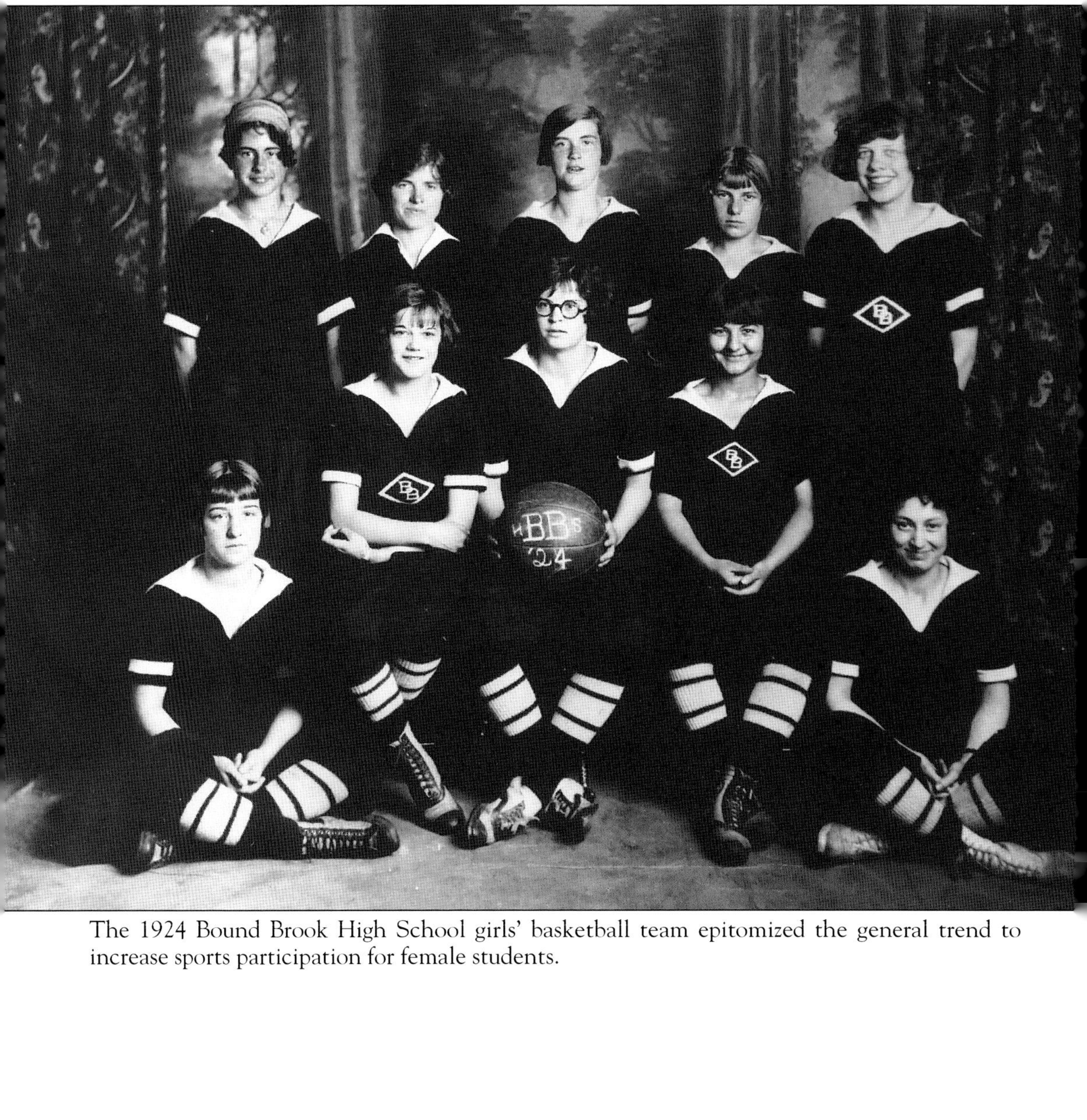

The 1924 Bound Brook High School girls' basketball team epitomized the general trend to increase sports participation for female students.

Three

Memorable Events

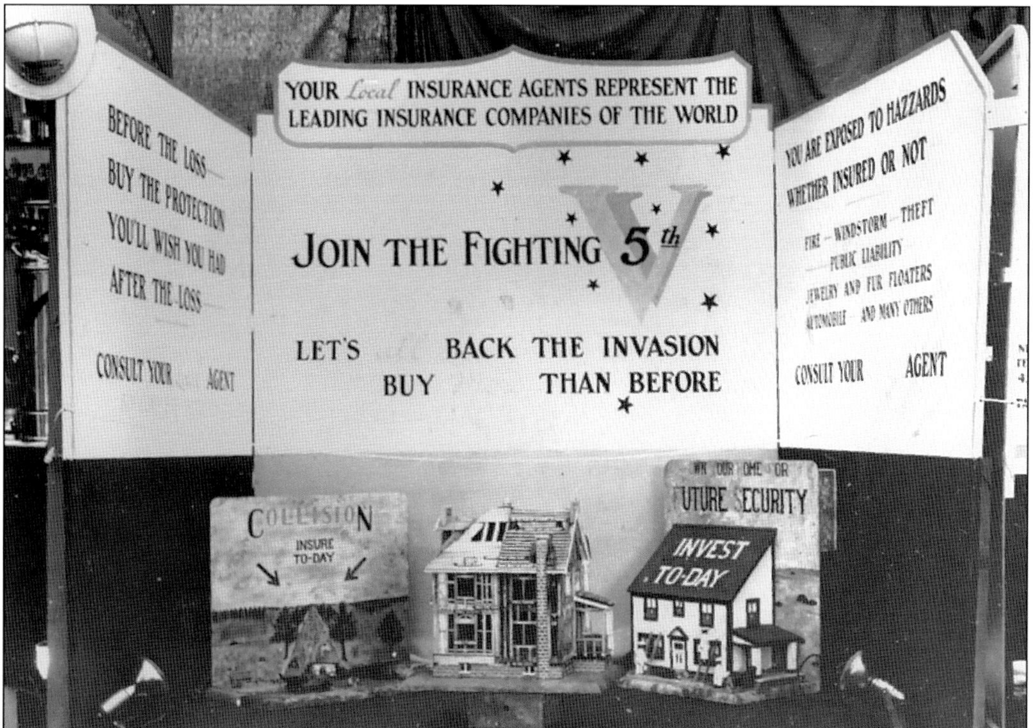

Local insurance agents banded together to produce this interesting exhibit at the 1944 Greater Bound Brook Exposition.

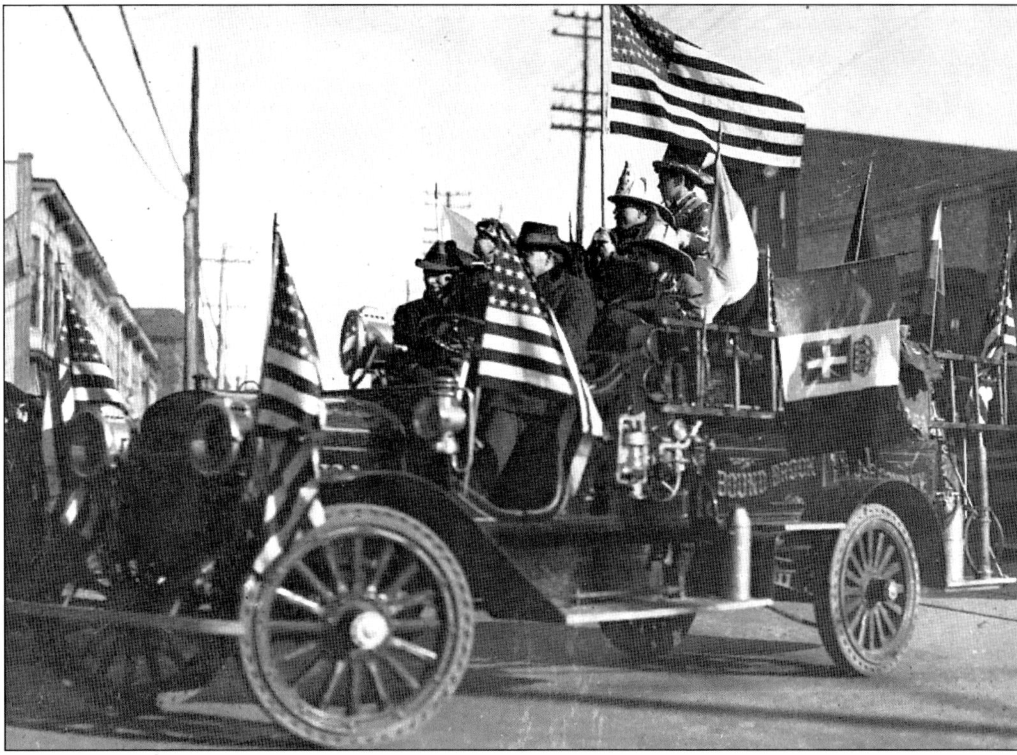

In 1899, a little over a decade after a destructive conflagration without a fire brigade, the town firemen parade with their fire engine at a municipal event.

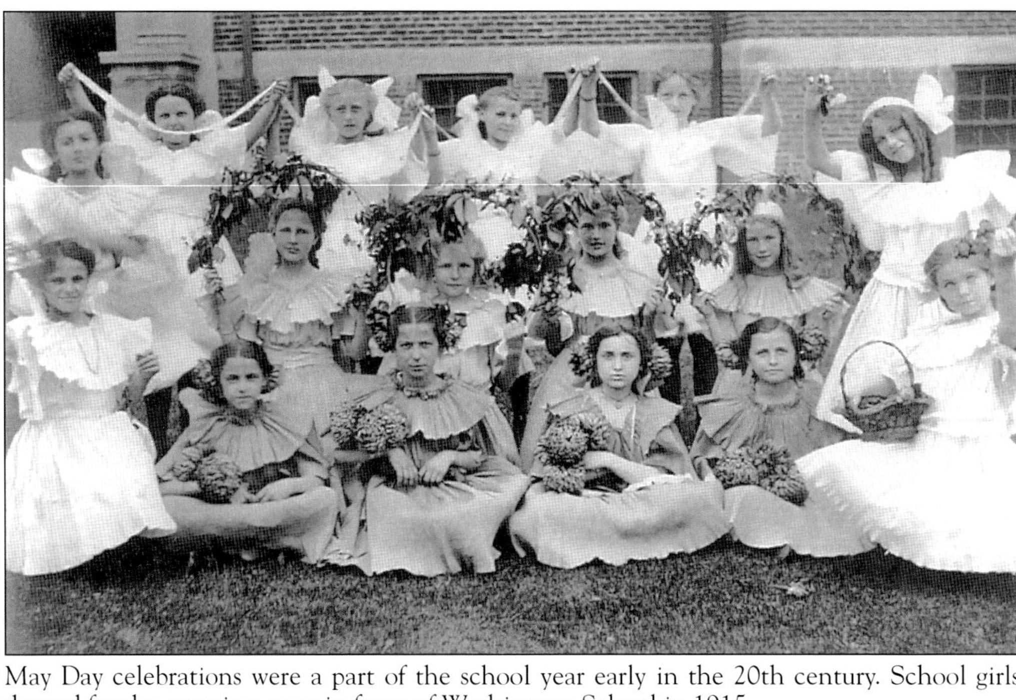

May Day celebrations were a part of the school year early in the 20th century. School girls, dressed for the occasion, pose in front of Washington School in 1915.

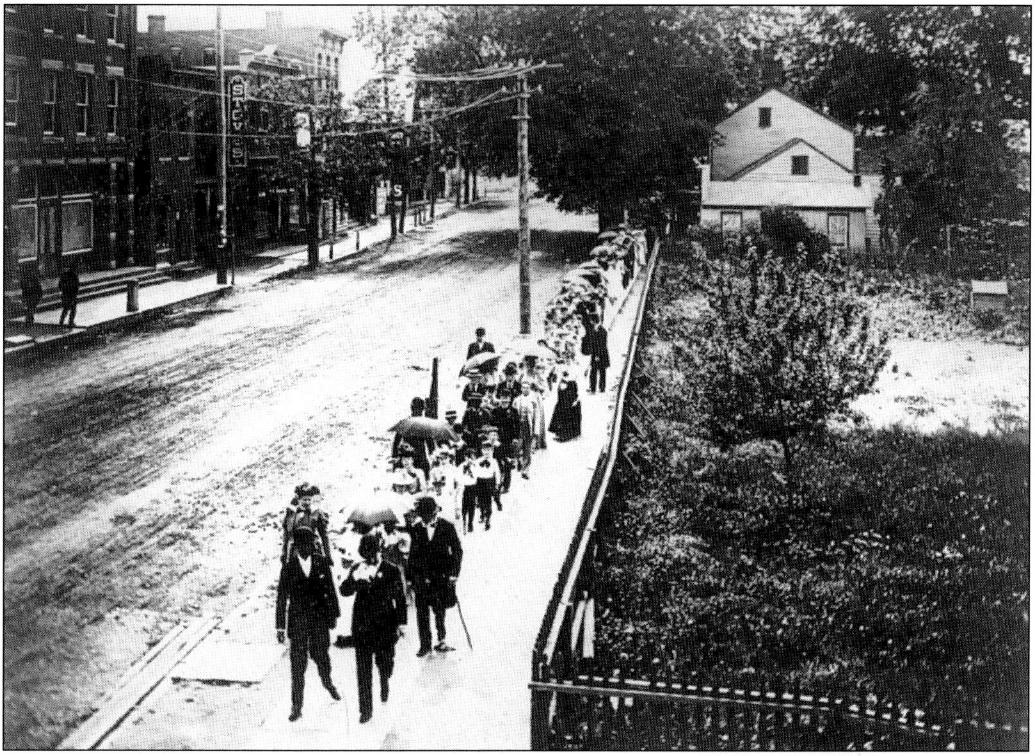

A Children's Day parade in the 1880s winds its way down Main Street toward the Presbyterian Church. Note the rural look of the fenced-in garden, the unpaved road, and the parasol-carrying adults.

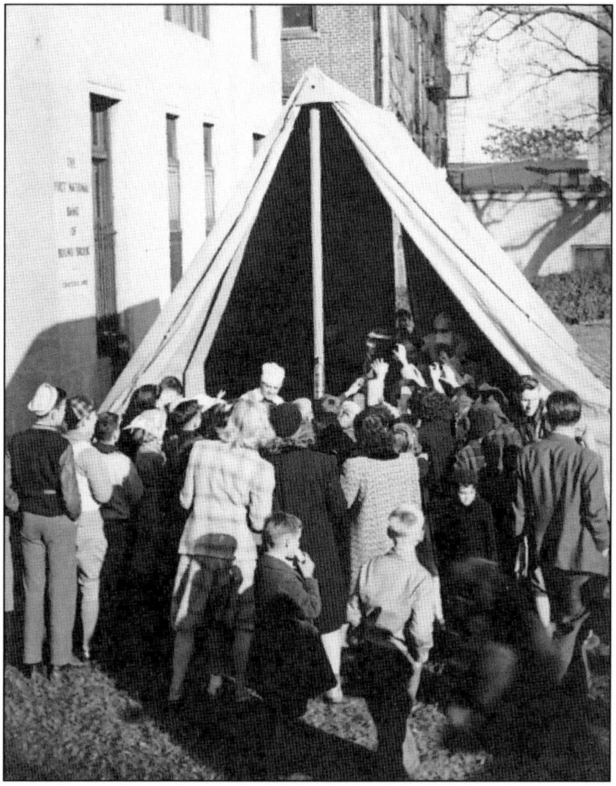

A U.S. Army cooking display was set up on the First National Bank property during WWII. It was one of the public attractions designed to educate the home front during WWII.

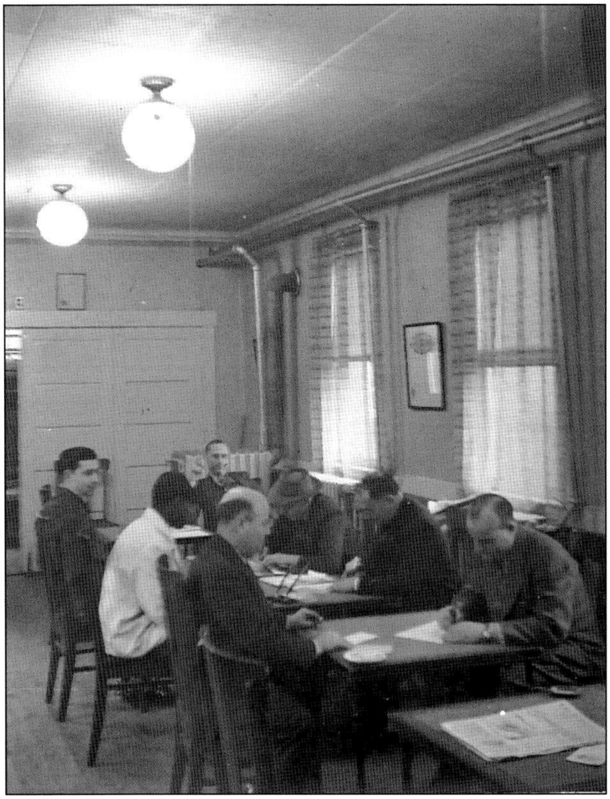

The draft and local draft board were facts of life in towns across the land during WWII, and Bound Brook was no exception. Here, eligible residents complete the required paperwork.

When Prohibition ended in 1933, the Bound Brook Hotel proudly announced the legal return of the availability of alcoholic beverages.

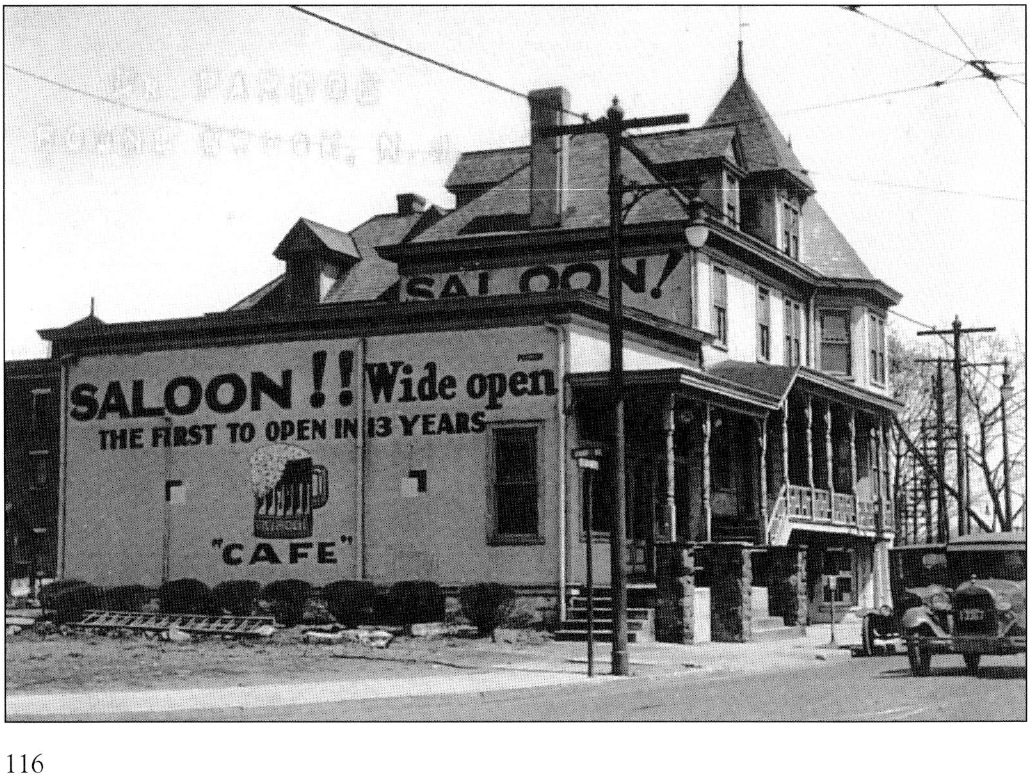

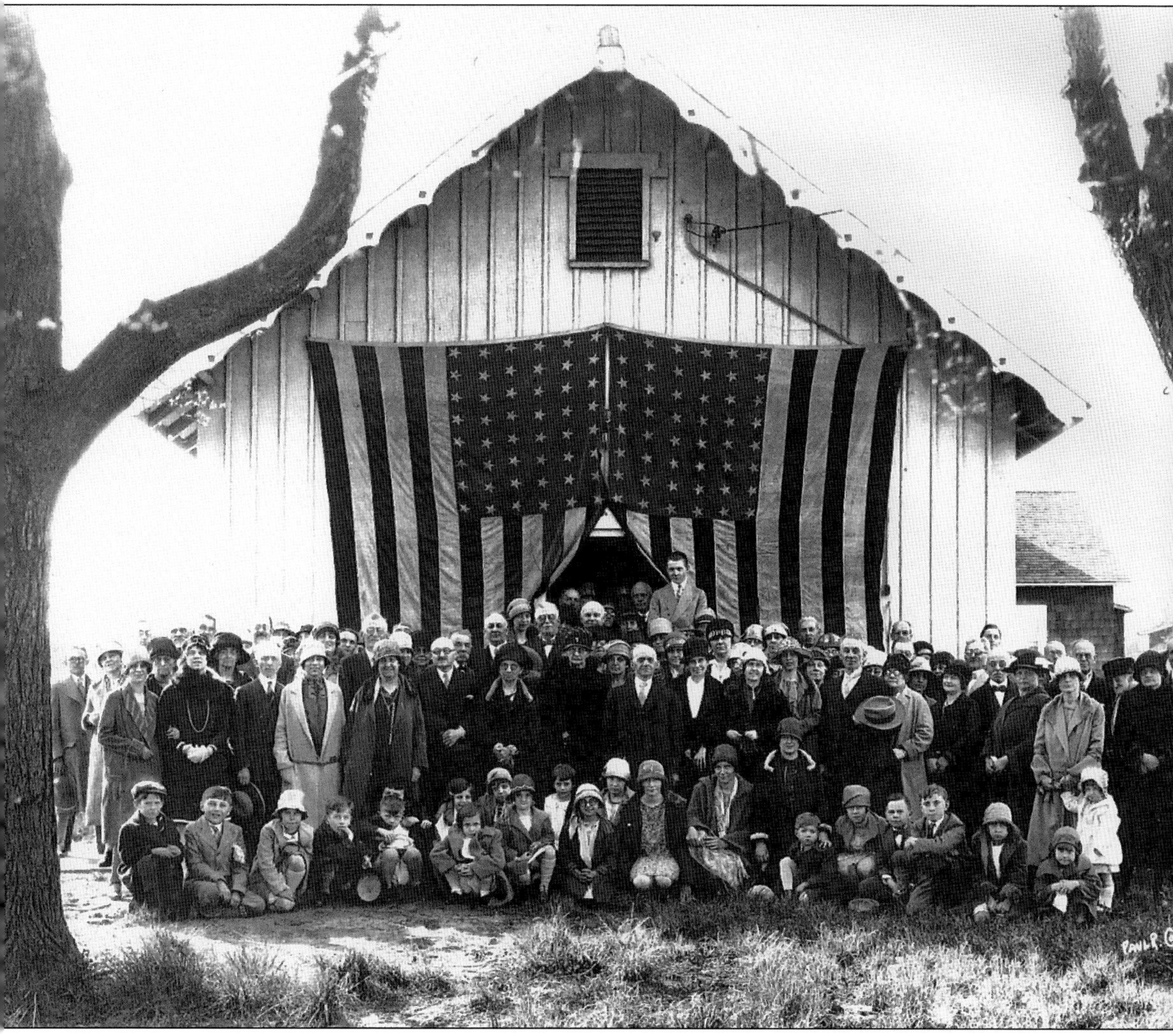

Celebrating their 100th anniversary in 1926, members of the Harris Avenue Sunday School posed for this photograph. Founded by members of the Bound Brook Presbyterian Church in 1826, services were held in the schoolhouse.

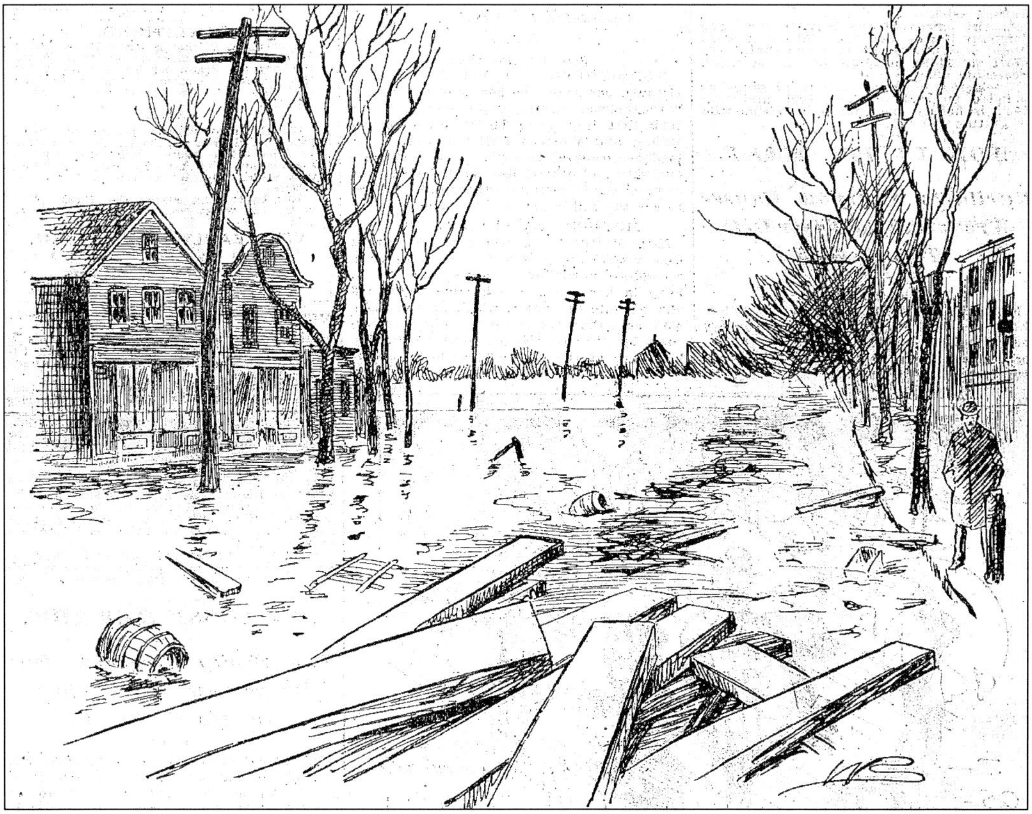

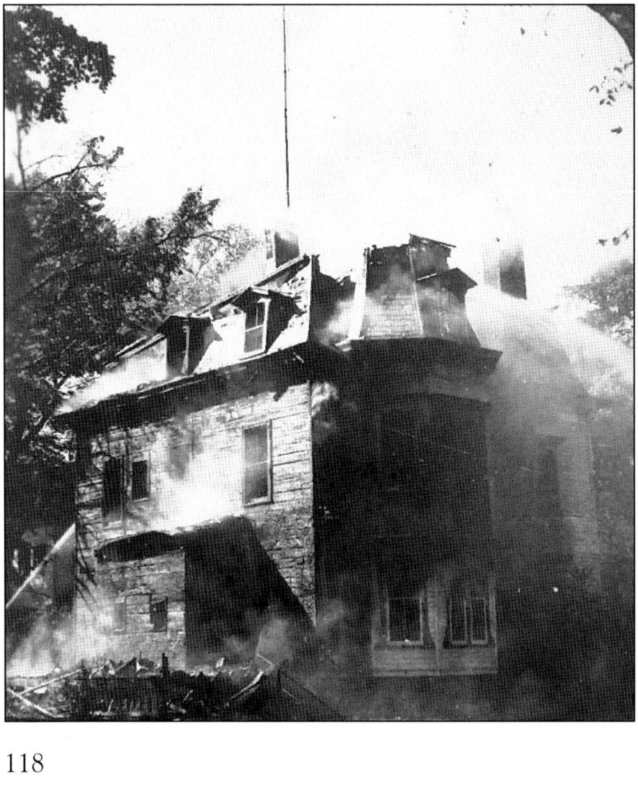

Bound Brook made the pages of the *New York Herald* in 1896, as the artist of that daily paper depicted the flood damage in town in this pen-and-ink sketch.

Fire in the 1950s destroyed Borough Hall, formerly the Lamb property on Hamilton Street and Somerset Street. This impressive Victorian home was originally the first in-town residence of George LaMonte, and was purchased by the borough from the estate of Ransom Lamb.

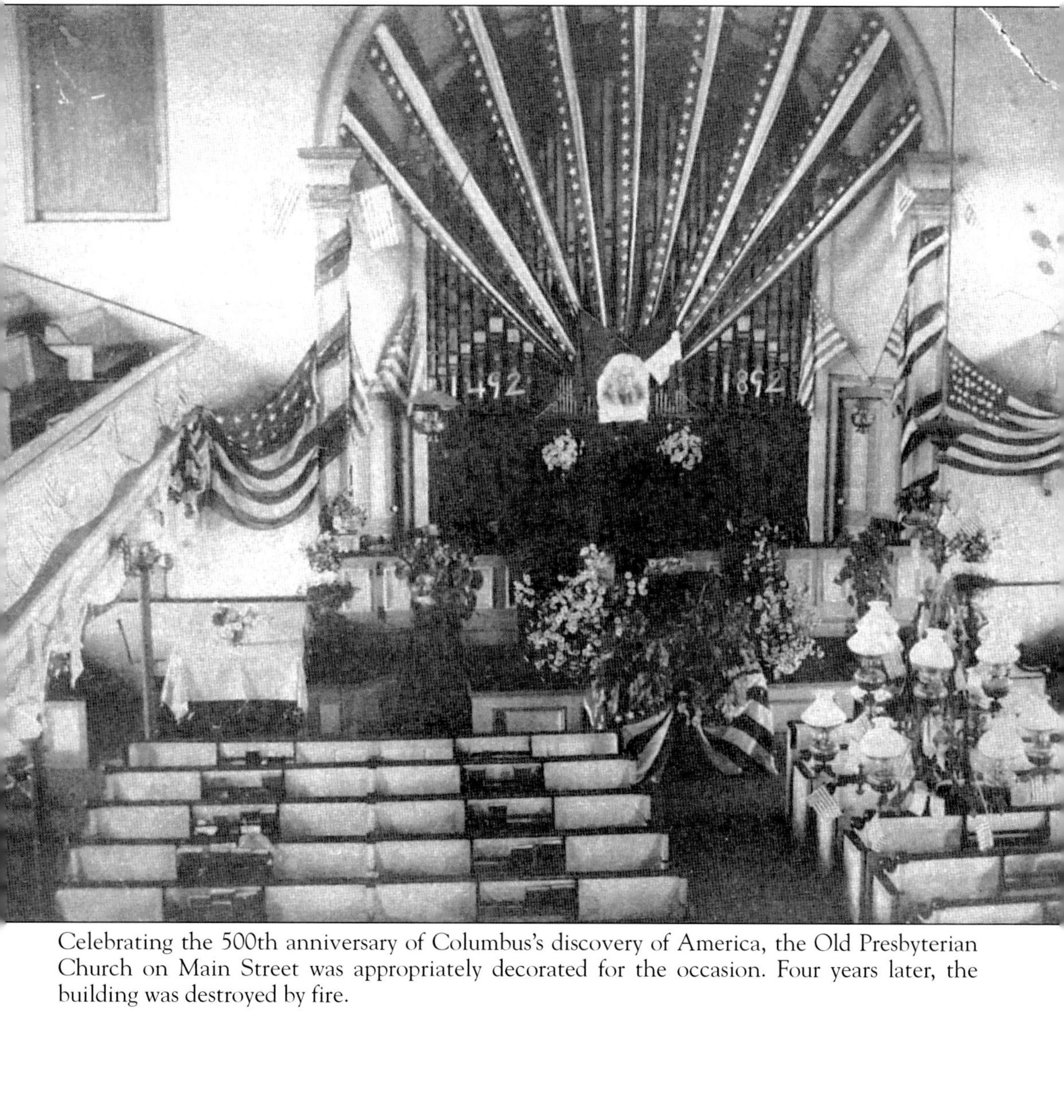

Celebrating the 500th anniversary of Columbus's discovery of America, the Old Presbyterian Church on Main Street was appropriately decorated for the occasion. Four years later, the building was destroyed by fire.

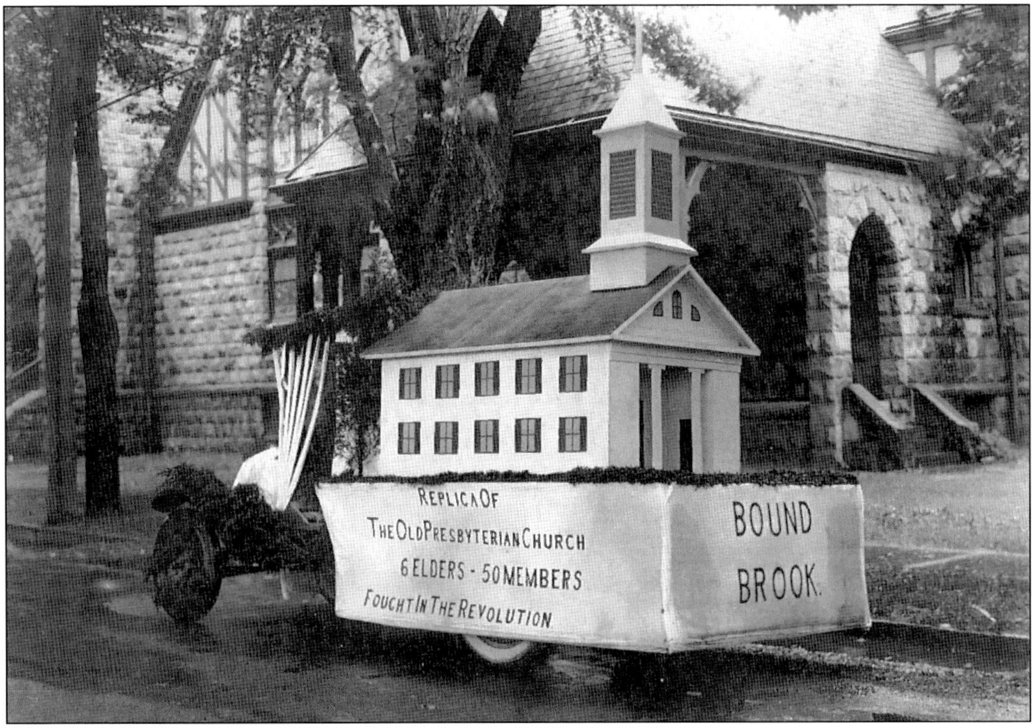

A grand three-day program celebrated George Washington's 200th birthday in 1932. This float, depicting the Old Presbyterian Church, was a parade entry. Nearly a half century went by before the Campground Association finally paid off the money borrowed to fund the event.

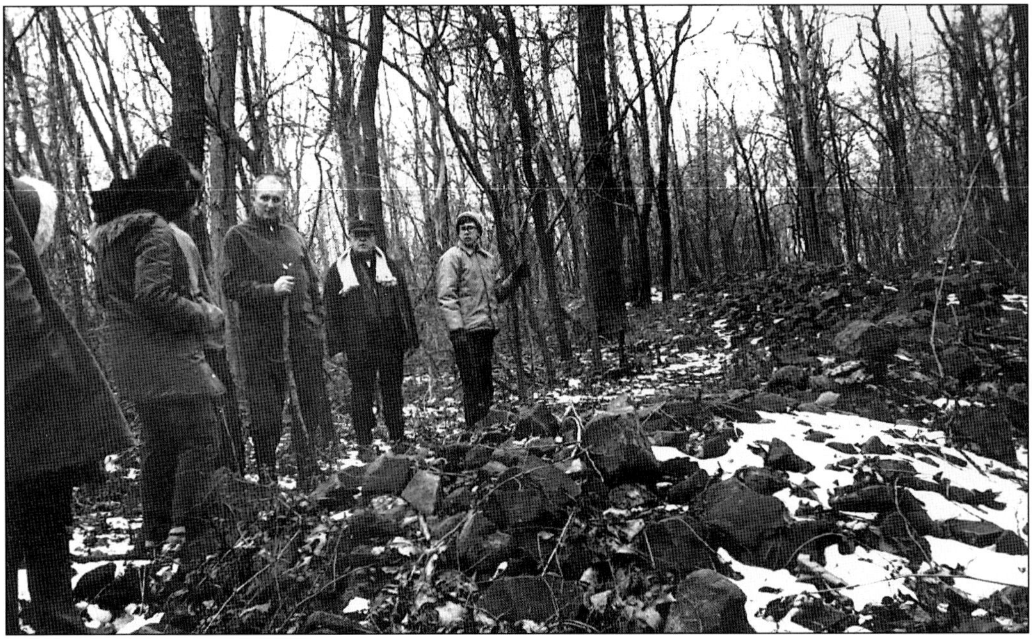

The late A.A. Boom, who resided just north of town, conducted walking tours of the Middlebrook Encampment on the heights above Route 22 as part of the county's bicentennial celebration in 1976.

Like July 4, Flag Day was an occasion for celebration in town in the early days of the 20th century, as this advertising poster of 1911 illustrates.

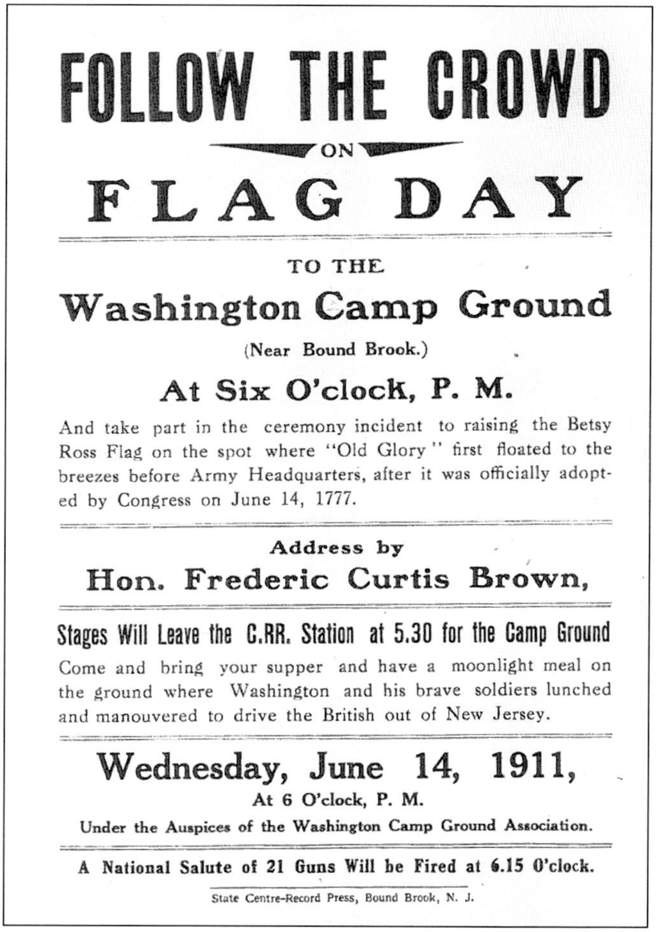

A WWI bond drive takes place on the veranda of the Berkeley Hotel, once located on the northwest corner of Main and Hamilton Streets. The hotel was one of the hubs of social activity for more than a half century before being destroyed by fire.

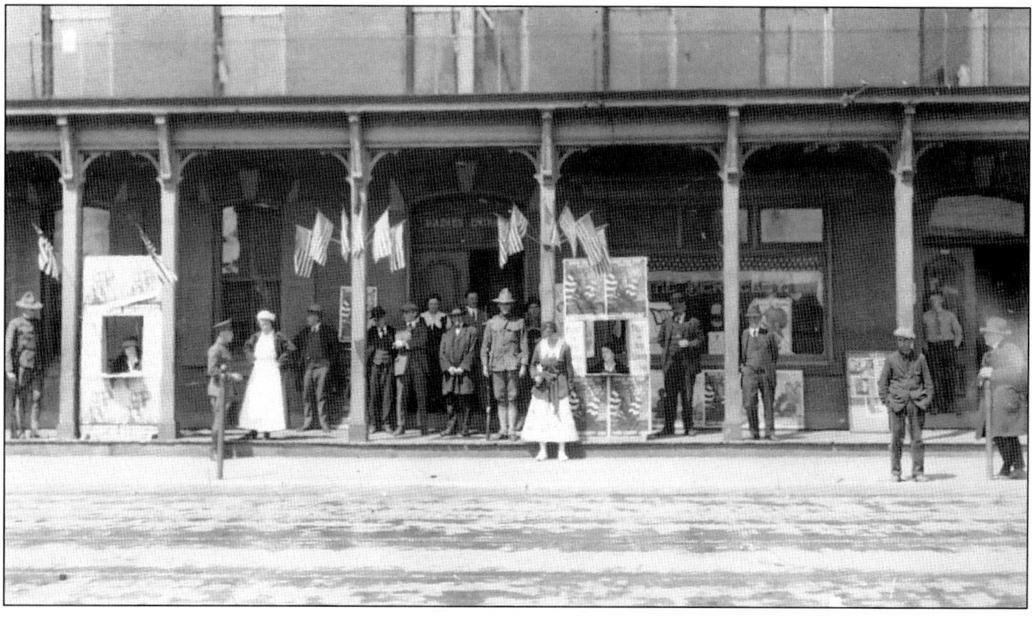

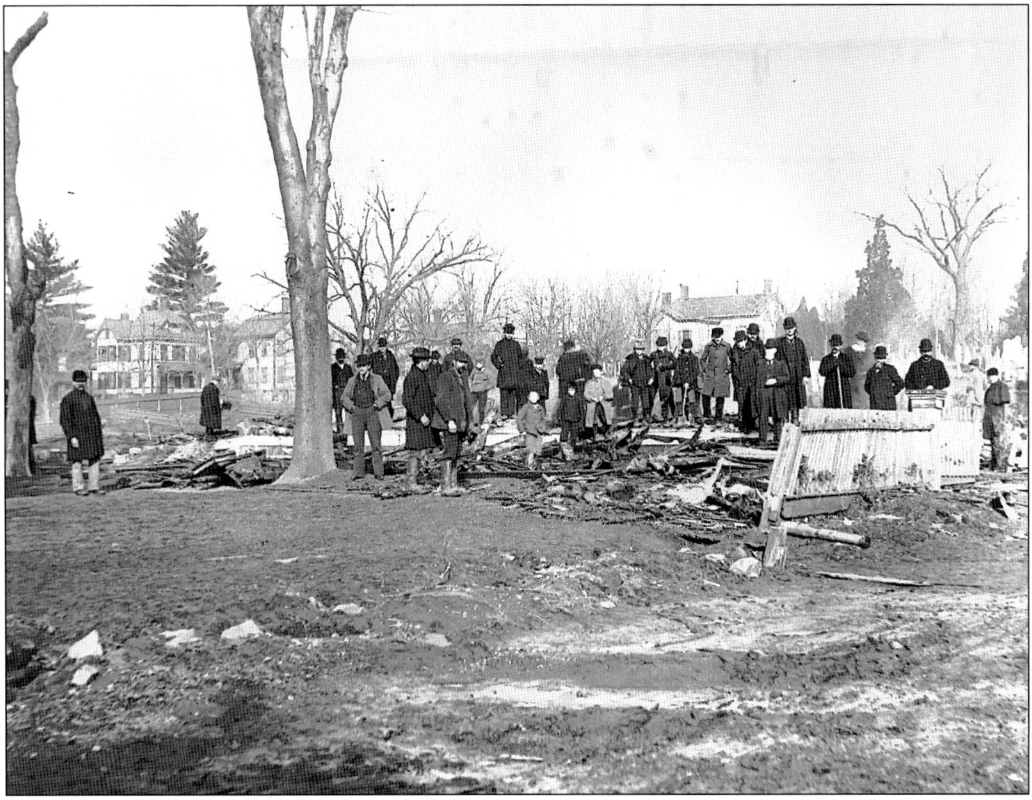

Residents inspect the remains of the old Presbyterian Church, which was destroyed by fire on the evening of February 6, 1896. The fire began in the adjoining lumberyard when floodwater ignited stored lime. Strong winds sent sparks onto the church roof.

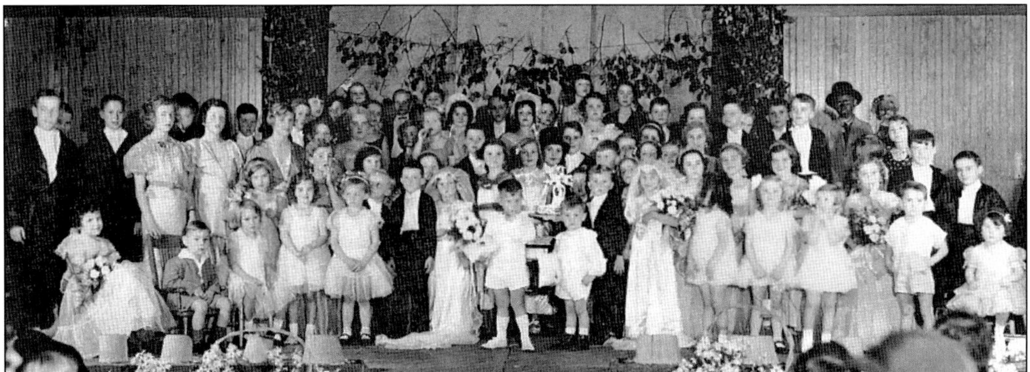

"Tom Thumb Weddings" were a popular form of fund raising in the early 20th century. The participants, members of the Presbyterian Sunday School, pose for this "wedding portrait."

On December 17, 1972, a devastating fire destroyed the education building adjoining the Presbyterian Church at Mountain and Union Avenues. Members and friends helped rescue many valuable artifacts threatened by the conflagration.

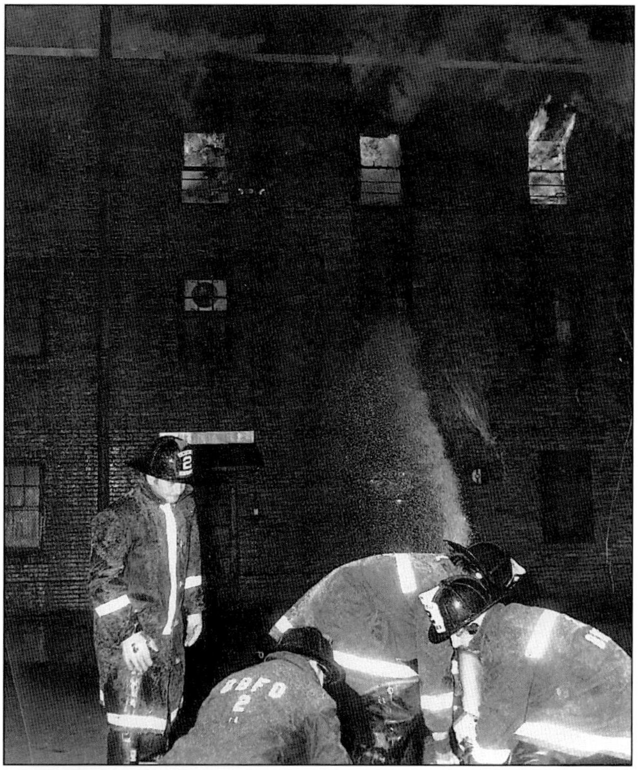

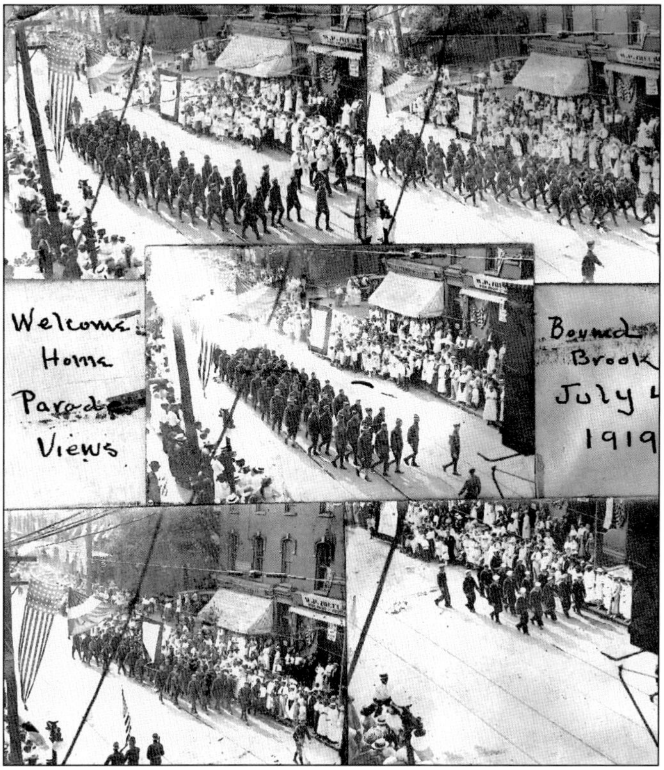

Homecoming parades following WWI were the order of the day in towns across the country. Bound Brook was no exception, as these views taken on November 19, 1919, demonstrate.

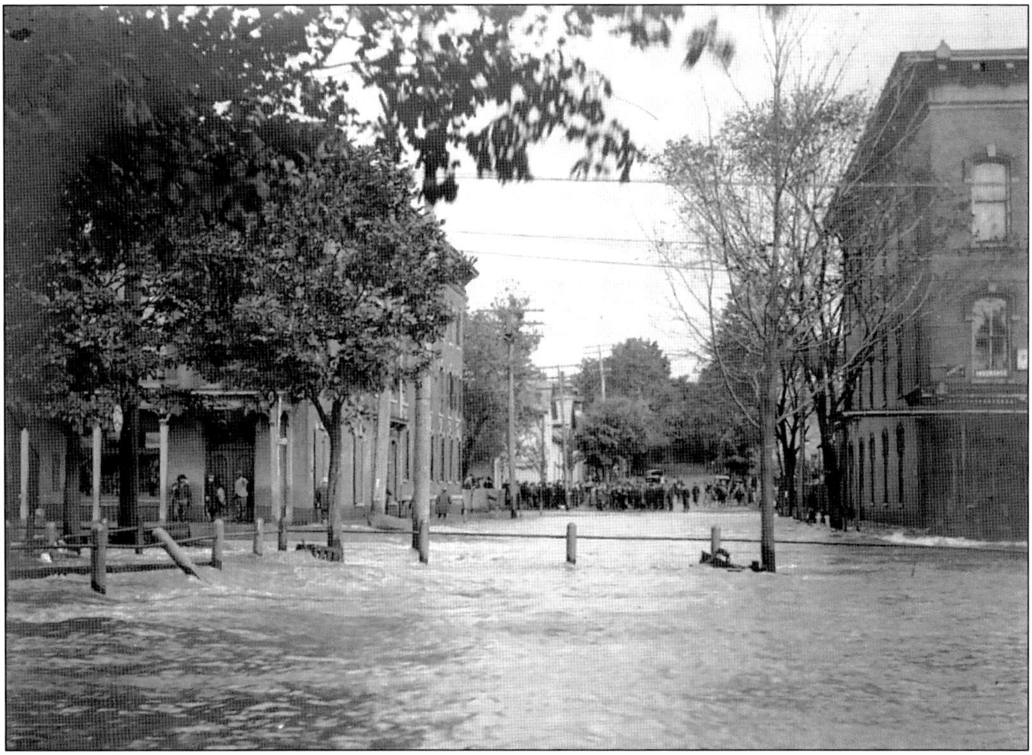

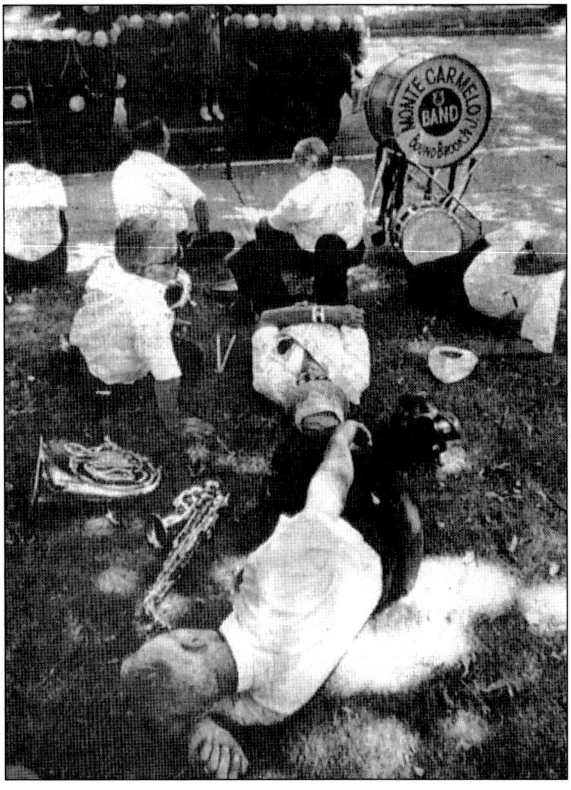

Always plagued by flooding, the downtown section of Main Street was a constant victim of high water. In this 1903 picture, bystanders view the damage on Hamilton Street from the safety of Second Street.

The Italian men of Bound Brook formed the Mount Carmel Society before the turn of the century. In the early years, the fraternal organization formed a band that frequently accompanied members' funerals to the cemetery. Here the band is part of the "Festa" held annually at the end of July.

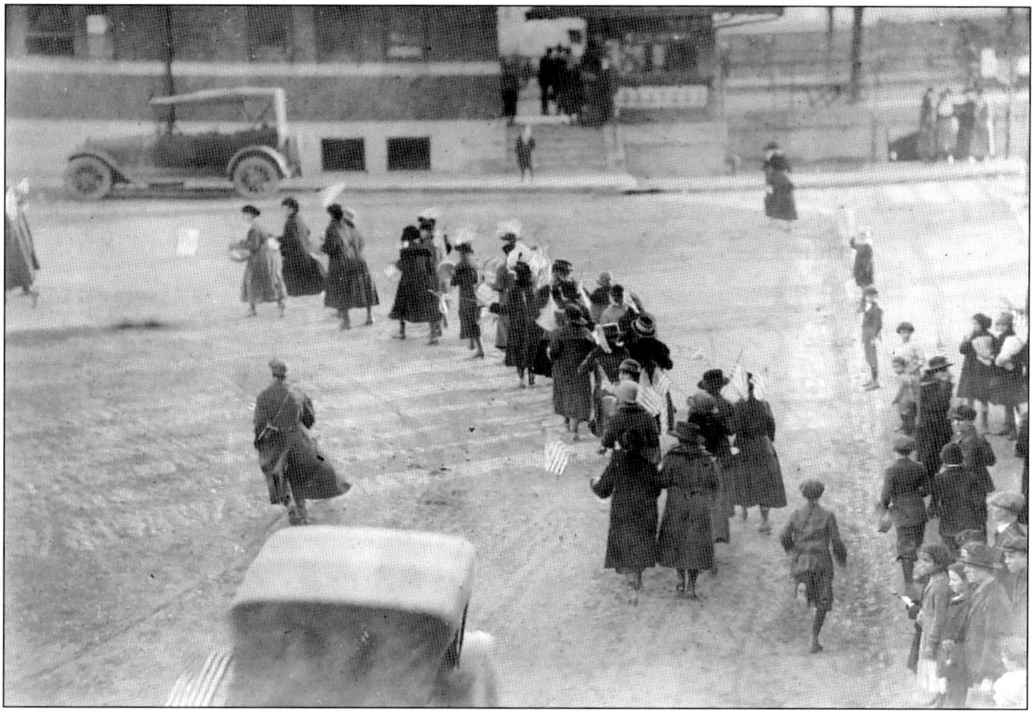

The campaign for women's suffrage found its way to town as it did throughout America in the post-WWI era. Local women demonstrate in front of the Central Railroad Station.

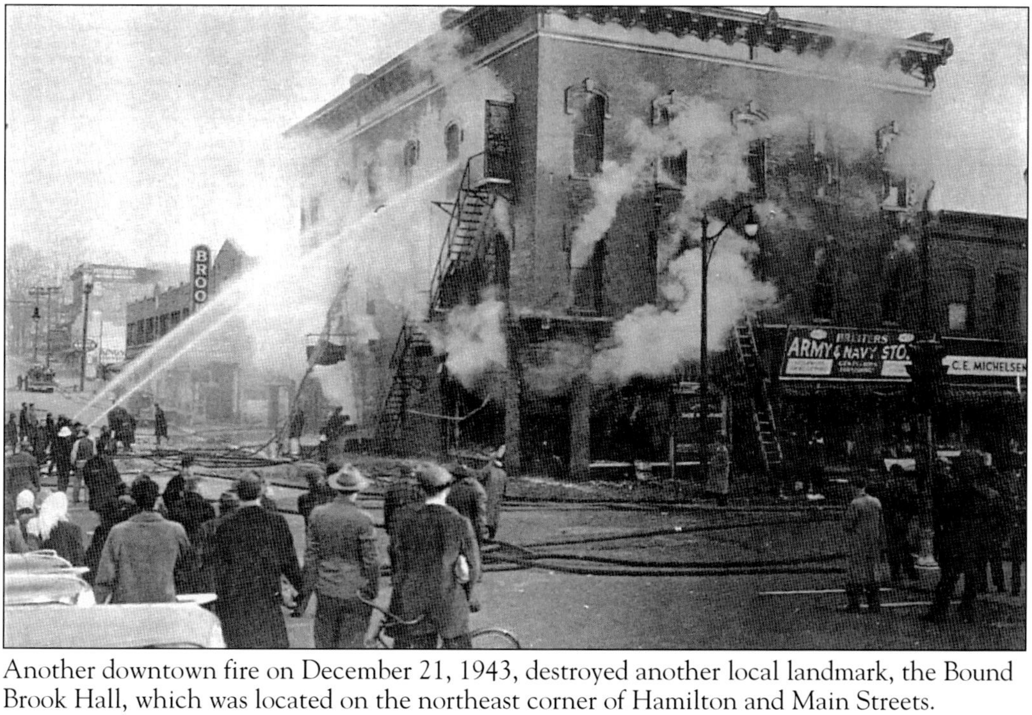

Another downtown fire on December 21, 1943, destroyed another local landmark, the Bound Brook Hall, which was located on the northeast corner of Hamilton and Main Streets.

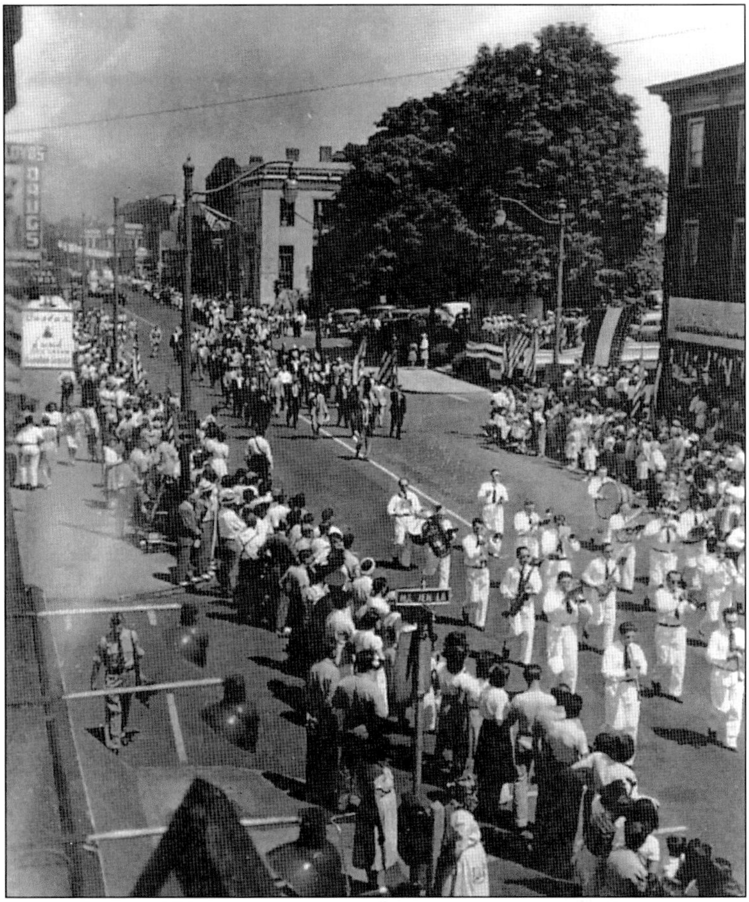

In 1946, the Welcome Home Parade for WWII service men and women filled Main Street with marching units, bands, and large numbers of onlookers.

School plays have always been one the highlights of the high school year, whether produced by the senior class or the Dramatic Club. Here we have a presentation of *Oklahoma* in 1955.

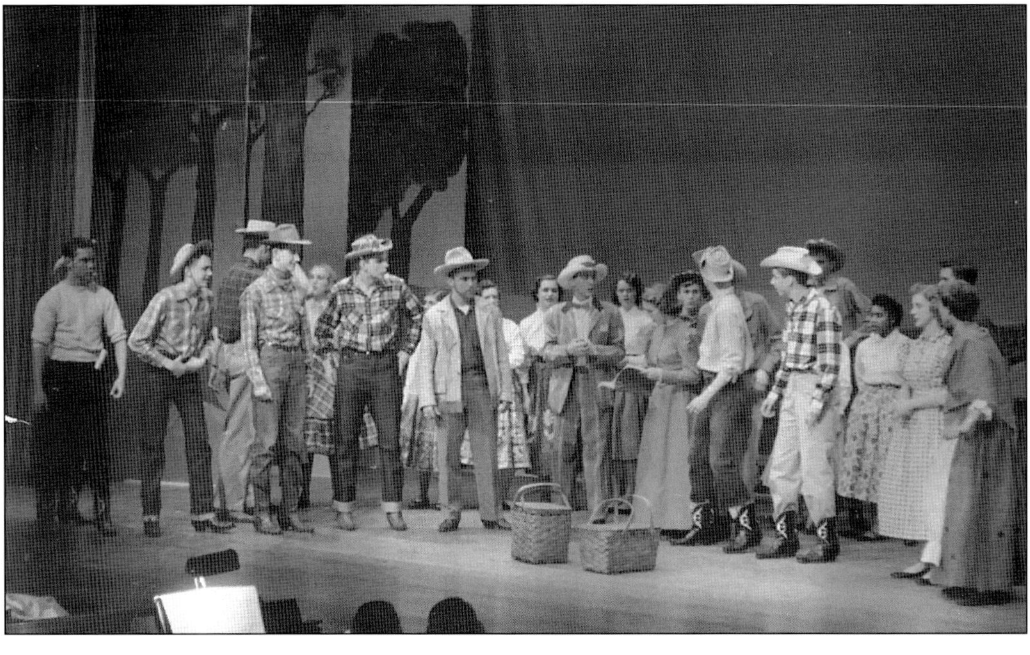

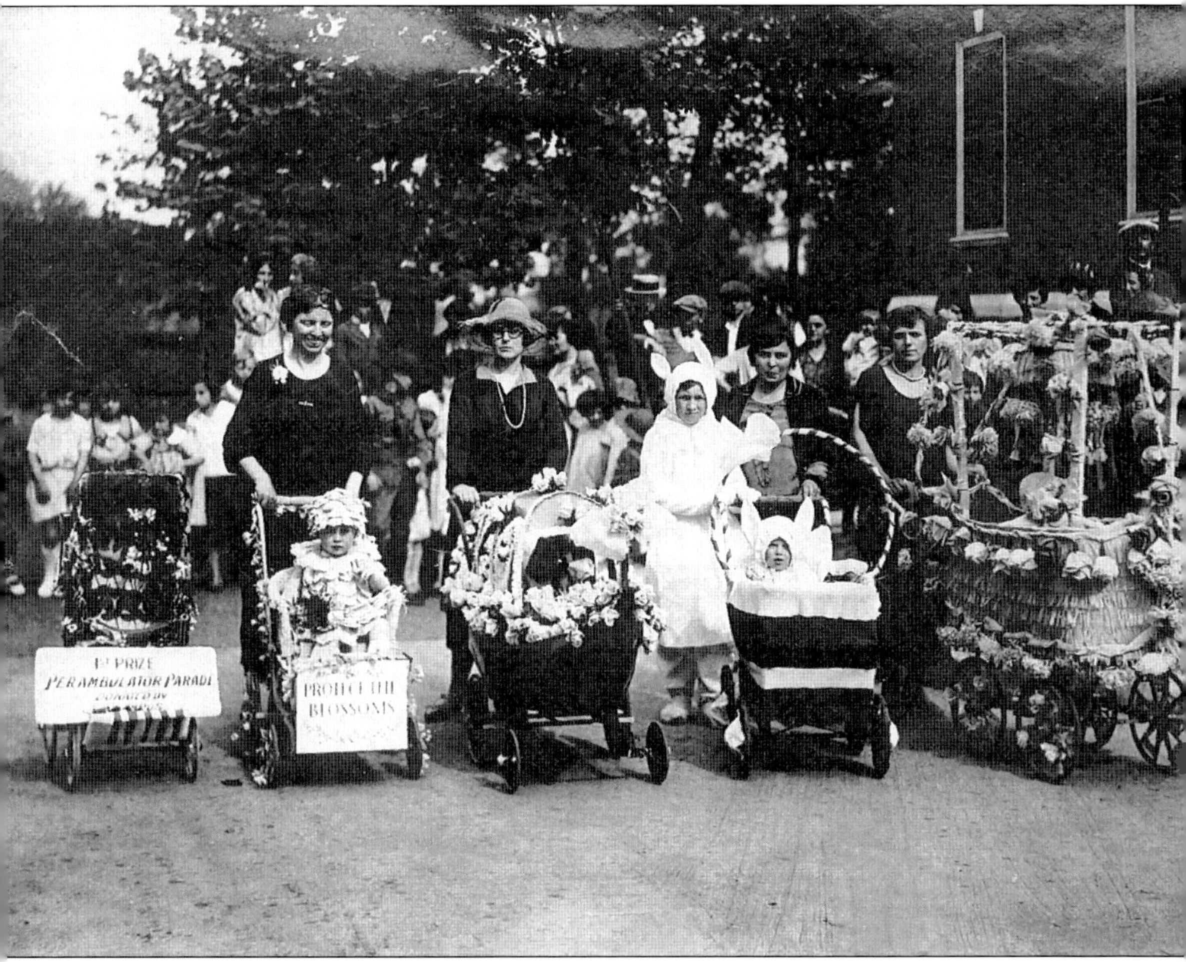

S. Klompus, a local store owner, donated the first prize of a baby perambulator for this 1925 Baby Parade Contest. The winner, on the left, was Mrs. Elizabeth Hall and her daughter Jane (now Mrs. Richard Spangler).

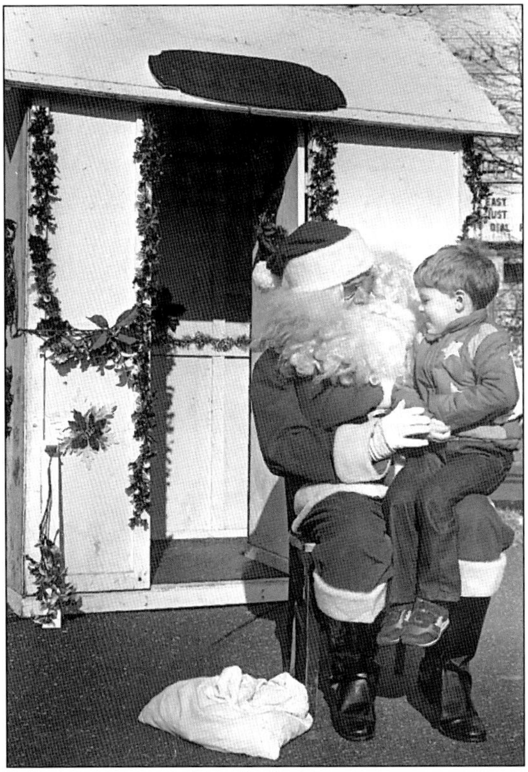

Even during the darkest days of the Great Depression, Santa Claus never failed to make his accustomed stop in town. The annual visits continued to hold true in 1987, when young Peter Hoffman paid this visit.

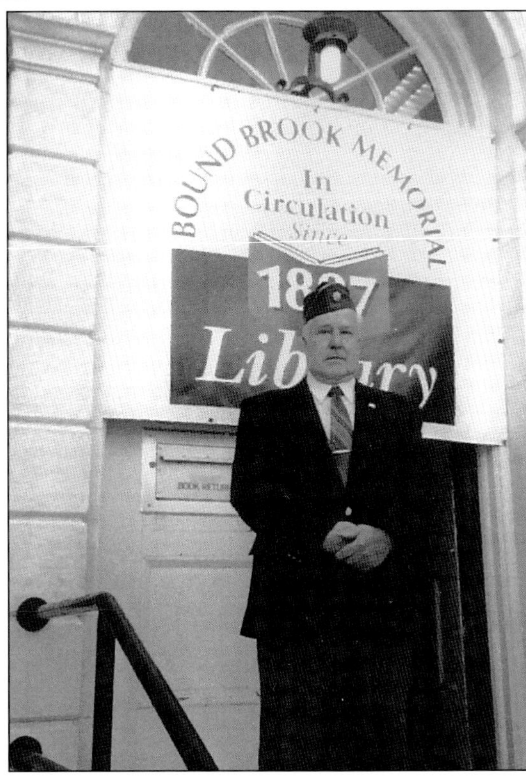

The Memorial Library conducted a year-long celebration for its 100th birthday in 1997. Posing beneath the celebratory banner on the library steps is current mayor, Frank Gilly.